# Vanity Economics

In memory of Professor Herschel I. Grossman

# Vanity Economics

An Economic Exploration of Sex, Marriage and Family

C. Simon Fan

*Professor of Economics, Lingnan University, Hong Kong*

**Edward Elgar**

Cheltenham, UK • Northampton, MA, USA

Published by
Edward Elgar Publishing Limited
The Lypiatts
15 Lansdown Road
Cheltenham
Glos GL50 2JA
UK

Edward Elgar Publishing, Inc.
William Pratt House
9 Dewey Court
Northampton
Massachusetts 01060
USA

A catalogue record for this book
is available from the British Library

Library of Congress Control Number: 2013951855

This book is available electronically in the ElgarOnline.com Economics Subject Collection, E-ISBN 978 1 78347 231 4

ISBN 978 1 78347 230 7 (cased)

Typeset by Columns Design XML Ltd, Reading
Printed and bound in Great Britain by T.J. International Ltd, Padstow

# Contents

PART IV   VANITY, HUSBAND–WIFE RELATIONSHIPS, AND
          INTERGENERATIONAL RELATIONSHIPS

PART V   VANITY AND INTER-FAMILY RELATIONSHIPS

# Preface

This book is based on my extensive research and teaching, most of which concerns the economics of family and social behaviour. It began with the PhD dissertation I wrote at Brown University, entitled 'A Theory of Intergenerational Transfers', for which I won an Alfred P. Sloan Doctoral Dissertation Fellowship in 1993. However, it took me many years to realize that the key idea of the thesis could best be summarized as follows: parents transfer wealth to their children to perpetuate the high social status (or vanity) of their grandchildren and future generations.

I have been much enlightened about family issues in general and the ground covered in my thesis in particular by many years of teaching an undergraduate course entitled 'Economics of the Family'. College students are naturally very interested in the issues of romance, marriage and the family. The lively discussions in the classes among the young and energetic students substantially improved my understanding of such issues. I gradually came to realize that 'vanity' is the key word in both male–female and intergenerational relationships.

Possibly because classical economists were motivated by a more naked type of capitalism over 100 years ago, they assigned vanity a central role in the study of people's economic and social behaviour and gave it a clear definition, as 'the mere desire of superiority over others by whatever criteria'.

I have lived and taught in Hong Kong for two decades, which has allowed me to observe unfettered local capitalism and that in Mainland China. Hong Kong has long been considered the freest economy in the world. China is at an early stage of capitalism in which its people's mentality is quite similar to that which the classical economists observed in Western countries 100 years ago. Moreover, the ever-vanishing ideology of communism and the lack of religious belief have turned China into a spiritual vacuum, in which vanity is manifested in the most conspicuous and unscrupulous ways. This book is also inspired by those observations. Indeed, as Albert Einstein insightfully pointed out, 'the whole of sciences is nothing more than the refinement of everyday thinking'.

This book has two main interrelated goals. First, it aims to reach a better understanding of numerous issues of marriage, sex and family by analysing them from the perspective of economics. Gary Becker (1991) made path-breaking contributions on family issues that have revolutionized economics and enriched other social sciences. This book intends to significantly extend Becker's work and related work in other studies.

Second, it tries to explore further the role of social status (or 'vanity') in social and economic behaviour, and thereby expand the frontier of economics and contribute to other social sciences. Thorstein Veblen (1899) advanced the idea that vanity plays an important role in consumption activities. This book applies Veblen's idea to the study of gender and family issues. In Veblen's theory of 'conspicuous consumption', vanity is obtained from the consumption of luxuries such as expensive handbags and brand-name cars. In this book, vanity is achieved from having a 'high-quality' spouse and children, in terms of beauty and intelligence.

This book contributes to both 'vanity economics' and the economics of the family from numerous angles. By thoroughly elaborating the crucial role of vanity in the study of male–female and intergenerational relationships, this book aims to contribute to the development of a new field in economics, in which social status is the main driver of a person's social and economic behaviour. This new field could be called 'vanity economics' or 'social economics'.

Moreover, at a more general and philosophical level this book implies that the 'survival of the gene' and hedonistic pleasures are not the only human motivations; vanity is another important driver that explains both individual behaviour and social and economic progress.

# 1.   Introduction

This book has two main interrelated goals. First, it aims to better understand numerous issues related to marriage, sex and family by analysing them from the perspective of economics. Second, it explores further the role of vanity in social and economic behaviour, thereby expanding the frontier of economics and contributing to other social sciences. The book introduces a large number of original ideas, presented in this chapter as a synopsis.

In his classic work, Adam Smith (1759) writes: 'For to what purpose is all the toil and bustle of this world? ... To be observed, to be attended to, to be taken notice of... It is the vanity, not the ease, or the pleasure, which interests us'. Alcott (2004, p. 767) provides a summary of studies by Smith (1759), Veblen (1899) and others in the classical economics literature, and notes that the meaning of 'vanity' is best described as follows: 'Vanity is "the mere desire of superiority over others' by whatever criteria".' My conception largely follows that definition of 'vanity'. Simply put, 'vanity' means social status plus self-esteem.

A dictionary may give other meanings, and our definition may be somewhat different from any of those. Thus our definition, which is in line with classical economists, may be at some risk of abusing the English word, but I stick to this word for its simplicity and for being in line with the writings of classical economists.

This book applies Veblen's idea to the study of gender and family issues. In the literature on 'conspicuous consumption', vanity arises from the consumption of luxuries such as expensive handbags and brand-name cars. In this book, vanity is achieved by having a 'high-quality' spouse and children, such as a beautiful wife, a tall husband and intelligent offspring. This book contributes to both 'vanity economics' and the economics of the family. It substantially expands the scope of vanity economics by showing that the vanity sources extend beyond materials such as handbags, cars and houses to the family. It also introduces vanity as an aspect to consider when examining both male–female and inter-generational relationships in the economics of the family.

The numerous chapters in this book approach the vanity economics of marriage, sex and family from various angles. Roughly, the first half of the book investigates the role of vanity in male–female relationships and marriage, and the second half examines its role in intergenerational relationships and family issues.

Chapter 2 summarizes the economics literature on vanity, and offers explanations for why vanity is often a major pursuit in most cultures and societies. Moreover, in addition to the idea of 'vanity by possession' that is widely accepted and studied in the literature, I posit that vanity can also be achieved through affiliation. I call this 'vanity by affiliation', which can help us better understand various family issues. For example, most people's 'closest affiliates' are their children and grandchildren. Hence they can fulfil their 'dreams' when their children achieve certain education or career development goals.

Chapter 3 briefly surveys some empirical studies on the 'conspicuous consumption' of material goods, particularly durable goods. It also presents a 'consumption ladder' hypothesis that extends the literature.

Chapter 4 summarizes and extends the literature on the marriage market in traditional and modern societies. In particular, it demonstrates the forces of competition in marriage outcomes.

Chapter 5 analyses why physical appearance is of paramount import-ance in marriage markets from the perspectives of both evolution and vanity. A certain standard of 'beauty' emerged due to its evolutionary advantage and became a part of social norms. Although the evolutionary advantage of the standard of beauty disappeared with the advent of economic development and technological change, it may remain import-ant because of the 'vanity' with which it is associated. The chapter also compares the relative importance of personality versus physical appear-ance. It implies that if vanity is not taken into account, then an individual's marginal utility from their spouse's physical appearance is very high at the beginning, but becomes less important than personality over time. However, when vanity is considered, the marginal utility is always very high, and can always dominate personality in importance.

Chapter 6 analyses the role of female virginity in marriage and male–female relationships. In ancient times, to the extent to which people valued the survival of their genes, there was a real value to female virginity in the marriage market. In modern societies, female virginity may continue to be very important because, from the perspective of a husband, whether his wife is a virgin or not may matter greatly to his vanity. The exact value of this 'vanity of possession' depends on a 'self-fulfilling prophecy', which explains why it is highly valuable in some societies and of little value in others. In addition, the application of economic theory, game theory and vanity economics in the chapter helps to better explain several factors that are often difficult to understand, such as the market for female virginity, acquaintance rape and the seclusion of women.

Chapter 7 is about premarital sex, cohabitation and marriage in the age of sexual liberation. It analyses three necessary conditions for widespread premarital sex. It then investigates the underlying forces in the social transition from a culture that emphasizes virginity to a culture of sexual liberation, and suggests the following three factors. First, a substantial decline in fertility and increase in marriage age during demographic transitions provide a material basis for sexual liberation. Second, today's media often belittle premarital female virginity and glorify sexual promiscuity. This considerably changes the culture, as people now often obtain a great deal of vanity from actively engaging in sexual activities and little vanity from having a virgin bride. Third, many women compete for 'high-quality' men in dating and romance.

Moreover, this chapter analyses people's intention to marry in the age of sexual revolution. While marriage limits a man's sexual freedom, it provides him with the vanity of possessing a family – a wife and children. Thus, even a man with a tendency to be sexually promiscuous may be induced to marry. Some men may be willing to trade promiscuity for vanity. However, in some societies, only a 'desirable' (e.g. good-looking) spouse can introduce an individual (positive) vanity, while an 'undesirable' spouse introduces an individual negative vanity. In this case, many people may choose to be single, and we may observe a large fraction of men and women in a society choosing not to get married.

Chapter 8 is about prostitution and commercial sex. It first discusses the demand factors, and shows that when income inequality is very large, commercial sex may take various forms. For example, in the 1990s, many Hong Kong men had one wife in Hong Kong and another wife across the border in Mainland China at the same time. Most Hong Kong men who kept a 'No. 2 wife' in China visited these women at weekends only. Thus, despite not receiving any sexual services on weekdays, they needed to pay these women for the time they spent waiting for them to return. This chapter explains that a 'No. 2 wife' provides a man with a strong sense of vanity of possession, from which he obtains much more vanity than from having sex with prostitutes.

It then discusses the supply factor of the sex industry. In particular, it presents a game-theoretical analysis, showing that there often exist multiple self-fulfilling equilibria. In one equilibrium many women engage in prostitution, whereas in the other they do not. There are two main reasons for multiple equilibria to emerge. First, interpersonal comparisons often considerably magnify vanity from material consumption. For example, if a woman sees that all her friends and colleagues have iPhones, she may feel embarrassed if she does not have one. Second, a woman feels ashamed to work as a prostitute if there are few prostitutes in her community. However, such a stigma (or negative vanity) greatly decreases if many of her friends work as prostitutes. Chapter 8 shows that, under some circumstances, many women will work as prostitutes, yet all of them would be better off if they made a commitment so that no one did so. Moreover, the chapter considers 'compensated dating', a practice somewhere between dating and prostitution. A theoretical analysis of 'compensated dating' is presented based on a logic that is similar to the theory of the 'compensating wage differential' principle in labour economics.

Chapter 9 analyses extramarital affairs. It first addresses why extramarital affairs are so devastating to marital relationships from both an evolutionary perspective and a new angle of vanity: the vanity of possessing a spouse. In Veblen's theory of conspicuous consumption, vanity is manifested in the possession of material goods such as delicate handbags and luxurious cars. In this book, a person's vanity is reflected by the possession of their spouse. Thus an individual would feel that this sense of possession had been seriously damaged or even ruined if their spouse engaged in extramarital affairs. The chapter then uses game theory to analyse an individual's strategic response when their spouse engages in an extramarital affair. A woman could threaten her husband with divorce, but the threat might not always be credible. This chapter shows that, under some circumstances, the only strategic equilibrium is that a man engages in low-level extramarital affairs and his wife tolerates such affairs.

Chapter 10 discusses homosexuality. First, to make sense of homosexuality in the context of evolution, it provides a new theory by suggesting a 'principal–agent' relationship between a living being and their genes. The aim of each gene (the 'principal') is to maximize the probability of its own survival. However, such a goal is not achieved by the 'gene' itself. Instead, it is directly achieved by a living being (the 'agent') such as a human. The gene induces a living being to achieve its goal of survival through a number of biological desires, particularly for food and sex. Homosexuality may be the product of intelligence in the evolutionary process, which results in a principal–agent problem between genes and humans. In particular, because some sexual acts (e.g. oral sex) can be performed by two persons of either the same or different sexes, homosexual activities may occur among a fraction of the human population. This chapter shows that vanity may be an important factor in explaining that, in different societies and at different times, the proportion of homosexuals in the entire human population may differ drastically.

Chapter 11 discusses classical population theory, and analyses the empirical relevance of its key assumptions in historical and modern times.

Chapter 12 presents Gary Becker's theory of population in which parents obtain happiness from the quantity and quality of their children. Moreover, it shows that vanity economics can help us better understand the underlying assumption of Becker's theories. It addresses why people are motivated to have children in modern societies. The new answer provided by this book is the vanity of possessing one's own children. If everyone believes that a society assigns a high social status to couples who have children, then, similar to the analyses of the previous chapters, it can be shown that this belief is self-fulfilling. On such a belief, those who do not have children have low social status, which motivates them to have children despite the high cost and hard work involved.

The chapter then addresses why parents care about the quality of their children. Some critics comment that the issue cannot be well explained from the perspective of evolution, as better-educated children tend to have fewer grandchildren. The chapter provides an alternative answer: if having children itself is a form of vanity for parents, the 'quality' of their children is naturally also a form of vanity.

Chapter 13 discusses the cost of raising and educating children in modern times. People often complain that children are expensive, but the chapter points out that the expense may largely stem from parents' vanity and their competition in increasing expenditure on the quality of their children.

Chapter 14 analyses several aspects of child labour: its determinants, impacts on children's education and welfare, and impact on fertility. Because child labour yields earnings, parents may send their children to work to increase their household income, which can be used to increase consumption and finance the children's education. For example, parents may arrange for some children to work so that other children can receive better education, which generates more vanity for the parents than the outcome that the children play at home but undergo few years of schooling due to the high cost of education. Moreover, working children may fully agree to such an unequal arrangement, as they consider their siblings their 'vanity affiliates'. This argument is well supported by the 'working daughters of Hong Kong' example from the 1960s and 1970s.

When children's earnings are sufficiently high relative to their cost, raising them is cheap but sending them to school is expensive. Thus parents may consider the quantity of their children a 'necessity' and the quality of their children a 'luxury' due to their 'price difference'. People demand more 'luxury' and less 'necessity' as they become richer, and fertility decreases and children's educational attainment increases as parental incomes rise. This new theory enriches the study of the interaction between the quantity and quality of children.

Chapter 15 examines children's contributions in traditional societies. In ancient times, people depended mainly on their children for support in their old age. It is argued that an 'implicit contract' exists in which parents invest in their children and in return obtain material support from them in their old age. This chapter shows that vanity can play an important role in enforcing this implicit contract. For example, in ancient China, filial piety was regarded as the most important virtue. A member who had the reputation of not being filially pious towards his parents was often ostracized by the society and could not be appointed as a government official. In other words, filial piety itself is a major source of vanity in some societies.

The chapter also examines the benefit of having children when the rule of law is not well established. When there is little legal protection, a household's income and welfare are determined not only by its members' productive capacity but also their abilities in combat and ability to protect the interests of the household. In such a setting, a household with fewer male members is likely to be exploited and bullied by other households. In contrast, a household with more grown-up sons is likely to be 'respected' by other households. Therefore the fertility rate tends to be higher in a society with a less well-established rule of law.

Chapter 16 considers some gender issues. It first addresses why a gender bias exists against girls in some cultures and societies, and finds that due to the problems of domestic violence and wife-beating, parents find that they obtain a higher status from their sons than from their daughters. This is particularly the case when they live with their children after their children are married. If a person has only daughters, they feel bad (negative vanity) when the daughters are abused and bullied by their spouses after marriage. Foreseeing this, people prefer to have male children. This chapter also shows a narrowing gender gap in wages in most developed countries due to the structural change from a manufacturing-oriented economy to a service-oriented economy. Consequently, women are generally bullied by their husbands less often as their 'bargaining power' rises, which may in turn reduce the gender bias.

Chapter 17 first identifies that 'superstars' find their way into many occupations in modern societies. Although real superstars represent only a tiny fraction of the population, the contemporary world has become a society in which winners take all. Based on this, and in line with Veblen's theory, this chapter puts forward a new concept, 'conspicuous career', which means that people may also achieve a high social status or vanity from a successful career. Therefore many people, especially better-educated individuals, tend to work hard for success. Moreover, the nature of 'work' has changed over time. Working is often pleasant in many occupations and may result in 'workaholism'. An immediate implication of overworking is that people have to compromise their most time-intensive activity at home: that of bearing and raising children.

Chapter 18 examines the value of time in consumption. With the rise of hedonism in modern societies, many people are busy at work and hectic in life, as the enjoyment of life often takes a great deal of time. This chapter presents two new arguments. First, the consumption of 'quantity' (or variety) is time intensive. Second, the consumption of 'quality' is money intensive. It then presents a theory that extends the study of the interaction between the quantity and quality of children. When people are poor, they are 'time abundant' and constrained only by their financial resources. Thus the fertility rate tends to increase as their incomes rise. When incomes increase, people become increasingly 'money abundant' and 'time scarce'. In this case, an increase in incomes results in three outcomes: (i) people consume more varieties of higher-quality material goods; (ii) many enjoy more 'conspicuous leisure'; and (iii) people have fewer children but try to improve the 'quality' of their children. This thus provides another explanation of demographic transition.

Chapter 19 analyses a 'population problem'. It argues that, from the perspective of social welfare, richer and better-educated parents often have too few children and poorer and less-educated parents may have too many children. In particular, because many well-educated people devote themselves to the constant pursuit of 'conspicuous careers' and enjoy the ever-expanding varieties of goods and services and 'conspicuous leisure', they often have little time and energy for family life and raising children. However, if better-educated parents had more children, the proportion of skilled individuals in the next generation would be higher, which would increase social welfare. The chapter also discusses various policies that mitigate the population problem.

Chapter 20 contributes to the study of divorce. As illustrated by most people's lack of enthusiasm in sperm or egg donations, people value a 'complete' family. In many societies, an individual achieves high social esteem if they have a spouse and children. If a person divorces, they lose the social status of possessing a spouse before they remarry. Meanwhile, they obtain much less of a social status from the children, as the family is now broken. However, divorce sometimes does occur. This chapter analyses the general causes of divorce from the perspective of vanity economics.

Chapter 21 shows that divorce is mainly a by-product of economic development. Indeed, the main causes of divorce are 'infidelity', 'physical abuse', 'emotional abuse' and 'incompatible personalities', factors that have been a part of husband–wife relationships throughout human history. However, divorce is only a problem of contemporary times, which implies that it is caused by economic growth. Meanwhile, divorce increases with a decrease of social stigma (i.e. negative vanity), which results from social development. Moreover, this chapter demonstrates the intriguing interactions between divorce, fertility and women's labour market participation. For example, the consideration of a possible divorce lowers fertility, which in turn increases the probability of divorce, which further reduces fertility and so on.

Children are their parents' closest 'vanity affiliates' and thus their major concern. Chapter 22 describes various channels through which family background affects children's education. First, to the extent that educational expenditures matter to student outcomes, a richer family tends to spend more on education and hence sees a higher level of educational attainment in their children. Second, intelligence may be genetically hereditary, which implies that better-educated parents tend to produce more intelligent children. Third, study effort is an important determinant of educational attainment. Moreover, effort and intelligence are often positively correlated. More intelligent children tend to find vanity in their studies, as they are often praised by teachers and envied by classmates. Consequently, they spend more time and effort on their studies, further enhancing their academic performance. In contrast, less intelligent children may find negative vanity in their schoolwork, and hence spend less effort on their studies and more on activities such as sports and socializing.

Chapter 23 investigates the effects of parental behaviour on children's 'quality'. In particular, it shows that an important incentive to participate in religious activities is to create an environment that is conducive to children's cognitive and emotional development. Under some reasonable conditions, it is shown that religious attendance rises with education for those whose educational attainment is below a certain level. However, this positive relationship may turn negative for those whose educational attainment is above that certain level. This result helps to explain an important stylized fact about education and religion in the USA.

Parental behaviour may affect children in many respects, and religion is not the only way to influence them. Evidence shows that, whereas fathers are more likely to participate in service-type organizations, church attendance and intergenerational family ties, non-fathers are likely to go to a bar or engage in other pleasure pursuits. Thus fatherhood may substantially change a man's lifestyle and induce him to develop good habits that both teach his children by example and increase his productivity. Thus the chapter provides a new explanation for the 'male marriage premium puzzle'.

Chapter 24 examines intergenerational relationships and financial transfers from both vanity economics and evolution theory. In the economics literature, it is commonly assumed that parents and children are linked by intergenerational altruism, meaning specifically that children's happiness is a part of their parents' happiness. Based on this assumption, parents are interpreted as giving money to their children because such an intergenerational transfer can increase their children's happiness. However, this implication is inconsistent with observed evidence, such as that of primogeniture in ancient times.

The chapter argues that parents and children are linked through their common concern for grandchildren. Given that grandparents do not beget grandchildren directly and that their life horizons are limited, concern for the survival of the gene and/or the perpetuation of social status (or vanity) into future generations induces grandparents to transfer some of their wealth to their children to induce them to have and raise grandchildren in order to maintain the social/economic status of the family line. This new explanation better accounts for the observed evidence. Moreover, it suggests that primogeniture and polyandry, which appear to be totally irrelevant, can in fact be well explained by the same theory.

Chapter 25 shows that vanity economics can help explain a number of important puzzles related to consumption, particularly from the perspective of intergenerational transfers. First, why do the rich in a country save more, but richer countries may have lower saving rates? Second, why do people consume significantly less immediately after they retire? Third, why do those who expect a higher income growth save more than those who expect a lower income growth?

Chapter 26 examines the relationship between vanity and social interactions. While vanity may exist even in the absence of explicit social forces, interpersonal comparisons amplify vanity substantially. The chapter shows that to increase their happiness, people may act in accordance with vanity in their choices of friends and social circles.

Chapter 27 investigates the relationship between vanity and the patterns of migration in relation to family. If an individual engages in a degrading job, they will have a strong incentive to work abroad to avoid the stigma (negative vanity) the job brings to family and self. However, if an individual has a successful career, they will be tempted to return to their home town to enjoy their 'conspicuous career' in the midst of family members and close neighbours. Moreover, an indiviudal may choose 'seasonal migration' by working in a rich country for part of the year and returning to the home country to enjoy 'conspicuous consumption' with their family.

Chapter 28 is an epilogue addressing the issues from a more general and philosophical perspective. It demonstrates the wide applicability of 'vanity economics'. Further, it argues that vanity may serve as another 'invisible hand' that induces people to work hard and raise and educate children, ultimately improving social welfare.

PART I


Background information

# 2.   Vanity economics: a survey and an extension

## 2.1  'ECONOMICS IMPERIALISM'

Over the past half-century, the boundaries of economics have been enormously expanded. In fact, the phrase 'economics imperialism' was coined to highlight that modern economics analyses virtually all social science subjects such as crime, politics, discrimination, social norms and, in particular, family.[1] Certain questions arise. What is the definition of economics? How does economics differ from other social sciences, say sociology, regarding research on family issues?

Economics distinguishes itself from other social sciences in its fundamental assumption of individual rationality. While other social sciences do not exclude this assumption in their methods, it is the cornerstone assumption in economics. Indeed, for at least the past half-century, mathematical methods have often been used to derive theoretical results in economics. Rigorous mathematics clearly matches the assumption of individual rationality perfectly. At this point, one may ask why the discipline of economics is based more firmly on the assumption of individual rationality than other disciplines such as sociology. There are two main interrelated answers to this question. First, in at least the early stages of economics development, the research focused on issues that were not very sensitive to people's emotions, such as the market, earnings, trade and production. Thus ideology and 'political correctness' were largely not an issue in economics. This tradition continued when economists turned to study more sensitive issues such as marriage, divorce and children. Second, 'utility theory' was developed in economics, establishing a starting framework for analysing people's behaviour. I briefly outline utility theory as follows.

In analyses based on the assumption that people make rational choices, the utility theory is used to examine ways to achieve maximal welfare when individuals make choices that are affected by multiple dimensions. In some special circumstances, an individual may be dominated by desire in one dimension. For example, a participant in the stock market may aim only to make more profit. In such a case, the individual's rational choice is only to maximize income. However, more often than not an individual makes choices that are affected by multiple dimensions. Consider a boy who loves to eat both apples and oranges. Given a certain amount of money, how would he choose the exact number of apples and oranges to purchase? He would first consider their prices. He would then ask himself how much pleasure he would get from eating the fruits in different combinations. In this case, pleasure is precisely the boy's utility. Without the utility theory, he may be stuck with the familiar saying that 'you cannot compare apples with oranges'. According to utility theory, there is a general index of happiness, called utility. For example, given the total expenditure on apples and oranges and their separate prices, the boy chooses the combination of apples and oranges that maximizes his index of happiness, or utility.

Note that when ideology and political correctness are important in debate, people often rebuke each other and argue that one cannot compare apples with oranges. In economics, it is argued that everything can in fact be compared. Further, to avoid the complication of ideology and political correctness, economics often emphasizes that it is a 'positive' discipline that aims to explain how the world is, rather than a 'normative' discipline that tries to argue how it should be. In this respect, this book follows the tradition of economics: it analyses people's social and economic behaviours from the angle of vanity, but it does not address whether people should care about vanity or how much they should concern themselves with vanity. In other words, this book is not a framework for morality.

What is the meaning of human life? This question is of fundamental importance to every individual. For most, however, it appears too deep and philosophical. Indeed, if we type this question into Google, most of the answers appear to be given from religious perspectives. In economics, the answer to this question is simple and straightforward: the meaning of human life is to maximize one's utility (i.e. the happiness index).

However, economists have paid relatively little attention to the description and analysis of utility sources (i.e. happiness and unhappiness). Such an abstraction is often innocuous in simple circumstances. For example, in choosing the number of apples and bananas to purchase, given a certain total budget, the utility sources are simply an individual's biological tastes for the two fruits. However, for a better understanding of complicated issues such as the choices of spouses and number of children, an economist should try to develop a deep understanding of human nature and needs. This is precisely the starting point of this book.

## 2.2 THE HIERARCHY OF NEEDS

In contrast to economics, psychology has a large literature that examines various dimensions of 'utility' or human needs. A classic piece of psychological literature on the sources of happiness and unhappiness is Maslow's theory of the 'hierarchy of needs'. Maslow (1943) identifies human needs as a hierarchy. From the bottom to the top, these needs include basic physiological needs, safety needs, needs for love and belonging, esteem needs and needs for self-actualization. Maslow's framework has been extremely popular and widely used in the study of social science issues. While it was developed 70 years ago, it is still often taught in introductory psychology and sociology courses.

However, Maslow's framework is clearly not the only way to describe people's hierarchy of needs, and neither is it always the best way. For example, in their influential psychology textbook, Gerrig and Zimbardo (2010) divide human motivation into three categories: eating, sexual behaviour and the need for achievement.

Among a person's basic physiological needs, the strongest is the desire to have enough food and water to stay alive. For example, Maslow (1943, p. 17) states:

> For our chronically and extremely hungry man, Utopia can be defined very simply as a place where there is plenty of food. He tends to think that, if only he is guaranteed food for the rest of his life, he will be perfectly happy and will never want anything more. Life itself tends to be defined in terms of eating. Anything else will be defined as unimportant. Freedom, love, community feeling, respect, philosophy, may all be waved aside as fripperies which are useless since they fail to fill the stomach. Such a man may fairly be said to live by bread alone.

In fact, it is only recently that most people in the world have not been concerned about hunger. When people do not have enough food for subsistence, no other desire is more important. Even today, a common greeting among older Chinese is 'Chi Bao Le Ma?', which directly translates as, 'Have you had enough food so that you are not hungry?'

Maslow's argument is vividly reflected in a story about King Zhou of ancient China's Shang Dynasty. This story, known as 'A pond of wine and a forest of meat', is perhaps the most famous story of luxury in ancient China. According to Wikipedia,[2] the story goes as follows:

> A large pool, big enough for several canoes, was constructed on the Palace grounds, with inner linings of polished oval shaped stones from the sea shores. This allowed for the entire pool to be filled with alcohol. A small

island was constructed in the middle of the pool, where trees were planted, which had branches made of roasted meat skewers hanging over the pool. This allowed Zhou and his friends and concubines to drift on canoes in the pool. When they thirst, they reached down into the pool with their hands and drank the wine. When they hungered, they reached up with their hands to eat the roasted meat. This was considered one of the most famous examples of decadence and corruption of a ruler in Chinese history.

The story reflects the ancient people's fantasy of utopia. Such a fantasy no longer exists from the perspective of most people in the developed world. For example, a typical student restaurant in an American university that has plenty of food and beverages for hundreds of people can really be considered 'a pond of wine and a forest of meat'. (It should be noted that people once chose to drink wine instead of water to ensure hygiene. Many bacteria that were fatal to humans could often be found in the water.)

In addition to food, sex is an important component of life. For example, according to a survey, 54 per cent of adult men and 19 per cent of adult women in the USA think about sex at least once every day.[3] Considering that many people are unwilling to make this confession, such percentages may be much higher in reality. This may be reflected in American television comedies such as *Friends*, in which sex is a common theme.

The motivation for sexual behaviour has a clear evolutionary basis: reproduction. Most animals are produced through male–female sexual intercourse, which is driven by sexual motives. Given that a species is reproduced sexually, the sexual desires of the members of the species are clearly crucial for the successful multiplication of its members and its long-term survival. Some animals, such as pandas, are facing extinction due to low sexual desire. One report from BBC News in 2011 stated:

> Out of their natural habitat more than 60% of male pandas exhibit no sexual desire at all. In a bid to encourage them to mate, the Chinese have experimented with everything from what has been dubbed 'panda porn' – explicit video of pandas mating – to traditional herbs.[4]

Fortunately, humans have no such problem of low sexual desire, and it is one of the reasons that they are the most successful species on the planet. Moreover, humans have sex not only to reproduce but also to experience pleasure. In fact, Sigmund Freud argues that the human sexual drive is so strong that it drives virtually every aspect of human behaviour.[5] As reflected in numerous love songs, a satisfactory romantic relationship is like a utopia, and acts as 'food' for a hungry man. Indeed, most songs in most cultures and societies are related to romance. Moreover, scientific research shows that sex is pro-evolution. For example, biological research shows that sexual reproduction makes a population better able to fight against parasites and cope with change compared with asexual reproduction.[6]

There is clearly no difference between humans and animals in terms of their motivations for food and sex. The essential difference between them lies in the spiritual aspect. For example, as summarized by Gerrig and Zimbardo (2010), humans have the motivation for personal achievement. Much of the psychology literature examines this motivation and its effects on people's successes and failures in work and life. For example, David McClelland and other psychologists designed ways to measure the level of this motive in a research experiment by asking participants about their fantasies in response to some drawings. McClelland (1973, p. 5) argues,

> If you want to find out what's on a person's mind, don't ask him, because he can't always tell you accurately. Study his fantasies and dreams. If you do this over a period of time, you will discover the themes to which his mind returns again and again. And these themes can be used to explain his actions.

In fact, the spiritual aspect of human desire is strongly emphasized by Adam Smith and other classical economists, who founded the discipline of economics. For example, in his classic work *The Theory of Moral Sentiments* (1759), Smith states: 'The wish to become proper objects of this respect, to deserve and obtain this credit and rank among our equals, may be the strongest of all our desires.' In particular, as noted in the Introduction, he assigns vanity a central role in economic incentives.

In a more concrete way, Thorstein Veblen advances the idea that vanity plays an important role in economics, particularly in consumption activities. In *The Theory of the Leisure Class* (1899), Veblen puts forward the theory of 'conspicuous consumption'. He argues that economic behaviour is socially determined and driven by the human instincts of emulation and social comparison. He further argues that, in consumption activities, people often try to impress others through conspicuous consumption. In other words, a major purpose of consumption is not to satisfy individuals' biological needs, but to gain and signal social status. Further, John Maynard Keynes (1930, p. 326) argues that an important aspect of our desires for conspicuous consumption consists 'in the sense that we feel them only if their satisfaction lifts us above, makes us feel superior to, our fellows'. Veblen's theory has had a profound effect on a number of social science and business disciplines, such as economics, sociology and marketing science.

At this point, we need to discuss more precisely the definition of 'vanity' used in classical economics literature. Based on a survey of the ideas of John Rae (1834) and Veblen (1899), Alcott (2004, p. 767) offers the following summary about vanity:

> Vanity is 'the mere desire of superiority over others' by whatever criteria; 'a perfect being' can achieve de facto superiority purely through 'pleasure in the good he does,' but it is the (vain) pleasure in 'surpassing others' that moves the rest of us ... Vanity is also the 'pride' moving a man to rise in the world, 'placing himself on an equality with those to whom he was once inferior' ... for Veblen it is 'to rank high' in 'invidious comparison' with our 'competitors' ... recalling Rae's 'desire ... to rank high in the estimation of the world' ... and 'It is invidious to run to expenses which others cannot follow' ...

## 2.3   'VANITY BY POSSESSION'

Based on the works by Smith (1759), Rae (1834) and Veblen (1899), this book defines vanity as the happiness of feeling superior over others and the unhappiness of feeling inferior to others. Also, in some contexts, we may more conveniently define vanity as the (spiritual) sense of success or failure. Simply speaking, 'vanity' means social status plus self-esteem.

First of all, vanity is self-esteem. Thus it exists even when there is no direct interpersonal comparison. For example, one may feel very happy if one wins a game against an electronic opponent on the Internet. In China, some computer games are created so that the users become more powerful when they purchase 'weapons' online. Many game lovers indeed pay substantial amounts of real money to buy these weapons, which help them obtain more points in the games. While the points they get from playing the games provide them with no value at all in their daily lives, they are willing to pay the money out of sheer vanity.[7]

However, interpersonal comparison is usually closely related to and often greatly enhances or intensifies vanity. Social comparisons matter not only to one's self-esteem but also to one's social status, dignity, honour and respect in a society. For example, in the opening statement of an influential book on envy and human nature, Schoeck (1987, p. 1) writes:

> Throughout history, in all stages of cultural development, in most languages and as members of widely differing societies, men have recognized a

fundamental problem of their existence and have given it specific names: the feeling of envy and of being envied. Envy is a drive which lies at the core of man's life as a social being, and which occurs as soon as two individuals become capable of mutual comparison.

In the writings of classical economists such as Smith and Veblen, vanity takes the form of possession of material resources. I refer to this as 'vanity by possession'. This book intends to extend the literature in two general ways. First, I posit that vanity plays a very important role in a number of sex and family issues such as mate selection, fertility choices, ways of raising and educating children, and bequests. This extension is natural. For example, in his pioneering research on the economics of fertility, Gary Becker (1960, 1991) argues that children can conceptually be considered as the 'durable goods' of their parents' consumption. His theory is widely accepted in economics today, and based on it I argue that people obtain vanity from possessing a spouse and children. In fact, for most people, the vanity from this source is much more important than the vanity obtained from possessing material goods such as cars and houses.

However, it should be emphasized that 'possessing' is a feeling, rather than ownership itself. For example, in a marital relationship, the husband has the feeling of 'possessing' a wife, and the wife has the feeling of 'possessing' a husband. However, neither the husband nor the wife is their spouse's slave.

The second extension is described in the following section.

## 2.4 'VANITY BY AFFILIATION'

In addition to the 'vanity by possession' that is widely accepted and examined in the literature, I posit that vanity can be obtained through affiliation, which I refer to as 'vanity by affiliation'. The closest affiliations are, of course, children, grandchildren and close relatives, and these are emphasized in this book's examination of family issues. For example, if a child attains certain education and career development goals, its parents often feel proud. In this case, I call the child the 'vanity affiliate' of the parents. Moreover, for many people, the vanity they obtain from their children is a very important concern in their lives. For example, well-known economist Esther Duflo was interviewed by the *Financial Times* shortly before she was due to deliver a baby. Talking about her baby, she remarked: 'People here are obsessed with doing everything perfectly. If you raise a child, it must be a perfect child. They must go to the perfect college and be the best at their job.'[8]

'Vanity by affiliation' has a wide range of applications. One example is the popularity of the US basketball team Miami Heat that began in 2009, when LeBron James and Chris Bosh joined Dwyane Wade on the team, turning it into the National Basketball Association's (NBA's) hottest championship contender. Many NBA lovers have become fans of the Miami Heat, revelling in the team's glorious victories and enjoying the associated vanity through all possible affiliations, down to having a distant uncle living in Florida. In fact, after the arrival of James and Bosh, a new item, 'Heat Index: Complete Coverage of the Miami Heat', was added to the NBA section of the cable TV channel ESPN's website.

A key ingredient in an individual's vanity by affiliation is the 'social distance'[9] between the individual and their vanity affiliate. The shorter the social distance, the greater the vanity by affiliation. For example, the NBA became much more popular in China after the 'Yao Ming effect', which shortened the social distance between the NBA and the Chinese audience and turned many people in China into enthusiastic fans of the NBA and particularly the Houston Rockets. The following article, taken from *Dime Magazine* in 2011,[10] illustrates the effect in some detail.

> During the past eight seasons, dozens of Chinese media members covering the Houston Rockets have swarmed into the depths of every NBA arena, outnumbering the beat writers, magazine journalists and national pundits. For that, they can thank Yao Ming. Tracy McGrady and Steve Francis benefited from Yao's stardom, too. Playing in only six games before the 2009 All-Star break because of injury, McGrady nearly had enough votes to become a starter on the All-Star team, all thanks to the millions of Chinese fans that had latched on to him as Yao's teammate …

Shortly after Yao Ming's retirement from the NBA, another sensational event was widely reported in the media around the world, particularly in the USA and China. At the beginning of the 2011–12 NBA season, people had high expectations of the New York Knicks, which had just acquired star player Tyson Chandler from 2010–11 season champions the Dallas Mavericks and already had superstars Carmelo Anthony and Amare Stoudemire in their line-up, along with some good supporting players. However, the Knicks' performance at the beginning of 2012 was very disappointing. The team lost 11 of its last 13 games before 3 February 2012. With the Knicks' key players out due to injuries, Jeremy Lin came off the bench for the team on 4 February against the New Jersey Nets, and played a key role in helping the Knicks win the game. Lin was afterwards promoted to the starting line-up, and led the Knicks to six straight victories.

While such stories are exciting in the NBA, they are not rare. It should be noted that Lin was waived several times by NBA teams during his short career. Thus he must have considered it a golden opportunity to be given plenty of time to play for the Knicks in an NBA game. As a player whose NBA career was at risk, Lin played extremely hard when given the opportunity to perform. Within a short time and with a little luck, a player's extremely hard effort and concentration may help him overcome his skill and athletic ability deficiencies and deliver a terrific perform- ance. However, it is reasonable to predict that such performances may not last long.

This story was a sensation around the world. Some Knicks fans gave Lin the nickname 'Linsanity', and a website, linsanity.com, has since been developed. The following newspaper story illustrates the frenzy of this sensation.[11]

> Not Magic and Bird, not Kobe or LeBron. Not even Michael Jordan. Nobody can match the buzz that Jeremy Lin has created in such a short amount of time, NBA commissioner David Stern said Thursday. 'I haven't done a computation, but it's fair to say that no player has created the interest and the frenzy in this short period of time, in any sport, that I'm aware of like Jeremy Lin has'.

The theory put forward in this chapter may provide a useful explanation of Linsanity. Lin has the following characteristics:[12]

- He is the first American of Chinese descent to play in the NBA.
- He came from a middle-class family.
- He went to college at Harvard, where he obtained a 3.1 GPA majoring in economics.
- He is a devout Christian and often expresses his faith in public.

Relative to that of most other NBA players, the social distance between Lin and the Chinese audience (in both China and other places) is short because Lin is ethnically Chinese. Moreover, these characteristics indi- cate a short distance between Lin and many people in the USA, particularly the better-educated class and conservatives. Thus many people find themselves at a much shorter social distance from Lin than from most other NBA players, and hence hope to realize an NBA dream through a vanity affiliation with Lin.

Finally, it should be noted that the feeling of 'vanity by possession' and 'vanity by affiliation' are not mutually exclusive. In general, the feeling of 'vanity by possession' is stronger if there are more social interactions between two individuals, and the feeling of 'vanity by affiliation' is stronger if there are fewer social interactions between two individuals. For example, before a girl comes of age, her parents may have a feeling of 'possession' towards her. When she grows up and has her own children, her parents' feeling towards her will increase through the channel of 'affiliation'. But even in this case, her parents' earlier feelings may not completely disappear. After all, she is still their child, no matter how independent she is or how far away.

## 2.5  VANITY AND HUMAN NATURE

This section discusses the following questions: why is vanity important, and why do people care about it? In the literature, it is often argued that vanity, which is largely a concern about one's social status, stems from evolution. For example, Frank (2011, p. 25) states: 'Since reproductive success has always depended most on relative resource holdings, it would be astonishing if the evolved brain didn't care deeply about relative position.'

Moreover, this section provides the following additional answers. First, vanity has an evolutionary basis in 'group selection'. For example, in ancient times, when a group of people had to fight a formidable and fierce animal such as a tiger, each individual in the group could choose one of two strategies: fighting bravely or being a coward. If everyone fought bravely, they were likely to kill the tiger. However, there was a chance that one or two members of the group would be seriously injured or killed by the tiger in the process. If a member of the group chose to be a coward and not actively participate in the fight while all the other members fought bravely, then the tiger would be killed and this certain member would not be injured. However, if all members chose to be cowards, then the tiger would not be killed and would instead kill most of the group. If the individual member was purely selfish in the sense that he cared only about whether he was injured, then his obvious strategy would be to be a coward, which would lead to the worst overall outcome for the group. This example illustrates the typical 'free-rider' problem in economics. To resolve the problem, which is detrimental to group survival, vanity (honour in this case) may evolve in the community. A community honours those who fight bravely, and humiliates and shames cowards. Clearly, every member of the community has a strong incentive to promote this social norm, and consequently vanity or honour becomes a cornerstone of the community. Over time, although technology has developed to the point that bravery in a fight with animals is no longer important for the survival of people, vanity has lingered as part of the community culture. Thus people may care about vanity even if its material foundation has largely disappeared.

Second, the pursuit of vanity is a way to banish idleness and boredom. In modern times, many people feel that they are overly busy. However, when people have nothing to do, they find idleness simply unbearable. In fact, we may argue from an evolutionary perspective that humans have an aversion to idleness: suffering from idleness motivates humans to work and think creatively.

This motive is related to the motive of self-actualization in Maslow's theory. For example, Maslow states:

> The need for self-actualization. – Even if all these needs are satisfied, we may still often (if not always) expect that a new discontent and restlessness will soon develop, unless the individual is doing what he is fitted for. A musician must make music, an artist must paint, a poet must write, if he is to be ultimately happy. What a man can be, he must be. This need we may call self-actualization.

However, most people have little need for such actualization. A peasant may not feel that he must toil the field; a construction worker may have little desire to work on a construction site for its own sake; a waitress may not be thrilled to serve rude and demanding customers and to clean tables *per se*; and a garbage collector may not be happy to collect garbage if there is no pecuniary reward. Indeed, throughout human history, creative artists and thinkers with strong intellectual curiosity have represented a small fraction of the entire population. What, then, is the object of most spiritual pursuits? In terms of the classical economists, the answer is vanity.

The pursuit of vanity may raise people's enthusiasm to engage in certain activities. For example, fat people are often advised to lose weight through exercise. However, many prefer to engage in competitive exercise such as playing soccer or basketball rather than 'simple' exercises such as running. The vanity related to competitive scoring induces them to expend effort in doing exercises that lead to losing weight. In fact, their concern for competitive scoring is so intense that they often forget that losing weight is the main purpose initially. In his best-selling book *How to Stop Worrying and Start Living*, Carnegie (1984, p. 163) quotes Harry Emerson Fosdick as saying, 'happiness is not mostly pleasure, it is mostly victory'.

Third, one main difference between humans and animals is that humans have the ability and tendency to contemplate their own death. When an individual has no other desires, the fear of death dominates their thoughts. Unless the individual is strongly religious, such a fear cannot be overcome. The following statement made by Steve Jobs (co-founder and former CEO of Apple Inc.) illustrates this point:

> No one wants to die. Even people who want to go to heaven don't want to die to get there. And yet death is the destination we all share. No one has ever escaped it. And that is as it should be, because death is very likely the single best invention of life. It is life's change agent. It clears out the old to make way for the new. Right now the new is you, but someday not too long from now, you will gradually become the old and be cleared away. Sorry to be so dramatic, but it is quite true.[13]

Thus, to the extent that the pursuit of vanity can distract people from contemplating their own death, it increases people's subjective well-being. In ancient China, many emperors had strong fears of death after conquering the known world, as it meant they had little further vanity to pursue. A notable example is Qin Shi Huang (259–210 BC), who was the first emperor of a unified China. Qin Shi Huang feared death so much that he spent an enormous amount of resources seeking special medicines to eat so that he could achieve immortality. In 219 BC, Qin Shi Huang sent an official named Xu Fu together with 3000 virgin boys and girls and numerous craftsmen and soldiers in a large fleet to retrieve the elixir of life in an ocean far away from China. Xu Fu and his crew did not return, and, according to some historians, he went to Japan and possibly became the first emperor of Japan.[14]

In ancient Egypt, to give another example, large amounts of resources were also spent to alleviate the fear of death. Egyptian pharaohs thought that the pyramids would allow them to continue to lead luxurious lives after death. Even commoners, who usually found it a very costly practice, hoped to live forever by being mummified immediately after death.

# 3. Vanity and the consumption of material goods/services

This book aims to examine the role of vanity in sex and family issues. However, as a benchmark for comparison, it is useful to discuss the existing literature on vanity economics, which has examined the role of vanity in the consumption of material goods and services. As noted in Chapter 2, Adam Smith emphasizes that vanity motivates people to work hard and pursue profits. Veblen puts forward the theory of 'conspicuous consumption', which simply means that people consume to demonstrate their social status, namely to gain vanity.[15]

## 3.1 VIVID EXAMPLES OF 'CONSPICUOUS CONSUMPTION'

This section provides some contemporary examples and evidence to illustrate Veblen's classical theory. The first story is based on my personal communications. Several years ago, a friend of mine went into a Louis Vuitton store in Hong Kong to buy a handbag for his girlfriend as a gift for her birthday. With the assistance of a saleslady in the store, he selected a handbag priced about HK$12 000. He then had a chat with the saleslady, and asked her about the difference in quality between that handbag and a cheaper handbag he could buy in the street for HK$200. The saleslady smiled, and kindly told him there was no difference. While this answer caught him by surprise, he bought the handbag immediately. He later told me that he did so not for its quality, but because his girlfriend cared only about the Louis Vuitton brand.

My friend's personal experience is well known to business people. For example, *The Economist* (1993, p. 93) quotes one marketing manager as saying 'Our customers do not want to pay less. If we halved the price of all our products, we would double our sales for six months and then we would sell nothing.'[16]

Another such story can be found in the December 2011 issue of *The Reader*, the most popular magazine in China. The author describes a friend whose son was studying hard to get into a prestigious high school.

To motivate their son, his parents promised to buy him a gift if he performed well in the entrance exam. The son asked for a sports bicycle. Although the bicycle cost the parents two months' salary, they agreed. After several months of diligent study, the son scored high in the entrance exam and consequently got into the prestigious high school. His parents indeed kept their promise and bought him the expensive bicycle. The author loved sports and exercise. After hearing the story, he visited the family, expecting to meet a teenager who loved the sport of cycling. However, to his surprise, he found the bicycle in a storage room, rarely used. The parents told the author that their son did not like cycling at all. The author asked the son why he had requested such an expensive and useless gift. The son replied that many of his classmates had expensive sports bicycles, and that without such a bicycle he would have no status. At the end of the article, the author comments that, upon reflection, such a story is common in China: people buy expensive things mainly to impress others rather than to satisfy their actual needs.

Gerke (2000) systematically examines consumption patterns in Indonesia, and also provides some interesting examples of the 'Veblen effects', noting (pp. 146–7):

> In Indonesia, it seemed, nearly everyone wanted to take part in 'modern' life. The socially palpable pressure to re-establish, constantly, middle-class membership led inevitably to demonstrative consumption … However, even before the 1997 crisis, only a small proportion of the Indonesian new middle class was able to afford a Western or urbanised lifestyle. The overwhelming majority was unable to consume the items defined as appropriate for members of the middle class … Thus, they engaged in substitutional activities to give their lives a middle-class 'touch'. As their consumption possibilities were limited, consumption assumed a mere symbolic dimension. For example, one could readily see young people and families spending hours sitting in strategic places, where they could be seen by all and sundry, at McDonald's or Pizza Hut drinking Coke or milk-shakes with a burger. They would take the empty hamburger bags with them, as they left the fast-food restaurant, so that everybody in the street could see where they had lunch or dinner. Students share one Benetton sweater with two or three others, wear second- or third-hand Hammer T-shirts and borrow jewellery from roommates to go shopping or hang around shopping centres.

In economics, there is a well-known paradox named after economist Richard Easterlin (1974), who finds that at any given time and in certain places, richer people tend to report being happier. However, over time, with an economic growth that allows people to become much richer on average, the average reported level of happiness does not vary much with the average income, at least in OECD countries. This puzzle can be easily explained if we consider that when an economy develops to a certain level, consumption activities are pursued mainly to demonstrate one's social status, namely vanity.

## 3.2  THE 'CONSUMPTION LADDER' HYPOTHESIS

This section is based on a study (Fan, 2000) in which I offer some evidence of the role of vanity in the determination of consumption patterns at different levels of economic development in China. More importantly, I put forward the 'consumption ladder' hypothesis.

In the study, I describe changing patterns of consumption in urban China. Before the country's economic reform, Chinese people spent most of their income on basic necessities such as food and cheap clothing. At that time, the most popular household goods, often referred to as the 'four big items', were sewing machines, watches, bicycles and radios. Economic reform has continuously improved Chinese people's living standards. In the 1980s, the former 'four big items' were replaced by the new 'six big items', including colour television sets, refrigerators, cameras, electric fans, washing machines and tape recorders. As income levels increased in the early 1990s, people focused their attention on luxury items such as video recorders, hi-fi systems and air conditioners. About a decade later, personal computers and private cars became the new 'big-item' fashions for Chinese households. More recently, the ownership of private apartments has become the major concern of most urban households, which to a large extent explains the skyrocketing housing prices in urban China.

These durable consumption goods were commonly called 'big items' not only because they introduced significant convenience to people's material consumption, but also because they conspicuously demonstrated the social status of their owners. Partly due to the legacy of communism, Chinese society has been a gregarious society in which people invite friends and colleagues to visit their homes. When only a small fraction of the Chinese people could afford such durable goods, the status related to whether a household possessed them, and to a lesser extent their qualities or brands, were important indicators of people's social and economic status. For example, in the 1970s and 1980s, most of these durable goods (such as sewing machines, refrigerators and washing machines) were often put in conspicuous positions in people's living rooms when they entertained guests. This phenomenon was pronounced in China not only during the current period of 'consumerism', but also the period of strong communist ideology before and shortly after the economic reform. Even under the strong ideology of communism, the motive of conspicuous consumption was maintained.

Based on these observations, I put forward a 'consumption ladder' hypothesis. It argues that, in developing countries, people's demand for durable goods often experiences *discrete* jumps. The logic of this argument is as follows. In a poor country, an ordinary worker's expenditure on a durable good often accounts for several years of their income. Further, in most poor countries, the financial markets for consumption loans are often not well developed. Thus a household in a poor country can consume a durable good only when its income reaches a certain threshold level. For example, if a household wants to purchase a television, it requires a certain amount of money that is at least the minimum price of a set. As a durable good is not divisible, a household cannot buy a fraction of a television. In addition, although it is theoretically possible, very few households pool money together to buy a set in common, which would result in many conflicts and tensions among households. Thus a household will buy a television only if its income reaches a certain level. This implies that, when the average household income is below that level, the demand for a television is very low, and that when the average household income reaches the critical level, demand suddenly becomes very large. When the incomes of most households exceed the critical level, most will possess televisions and consider the next level of durable goods in their consumption ladder, such as motorcycles and cars.

In Fan (2000), I provide a summary of the changing patterns of consumption of durable goods in urban China from 1982 to 1997. Consistent with the consumption ladder hypothesis, this shows that the possession rates of almost every kind of durable good increased considerably, with one exception: the ownership of sewing machines per household decreased over time in China. Chua (2000) provides an explanation for this phenomenon using an example from Singapore. He notes that, until the late 1970s, a significant proportion of clothes in Singapore were home-made. At the time, the possession of a sewing machine was important for a Singaporean household, and in fact a sewing machine was often a part of a bride's marriage dowry. By the late 1980s, however, most people were buying clothes in stores rather than making them at home. Consequently, few households now possess sewing machines. This example illustrates that conspicuous consumption may often have a material basis, and that what constitutes a luxury good at one time may lose its function of signalling one's social status as the economy develops.

# 4. Marriage markets

This and several of the following chapters examine the economics of mate selection for marriage. Economists assume that there is an explicit or implicit market for the selection of marital partners.

As with any other type of market, a marriage market has two basic components: supply and demand. The supply in a marriage market is defined as the group of men and women who seriously and actively look for a spouse at the same time and usually in the same place. With increasing globalization, decreasing telecommunication costs and the introduction of Internet applications such as Skype, people can look for marital partners in different locations. However, most continue to choose their spouses through face-to-face interactions.

An individual's demand in a marriage market refers to the kind of spouse they are looking for. While this can be complicated in modern societies, at a deep theoretical level the factors that determine demand in a marriage market are the same as those in any other type of market. These factors are preferences and endowments.

For example, consider the fruit market. A person has a certain preference for fruit, such as apples and bananas, and a certain amount of endowment (money) for purchasing them. Given the prices of the fruit, the person's demand for apples and bananas is derived from their preferences and the amount of money they have for the purchase. If the person prefers apples, they tend to buy more apples; if the person prefers bananas, they tend to buy more bananas. In the marriage market, preferences and endowments also interact closely to determine demand. A person's preference for their spouse's characteristics usually comprises multiple dimensions such as physical appearance, income, education and personality. People care about these dimensions to different degrees. The endowment of a participant in the marriage market also comprises these dimensions. As such, a marriage market differs from other markets, whose buyers' endowments usually comprise only money.

The main innovation of this book is that it highlights and carefully analyses the role of vanity in mate selection. However, vanity is not the focus of this chapter. Based on the economics literature, this chapter analyses two types of marriage markets: traditional and modern. They differ mainly in that parents are the main decision-makers in the marriage markets in traditional societies, but individuals can make their own decisions in modern societies.

## 4.1  MARRIAGE MARKETS IN TRADITIONAL SOCIETIES

This section presents an analysis of marriage markets in traditional societies, where marriage is determined by the parents of the bride and groom. It shows that vanity may play a relatively less important role in this type of marriage in comparison with modern marriages, where romance and love play the key roles. However, this is a useful starting point, and in fact this type of marriage may clarify how competitive economic forces function in the determination of marriage outcomes. It should allow us to better appreciate the role of competition in modern marriage/romance markets, which is usually more subtle and implicit and takes more forms.

In traditional societies, money usually changes hands between the families of groom and bride when (or shortly before) a marriage take place. For a newly wed couple, if the groom's family pays the bride's family, then the amount of money paid is called a 'bride price'; if the bride's family pays the groom's family, then the amount of money paid is called a 'dowry'. The interesting question is why bride prices and dowries exist in traditional societies. For example, substantial dowries exist in India today. In ancient China, large sums of money were needed to pay bride prices. Becker (1991) offers a simple and insightful answer: bride prices or dowries arise when there are uneven numbers of men and women in a marriage market.

To understand Becker's insight, let us consider the following analytical and numerical example. Consider a small community such as a village in which there are five households. Each of three families has a son to marry off, and each of the remaining two families has a daughter to marry off. Every family would be much happier if their child married. The happiness index ('utility' or 'utility function' in economics) of each family is as follows. First, if the child of a family is not married, then the family's happiness index is simply its total wealth. Second, if the child of a family is married, then the family's happiness index is simply its total wealth plus a fixed number such as 100. Suppose that each family's (initial) total wealth is $300. What is the marriage outcome? Is there a 'bride price' or 'dowry' in the marriage market? How much is it?

The answers to these questions are as follows. Let us denote the three families that have a son to marry off as A1, A2 and A3, and the two families that have a daughter to marry off as B1 and B2. Suppose that, at the beginning, A1 proposes to B1 and A2 proposes to B2 without any dowry or bride price. What will happen? In this case, A3 will propose to B1 (or B2) for $1 as the bride price. B1's (or B2's) utility will clearly increase. What will A1 (or A2) do? He will pay a greater bride price. When the bride price increases to $100, the happiness index of the family whose son is married is:

$$100 + 300 - 100 = 300$$

The happiness index of the family whose son is not married is 300.

In this case, the marriage market reaches an equilibrium. If it is less than 100, the left-out family will offer a higher price. If it is above 100, the families with sons will prefer not to have their sons married.

Based on the same logic, we can easily answer the following two questions.

(1) Suppose that there are 10 000 001 families that have a son to marry off, and 10 million families that have a daughter to marry off. What is the marriage outcome? In this case, the bride price is clearly $100.

(2) Suppose that there are 10 million families that have a son to marry off, and 10 million and one families that have a daughter to marry off. What is the marriage outcome? In this case, the dowry is clearly $100.

In the above examples, an implicit assumption is that every family has perfect information about all the other families, which may not be true in reality. However, the force of competition in the marriage market is revealed in all the above examples.

Sometimes we may observe bride prices and dowries simultaneously for a number of reasons. For example, in a marriage, one's relative status may depend on the amount of money and resources one brings into the new family. If the parents care about their children's welfare, then they have an incentive to give money and resources to their children, even when such a wealth transfer is not necessary for the marriage contract. It may also simply be a social custom that a family needs to at least symbolically give money to the in-law's family for their child's marriage. In such a case, we need to see only the net amount when we conduct an analysis similar to the preceding. If the bride price is greater than the dowry, then we say that the bride price clears the marriage market; if the bride price is less than the dowry, then we say that the dowry clears the marriage market.

This presents purely theoretical reasoning. – Yet, as the following examples indicate, there is empirical evidence that supports the theory.

Rao (1993) examines the issue of dowries in India, and finds that they often comprise 50 per cent of household wealth. While this is obviously a high number, it is not really surprising in light of the preceding theoretical analysis. If a household obtains a great deal of happiness from marrying off a child, then the market price must reflect the magnitude of that happiness. Moreover, Rao provides an explanation for the Indian dowry statistics. If we look at the absolute number of men versus that of women for any given age range, we may observe that there are not more women than men; in fact, the opposite may be true. However, the problem is that there are always more women in the marriage market. Why? Rao suggests two reasons. First, women tend to marry at a much younger age. Second, India experienced a sudden significant growth in its population due to high fertility and low mortality rates after the Second World War. In both contemporary and historical times, the fertility rates of poor countries are usually high. However, after the Second World War, there was a sudden drastic improvement in hygiene and medicine that made it available even to poor people, which significantly reduced the infant mortality rate. Consequently, the proportion of women in the Indian marriage market increased greatly, which led to a rising price of husbands.

In ancient China, paying an expensive bride price was the norm in the marriage market. This was caused by the practice of polygamy, in which men were permitted to have more than one wife. The uneven income distribution resulted in a substantial difference in ability to pay for a wife among rich and poor people. In addition, because the marriage decision was made by the brides' parents rather than the brides themselves, the parents were often willing to marry off their daughters to those who were willing to pay a high bride price. Thus a rich man in ancient China often had a large number of wives, which is conceptually equivalent to that man appearing in the marriage market as multiple participants, creating the impression that there are many more men in the marriage market than women and in turn leading to a high bride price. This theoretical implication is supported by empirical evidence. For example, Tertilt (2005) shows that, in Sub-Saharan Africa, polygamy is an important reason for high bride prices.

In modern China, due to the one-child policy and the practice of sex selection, there are more men than women in the new generation coming of age. Wei and Zhang (2011) provide evidence showing that this is an important reason for the high savings rate in China. They also report that the Chinese national savings rate has been about 50 per cent of GDP in recent years, and that household savings as a share of disposable income nearly doubled from 1990 to 2007. They conclude from their careful empirical analysis that the best candidate for explaining this high and variable savings rate is the country's unbalanced sex ratio and the consequent 'competitive saving motive': 'As the sex ratio rises, Chinese parents with a son raise their savings in a competitive manner in order to improve their son's relative attractiveness' (p. 511).

## 4.2  MARRIAGE CONTRACTS IN TRADITIONAL CHINA

This section provides a description and analysis of some practices related to marriage in ancient Chinese society, based on an article by Steven Cheung (1972). Moreover, it shows that vanity economics can help us better understand some of the social norms related to traditional marriage.

At the start of his article, Cheung describes the parent–child relationship in traditional China as follows: 'Just as dogs were raised to hunt for their masters before they were pets, so in early traditional China, children were raised as a source of income and a store of wealth' (p. 641). He points out that, in traditional China, children were effectively their parents' assets. Thus they could be 'sold' by their parents in the marriage market. In other words, every marriage involved an outright transfer of property rights. In traditional China, after a girl's marriage she usually lived with both her husband and her husband's parents, and her childhood home was referred to as her 'mother's home'. (Cheung translates it as 'foreign' home.)

Cheung makes a number of interesting observations about the concrete arrangements of marriage contracts in traditional China. First, the Chinese mainly retained sons and married off daughters. He explains that, while children were assets for their parents, they had a special feature apart from physical assets: they could run away. They might have done so because they and particularly their spouses were often abused by the parents, who had absolute power over them. It was less costly to prevent one's own child from running away. The parents usually treated their own children much better than their children's spouses, and there was a strong social norm of filial piety in traditional China. Thus it made economic sense for the parents to retain their sons and marry off their daughters, mainly because a woman was physically much weaker than a man and hence much easier to 'tame' (a word used by Cheung). Moreover, a woman could be easily 'tamed' in traditional China by having her feet bound, making it difficult for her to run away. In fact, Cheung finds evidence that girls were subjected to foot binding at about five years of age in traditional China.

Why did a Chinese family bind the feet of its daughters? The direct answer is that the price (i.e. the bride price) was higher for girls with bound feet in marriage markets, holding other things constant. Cheung (1972, pp. 645–646) suggests the following answer: 'To the groom's parents, the physical handicap thus imposed was more than counter-balanced by the girl's lessened ability to run away … In such activities as weaving, sewing, cooking, and other domestic work, bound feet were not a great impediment.'

Vanity economics offers an alternative answer. If a woman had bound feet, she would not be able to work on the farm. Thus a family willing to choose a woman with bound feet as a wife for their son signals to others that the family is relatively wealthy. Indeed, the bride had to perform farm work after marriage if the family was poor. In such cases, bound feet were a great disadvantage. Thus poor families experienced much less demand for their brides to have bound feet. Therefore the wife's bound feet reflected the status of the groom's family.

In fact, Veblen (1899, p. 118) provides a very similar answer in his discussion of women's dress and, in particular, 'high heels':

> The dress of women goes even farther than that of men in the way of demonstrating the wearer's abstinence from productive employment. It needs no argument to enforce the generalization that the more elegant styles of feminine bonnets go even farther towards making work impossible than does the man's high hat. The woman's shoe adds the so-called French heel to the evidence of enforced leisure afforded by its polish; because this high heel obviously makes any, even the simplest and most necessary manual work extremely difficult. The like is true even in a higher degree of the skirt and the rest of the drapery which characterizes woman's dress. The substantial reason for our tenacious attachment to the skirt is just this; it is expensive and it hampers the wearer at every turn and incapacitates her for all useful exertion. The like is true of the feminine custom of wearing the hair excessively long.

Moreover, according to vanity economics, the main reason for the social custom that Chinese tended to retain sons and marry off daughters was the parents' concern for their absolute authority in the family. If, instead, the sons were married off and the daughters were retained at home, the parents' authority might have been seriously challenged by the daughters' husbands, who were younger and hence probably physically stronger.

Another interesting observation of Cheung's (1972) is that marriage was blind in traditional China, in the sense that the groom was allowed to see the bride's face for the first time only after the wedding. He provides an economic explanation for this from the perspective of intergenerational conflict. It is human nature for a man to appreciate the beauty of his spouse's looks. Thus the groom put a great deal of emphasis on the appearance of his bride. However, the bride's looks were not a major concern to the groom's parents. Note that the decision-makers of the groom's marriage were his parents, who tried to exercise their wills rather than the groom's will in the selection of the bride. To avoid potential conflicts between grooms and their parents, a social norm emerged in China that marriage was blind for the grooms.

Partly because brides' faces could not be seen in 'blind marriage', the beauty standard for women in traditional China focused on foot size. It is reflected in the following story, which I heard several years ago while watching Phoenix TV, a Hong-Kong-based television channel that serves mainly the Chinese Mainland and Hong Kong. The story was told by an old woman. She got married in the 1920s, when she was still a teenager. According to the tradition at the time, on her wedding day she was carried in a marriage litter from her parents' home to her husband's home. As just described, her face was covered according to the Chinese custom of 'blind marriage'. However, when she stepped out of the marriage litter, all the people surrounding her applauded loudly. Why? Because people saw that her feet were very small.

## 4.3 ASSORTATIVE MATING IN MODERN MARRIAGE MARKETS

This section describes the patterns of marriage in contemporary times, when men and women (rather than their parents) choose their own marital partners. At the outset, one may ask why most people in modern societies and particularly men choose to get married. Indeed, some may think that a man would feel happier being single and having multiple sexual partners than he would being married and having sex only with his wife.

I will address this question at many points throughout the rest of this book, but, in short, people get married for the vanity of possessing a spouse and children. In other words, many people choose to get married out of the vanity of possessions (i.e. possessing a family). The argument here is essentially the same as that of Veblen (1899), who emphasizes the vanity of possessing material goods such as luxurious handbags, cars and houses. Indeed, for most people, the vanity they obtain from their spouses and children is much more important than the vanity they obtain from the possession of material goods. For example, a middle-aged female may feel a lack of social status if she tells others that she has no husband or children.

This chapter analyses the ways that people choose marital partners when they decide to get married. (For the time being, we will leave aside more detailed discussions on whether a marriage should occur.)

As described at the beginning of this chapter, supply in a marriage market is defined as the group of men and women who seriously and actively look for a spouse at the same time and usually in the same place. The key words in this definition are 'seriously' and 'actively'. Recall that in Section 4.1 we discussed the example of the Indian marriage market, where there is a large surplus of females and a shortage of males. In fact, for any demographic group below the age of 40, the absolute number of men is greater than that of women in India. Indeed, the problem of 'missing girls' caused by female foeticide, neglect or even murder is well known in India.[17] However, there have been more women than men in the Indian marriage market since the Second World War. The number of young men not entering the marriage market is much greater than that of women. This is also true for developed countries, though to a lesser extent. Many young men today want to have girlfriends, but are not thinking about marriage. As a result, there are often more women than men in developed countries' marriage markets, particularly in large cities.

In reality, the operation of a marriage market can be very complicated. However, regardless of the exact form a marriage market takes, competitive forces always play important roles in the determination of marital selection outcomes. To discover the essence of how competitive forces work in a contemporary marriage market, we examine the following simple example.[18]

Suppose that people care only about the wealth of their partners in the marriage market. Consider three men and three women in the marriage market with the endowments as shown in Table 4.1.

Who will marry whom? In this simple example, the supply of the marriage market is three women and three men. The people's preference is wealth, and their endowments are their income. The men are ranked according to their incomes in descending order in Table 4.2.

*Table 4.1   An example of a marriage market*

| Men | Income | Women | Income |
|---|---|---|---|
| David | 6 | Carole | 5 |
| John | 9 | Karen | 1 |
| Michael | 4 | Michelle | 3 |

*Table 4.2   Men's ranking*

| Men | Rank |
|---|---|
| John | 1 |
| David | 2 |
| Michael | 3 |

Then, in descending order, women are ranked according to their incomes in Table 4.3.

*Table 4.3   Women's ranking*

| Women | Rank |
|---|---|
| Carole | 1 |
| Michelle | 2 |
| Karen | 3 |

The only equilibrium in the marriage market is:

- John marries Carole
- David marries Michelle
- Michael marries Karen

It should be noted that other matches cannot be supported by market equilibrium. For example, consider Michelle dating Michael first and then meeting David. Because everyone cares only about wealth in their pursuit of happiness, Michelle will leave Michael for David. Michelle and David will marry because neither of them has a better option.

In this example, people care only about wealth. However, the same logic holds if we replace wealth with other desired marital partner characteristics such as height, physical appearance, education level or an aggregate index of overall attractiveness.[19] As simple as it is, this example illustrates that the marriage market is not romantic at all. Instead, it showcases the fundamental principle of economics for marriage. A person tends to marry someone who shares a similar level of attractiveness in aspects such as income, education, height or an aggregate of these characteristics.[20] In other words, 'assortative mating' is the rule of marriage.

This theoretical prediction is consistent with observed evidence. In the economics literature, empirical studies consistently show that a man tends to marry a woman with a similar level of education and income. Moreover, marital homogamy also applies to physical attractiveness. For example, Murstein and Christy (1976) examine a group of couples aged between 28 and 59 in the USA. They assess three aspects of the physical attractiveness of the men and women in the group: self-assessment, or how the men and women assess their own looks; spouse-assessment, or how one's spouse rates one's looks; and objective assessment, defined as the rating of five independent judges based on photos of the participants. According to their measurements of these three aspects, more attractive men tend to marry more attractive women. In addition, Terry and Macklin (1977) present a study in which participants were given a series of photographs. Each set of photos consisted of one man and four women. The participants were asked to guess which woman was the man's wife. The participants guessed correctly about 60 per cent of the time. If the guesses had been random, the participants would have been correct only 25 per cent of the time. The participants showed a higher percentage of correct answers based on the rule of assortative mating in terms of looks.

When an individual looks for a spouse, they usually have a number of criteria. Physical appearance is usually an important concern, but many factors are often considered relevant in marriage markets, such as income, intelligence, education and personality. For example, a woman will have more money to spend if she marries a richer husband. Thus some men show off their wealth in order to attract women. The following report is an illustration.[21]

> It is often said that money can't buy love. But trying telling that to a wealthy Indian man who splashed out £14,000 on a solid gold shirt in the hope it will attract female attention. Money-lender Datta Phuge 32, from Pimpri-Chinchwad, commissioned the shirt which took a team of 15 goldsmiths two weeks to make working 16 hours a day creating and weaving the gold

threads… 'I know I am not the best looking man in the world but surely no woman could fail to be dazzled by this shirt?' he explained.

Also, education is often a consideration in the marriage market. Although the starting salary for a more educated individual may not be much higher, a person's income growth is strongly positively correlated with education. A poor young man with more education may become rich in the future. Moreover, a couple spends leisure time together. An educated person is usually a better speaker and listener, making their partner happier. Further, there is an intergenerational effect. A child's educational attainment is often strongly related to their mother and father's educational attainment. So, if you find a better-educated wife/husband, your children will probably be more intelligent. Finally, personality also matters to happiness.

Chiappori et al. (2012) estimated the degree of substitutability between physical attractiveness and socioeconomic characteristics, using a large dataset in the USA. They find that: (i) for men, a 1 per cent salary increase can compensate for 1.3 units' increase in the body mass index (BMI); (ii) for women, an additional year of education can compensate for three units' increase in BMI.

People have to consider multiple traits in their future spouses, and may have different and complicated preferences. There is a saying that 'beauty is in the eye of beholder'. If 'beauty' literally meant physical appearance, this would probably be only partly or even only slightly true. If we modify the saying to 'attraction is in the eye of beholder', where attraction is defined as an aggregate index of attractiveness in the marriage market that includes income, intelligence, education and personality in addition to physical appearance, then the saying may hold much more truth. This is an important reason why the operation of a marriage market is highly complicated in reality. To better understand it, let us consider the following simple example of two men, John and Scott, and two women, Mary and Jennifer. We make the following assumptions:

- John thinks Mary is a more desirable marital partner for him.
- Scott thinks Jennifer is a more desirable marital partner for him.
- Mary thinks Scott is a more desirable marital partner for her.
- Jennifer thinks John is a more desirable marital partner for her.

These assumptions can be justified by various practical scenarios and considerations. For example, John thinks Mary is more attractive simply because she looks better than Jennifer. Mary prefers Scott because he is wealthier than John. Scott thinks Jennifer is a more desirable marital partner because she is more intelligent than Mary. Jennifer, however, loves a man with good looks, and John is better looking than Scott. Who will marry whom in this scenario? The answer can be analysed in the following way:

John asks Mary, 'Will you marry me?'
Mary answers, 'Wait'. Then Mary asks Scott, 'Will you marry me?'
Scott answers, 'Wait'. Then Scott asks Jennifer, 'Will you marry me?'
Jennifer answers, 'Wait'. Then Jennifer asks John, 'Will you marry me?'
John answers, 'Wait'. Then John asks Mary, 'Will you marry me?'

This marriage market clearly does not have equilibrium. If no one compromises, nobody will get married. This example illustrates that, although the rule of assortative mating may be clear, sometimes the marriage market may reach a stalemate. Therefore it may take a long time for people to find the right marital partners.

# PART II

# Vanity economics of sex and marriage

# 5.  Vanity in romance and marriage

## 5.1  WHY IS PHYSICAL APPEARANCE SO IMPORTANT IN MARRIAGE?

I visited London in the summer of 1997. At the entrance to a Tube station, I saw a poster enticing men to join a fitness club. The advertisement promoted short-term exercise training to reduce weight and build muscle. Although it targeted men, most of the poster space featured a picture of a beautiful woman in a sexy dress. A line of large text, the poster's only other content, made the following declaration: 'If you join the club, you will get a body like this!'

This advertisement illustrates two points highlighted in this book. First, as discussed in Chapter 4, assortative mating is a rule in the selection of marital partners. Second, physical appearance is of paramount importance in marriage markets. Indeed, among the numerous factors that matter to one's 'endowments' in the modern marriage market, the single most important factor determining one's overall attractiveness is physical appearance. (This is in sharp contrast with some traditional societies. Recall that, in traditional China, marriage was blind in the sense that the groom was allowed to see the bride's face for the first time only after the wedding.)

Appearance is particularly crucial for women. For example, Stannard (1971, p. 124) states:

> The ideal beauties teach women that their looks are a commodity to be bartered in exchange for a man, not only for food, clothing, and shelter, but for love. Women learn early that if you are unlovely, you are unloved. The homely girl prepares to be an old maid, because beauty is what makes a man fall in love ... A man's love is beauty deep. Beauty is man's only and sufficient reason for lusting, loving, and marrying a woman. Doesn't a man always say you're beautiful before he says I love you?

The question, then, is why are looks so important? The most direct answer is 'animal instinct'. Like other animals, humans have a natural instinct to select the most physically attractive member of the opposite sex available in mate selection and for sexual intercourse. This argument has a strong evolutionary basis. In the survival of the fittest, sexual selection is an important aspect of natural selection. Males tend to select females who are more fertile, and females prefer males who can produce healthier, more productive and more competitive offspring. 'Beauty' emerges in providing signals of these features. For example, those whose faces are more symmetrical tend to be healthier, holding other things constant. As a result, men and women with higher degrees of facial symmetry are often considered better looking. It is also often observed that men appreciate women who have large, firm, symmetrical breasts and fleshy, rounded buttocks. This observation can also be explained from an evolutionary perspective, as women with these features tend to have high fecundity. As for men, those who are taller and stronger are often considered better looking, as evolution dictates their ability to raise and protect offspring, be more productive at obtaining resources and be more competitive in combat.

After examining the importance of physical appearance or beauty from an evolutionary perspective, we now discuss the origins of beauty in the context of cultures and societies. While a beauty standard usually has a material foundation, it may not always be related to the 'survival of the gene'. That women with small feet were considered beautiful in traditional China, as discussed in Chapter 4, serves as a convenient example.

Moreover, a beauty standard may change over time as economic fundamentals change. In ancient Europe and the Wild West of the USA, the men who were tough, tall, muscular and strong were considered the best looking. The men of this type were most able to obtain resources, either through production when physical strength was the most important factor or through fights when the rule of law was not well established. For example, in a society where the major economic activity is hunting, bigger and stronger men can usually hunt more animals. Further, when the rule of law is not well established, bigger and stronger men can better protect themselves and their family members.

This argument is well illustrated by the following examples. The first is a story about the origin of the tie. A man usually wears a tie together with a suit when dressing formally. When and why did men begin to wear ties? There is no historical record that provides a definite answer. However, the following story appears interesting and convincing. It has been said that, in some tribes in ancient times, if a man killed a fierce animal such as a tiger or wolf, he would put a piece of the animal skin around his neck. He did so because it showed clearly that he had killed the animal and therefore signalled his strength and bravery. Over time, with the development of the modern economy, it was discovered that replacing the animal skin with silk cloth was both cheaper and more attractive. Further, with a better-established rule of law and other social developments, men had less of an incentive to show off their toughness. Consequently, the animal skins around their necks became the ties they wear today.

Another vivid example to illustrate the importance of men's toughness and physical strength is the 'duel'. Wikipedia provides the following description of a duel:[22]

> A duel is an arranged engagement in combat between two individuals, with matched weapons in accordance with agreed-upon rules. Duels in this form were chiefly practised in Early Modern Europe, with precedents in the medieval code of chivalry, and continued into the modern period (19th to early 20th centuries) especially among military officers. During the 17th and 18th centuries (and earlier), duels were mostly fought with swords (the rapier, later the smallsword, and finally the French foil), but beginning in the late 18th century and during the 19th century, duels were more commonly fought using pistols, but fencing and pistol duels continued to co-exist throughout the 19th century ... The duel was based on a code of honour. Duels were fought not so much to kill the opponent as to gain 'satisfaction', that is, to restore one's honour by demonstrating a willingness to risk one's life for it ... Most societies did not condemn duelling, and the victor of a duel was regarded not as a murderer but as a hero; in fact, his social status often increased. During the early Renaissance, duelling established the status of a respectable gentleman, and was an accepted manner to resolve disputes. Duelling in such societies was seen as an alternative to less regulated conflict ... According to Ariel Roth, during the reign of Henry IV, over 4,000 French aristocrats were killed in duels 'in an eighteen-year period' whilst a twenty-year period of Louis XIII's reign saw some eight thousand pardons for 'murders associated with duels'. Roth also notes that thousands of men in the Southern United States 'died protecting what they believed to be their honour'.

When the rule of law was not well established, a duel was an efficient way of resolving conflicts, serving as an alternative to other forms of conflict that were less regulated and larger in scale. Consider the example of a major dispute erupting between two large families or clans. When a dispute could not be resolved in a legal court because the rule of law was not well established, a natural impulse for both families and clans was to resolve the dispute through war. However, such a war could be very destructive. Over time, a social norm emerged in this kind of scenario that resulted in far fewer destructive consequences. For example, if a conflict emerged between two large families, each family could select a single member, such as its best fighter, and settle it via a duel between the two selected members without harming any other family members. This reasoning may explain the origin of the 'duel'.

The example of the 'duel' tells us that, not too long ago, and even in societies with relatively good legal systems and economic development, violence could be legal on some important occasions. On those occasions, men's toughness and physical strength were clearly of paramount importance. A taller, stronger and tougher man was better able to protect the interest and honour of his family and clan. Thus, not surprisingly, a social convention emerged that tall, strong and tough men are considered good-looking.

The rule of law has become much better established. In particular, duels are no longer legal. Modern economic developments have led to substantial changes in economic structures, so that the need for brain-power has increased and that for physical strength has decreased. For example, most high-paying professions such as doctor, lawyer, business-man, investment banker and senior government official require brains rather than strength. However, once a social norm is established, it does not disappear easily. The long-established social convention that tall and strong men are good looking persists to a large extent. Consequently, a man's height remains a major factor in determining his attractiveness in the marriage market. In contemporary times, vanity is the major concern in most people's pursuit of happiness. For a woman, the most important aspect of her vanity includes her husband's physical attractiveness, which to a large extent is determined by his height.

Moreover, the concern for men's physical appearance may even be far greater than before. As a general rule, when people become richer, their demand for luxury increases. For example, richer people develop more of an incentive to purchase Louis Vuitton handbags and BMW cars as vanity becomes more of a concern. Thus, by the same logic, when women become richer in both absolute and relative terms compared with men, their demand for beauty in a man, which is largely related to his height, increases substantially. Thus, although a man's height matters little in modern production activities so that it affects little his earnings, it is possibly even more important today than in ancient times, when it mattered greatly in obtaining material resources and protecting the family.

Although such changes are usually gradual, the beauty standard for men may change over time as economic fundamentals evolve into a knowledge-based economy. For example, while Tom Cruise and Leon-ardo DiCaprio are famous international movie stars and male sex symbols, Cruise is shorter than the average American white male, and DiCaprio is not muscular. In fact, the beauty standard for men and women seems to have converged. While many male celebrities are short, many female supermodels are quite tall. Such a convergence is illustrated by the different applications of the word 'beautiful'. 'Beautiful' was a word used only to describe females before the 1980s; men of the time would have considered it an insult. However, the word has been used to describe both American men and women since the 1990s.

We now turn to consider women's beauty. Early on I explained from an evolutionary perspective why women with symmetrical breasts and fleshy, rounded buttocks are considered good looking: the women with these features tend to have high fecundity. However, the fertility rate in most developed countries is currently low. In many countries and regions, a couple tends to have only one or two children and sometimes no child at all. What happens to the beauty standard for women in this case? When nature creates men and other animals, it also creates their incentive to have offspring through the operation of sexual desires. Thus, as long as men continue to have sexual desires, they will tend to consider women with symmetrical breasts and fleshy, rounded buttocks as sexy and hence beautiful. The very nature of men and women is hardwired into their beings.

However, when the fertility rate is low, the beauty standard for women is indeed diverse. For example, in the 1990s, many thin women with small breasts and skinny buttocks were considered beautiful. Kate Moss is such an example. Thus the media and mass culture can create a beauty standard. The attractiveness of blonde women is another example. While a woman's blonde hair does not increase her fecundity, many men prefer blonde hair on a potential spouse.

The bottom line is that once a beauty standard is formed, regardless of whether it has a material or evolutionary foundation, people tend to seek spouses who are strictly in line with that standard, as they are essentially seeking vanity. A person may obtain vanity from luxury items such as expensive bags and cars. However, much more vanity can usually be obtained from the 'quality' of a spouse than from any consumption good, no matter how luxurious. Physical appearance indicates a spouse's quality in terms of vanity, at least in most modern societies.

## 5.2 LOOKS VERSUS PERSONALITY

The previous section discussed the importance of physical attractiveness in marriage, which may stem from both animal/human instinct and vanity. To the extent that the importance of physical attractiveness is driven by human instinct, a person tends to pursue a sexual partner who is physically attractive. This implies that an individual may obtain more pleasure from having sex with a better-looking partner.

However, it is common knowledge that a person's interest in having sex with the same partner declines over time. This is particularly true of men, which can be explained by the theory of evolution as follows. After a male has had sex with a female continuously for a certain period (e.g. a couple of weeks) without using any contraceptive measures, the chance that the female is pregnant is very high. Thus, from the perspective of the survival of the fittest, it is a waste of energy and resources for the male to engage in additional sexual intercourse with that partner. (It should be noted that, during most of the history of human evolution, contraceptive measures neither existed nor presented a temptation.) Thus it is simply an evolutionary advantage for a male to lose sexual interest in a female after having had sex with her for a short period of time. From an evolutionary perspective, physical appearance is extremely important in sexual attraction at the very beginning of mating, but becomes increasingly less important over time and may quickly become completely unimportant.

It would be useful to introduce an economic theory to further analyse the issue. Recall that Chapter 2 presents a concept in economics known as 'utility', which refers to an index of happiness. In relation to this concept, we introduce another, known as 'marginal utility'. Marginal utility refers to a certain consumption good, and is defined as the amount of increase in utility (i.e. happiness) from the consumption of the last unit of the consumption good. (In more intuitive terms, we may refer to 'marginal utility' as 'instant happiness'.)

In economics, an important property of marginal utility is the 'law of diminishing marginal utility'. The more one consumes a certain commodity, the less utility (or pleasure/happiness) one obtains from the consumption of the last unit of the commodity. For example, if one feels very thirsty, drinking a cup of water will increase one's well-being (utility) tremendously. Drinking a second cup of water, however, will offer less utility, as one's thirstiness has decreased after drinking the first cup. A third cup of water will offer even less or zero utility.

The law of diminishing marginal utility is exemplified by an experience that a friend of mine had. He had never eaten potato chips before he went to the USA to study in the early 1990s. When he first tasted potato chips, he loved them. (His marginal utility from eating potato chips was very high.) He began buying them every time he went to a supermarket. As soon as he left the supermarket, he would open the bag, unwilling to wait until he arrived home. However, after he had lived in the USA for two years, his passion for potato chips disappeared. The law of diminishing marginal utility applied to his consumption of potato chips: his marginal utility from eating potato chips became very low after eating large amounts of them.

The law of diminishing marginal utility also applies to sex. Love and sex are very passionate at the beginning of a romantic relationship. This kind of passionate love is often reflected in popular love songs. Indeed, in most cultures and societies, passionate love is a constant theme of popular music. However, it is common knowledge that passionate sex does not last very long, usually no longer than three months. The familiar expression 'seven-year itch' literally means that a couple's sex life will become stale and boring after seven years of marriage or cohabitation. This saying was vividly portrayed and popularized by the movie of the same title starring Marilyn Monroe.

In fact, a couple's exciting sex life is usually much shorter than seven years. Although it varies across couples, it can be as short as a few months. The bottom line is that a couple's marginal utility (or instant happiness) from its sexual activities tends to decrease substantially over time. Further, as described earlier, this can be explained from an evolutionary perspective, particularly for men.

It has been argued that looks are important due to 'human nature'. Such human nature is clearly related to sexual activities. If sex becomes less important over time, then it is reasonable to argue that the importance of looks decreases considerably. Thus, if vanity is not taken into account, the importance of looks will decrease considerably in a marriage over time.

Here, we discuss the importance of personality in a marriage. An individual's happiness clearly depends on the way they are treated by their spouse. Plenty of media, movie and real-life examples indicate that an individual leads a happy and peaceful life if they have a spouse with a nice personality, and that the individual's life can be a living hell if they are treated badly by their spouse. Posner (1992, p. 435) described the modern norm of marriage as 'companionate marriage', in which the husband and wife are 'best friends, social and emotional intimates, and close companions'. Intimacy determines psychological well-being to a large extent. An individual with a better personality makes their spouse happier.

If vanity is not taken into account, we can draw the following conclusions. An individual's marginal utility from their spouse's physical appearance is very high at the beginning, but decreases quickly and drastically over time. The marginal utility an individual gains from their spouse's personality is moderate at the beginning, but remains stable and even increases over time. These conclusions are illustrated by Figure 5.1.

However, once we add the vanity of beauty into the picture, we may reach different conclusions. Recall Veblen's forceful argument that vanity matters greatly in conspicuous consumption. Nothing appears to be more

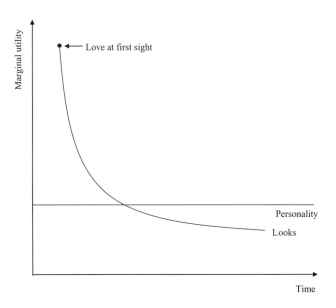

*Figure 5.1   When vanity is not considered*

conspicuous than the beauty of one's spouse as a reflection of their social status. When vanity is taken into account, looks may always be extremely important in a marital relationship. For example, marital partners often appear together and interact closely on social occasions. On such occasions, a person's social status is usually reflected more by their spouse's looks than the brand and quality of their watch or handbag. For example, a man with a beautiful wife is often described as a 'lucky guy'. Thus we may need to modify the preceding conclusion on physical appearance as follows. Where vanity is considered, the marginal utility an individual gains from their spouse's looks is always very high, and reaches its peak at the beginning of the marriage. As such, Figure 5.1 can be modified as Figure 5.2.

Indeed, empirical evidence shows that marriage is more stable for couples with similar physical attractiveness. For example, Peterson and Miller (1980) find that even elderly couples between 64 and 86 years of age show positive correlations of shared physical attractiveness. Maria Watkins and Arlen Price wrote an interesting study that was reported in the *Wisconsin State Journal* on 9 January 1983. (It is also described by Hatfield and Sprecher, 1986.) They surveyed 215 couples in California in 1974 and 1975. In particular, the couples were asked to take an IQ-type

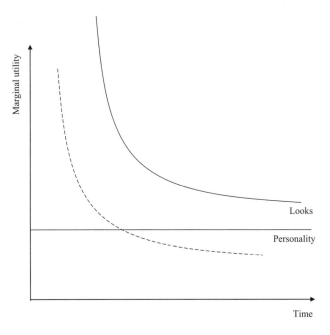

*Figure 5.2  When vanity is considered*

test on vocabulary and reasoning. They were asked about their height, which is an important aspect of beauty. In 1982, Watkins and Price managed to track down 167 of the original 215 couples. Of these couples, 52 had broken up and 111 had stayed together. The researchers found that those who had stayed together shared greater similarities in height. Further, they found that this beauty difference was more import-ant than the differences presented by the IQ tests in the dissolution of the marital/sexual relationships they examined.

Thus the analysis in this chapter implies that people may often downplay the importance of personality in their marriage decisions, although they may be fully aware that personality is most crucial for a harmonious relationship.

An observation is in order. In the preceding discussion, we implicitly assumed that personality can be perfectly ranked from good to bad. This is not entirely true. Sometimes the quality of a marriage match is bad simply because the couple's personalities do not complement each other. The following paragraph provides an example.[23]

Go Hyun-jung is a famous actress in South Korea. In 1989, she was a runner-up in the Miss Korea Pageant. In 1995, she starred in a highly popular television drama known as *Sandglass*, and her fame in Korea peaked. In May 1995, Hyun-jung married a rich young man named Chung Yong-jin, a grandson of Samsung founder Lee Byung-chull, a rich and powerful person in Korea. It was not a happy marriage. Whereas most of Yong-jin's family members spoke English or Spanish to show off their status, Hyun-jung had little education and spoke poor English. As a result, her husband's family often looked down on her. In November 2003, the couple took part in a nasty divorce.

# 6.  Vanity and virginity

## 6.1  THE IMPORTANCE OF FEMALE VIRGINITY

This chapter begins with four real-life stories.

**Story 1**[24]

1 January 2012 was the first day of the Year of the Dragon, and was supposed to be a very happy occasion for the Chinese. However, on this day, major Chinese newspapers and websites reported a tragic story. A beautiful 23-year-old bride named Shan-Shan Guo was seriously injured by her husband. Even more surprising, the couple were still in their honeymoon period, having been married for only four months. He attacked her with a kitchen knife with apparent hatred, seriously wounding her. Guo suffered more than 40 wounds, including some to her face and hands. Pictures of her taken before and after the attack were released, showing that the scars left on her face from the attack seriously damaged her physical appearance. Guo's husband had discovered that she had lost her virginity before their marriage, and burst out in fury at the thought that he was not his bride's sole sexual partner.

**Story 2**[25]

A similar story, perhaps even more tragic and shocking, occurred at one of the best universities in China. On the evening of 29 October 2008, Cheng-Li Fu, a 23-year-old male undergraduate student, burst into a classroom where a professor of the university, 43-year-old Chun-Ming Cheng, was delivering a lecture. Fu chopped Cheng in the neck with a meat cleaver, and Cheng died immediately. The tragedy stemmed from an obsession with female virginity. Not long before the incident occurred, Fu had dated a girl he fancied very much. When the girl began to accept Fu as her boyfriend, she confessed that she was not a virgin and had in fact lost her virginity to Cheng.

While the killing was premeditated, Fu had never planned to escape, and in this sense the event resembled a suicidal attack. Fu immediately surrendered himself to the police after the killing. He was given the death penalty with a two-year delay in implementation, which basically meant life imprisonment. (This is a rather unusual criminal penalty in China, as it effectively imposes a life sentence on the prisoner while carrying the implication that the prisoner deserves the death penalty.)

## Story 3[26]

Indian brides underwent 'virginity tests' (Monday, 13 July 2009): All the women who took part in a state-run mass wedding last month were forced to take the test, witnesses say. Several of the women later complained that they had found the exercise shameful and humiliating... In India, a bride's virginity is highly prized and pre-marital sex is frowned upon.

## Story 4[27]

A husband left his non-virgin bride (5 June 2008): A HUSBAND who found out his bride was not a VIRGIN when they wed has had the marriage ANNULLED. The man, who has not been identified, claims the bride said she had never had sex before. However, when he discovered that was a lie, he went to court to annul the marriage and a French judge agreed. The ruling ending the Muslim couple's union has stunned France. The decision also exposed the shame borne by some Muslim women who break long-held customs demanding proof of virginity on the wedding night.

These events vividly illustrate the importance of female virginity in many men's minds, even during an age of sexual freedom. Moreover, while these examples are somewhat extreme, the concern and even obsession with female virginity is fairly general. For example, in February 2012, a 38-year-old single female named Shi-you Tu set up a website in China that caught the attention of the whole nation. The website strongly promoted the idea of premarital female virginity. In particular, Tu uploaded a medical certificate of her virginity to the website. This very simple website turned Tu from a nobody into a national sensation overnight. Information about Tu can now be found on many major Chinese websites and Wikipedia.[28] This event was also reported in overseas media, and one report entitled 'Chinese woman sparks net craze with virgin website' reveals the following:[29]

'I have set up the website because I am quite successful in keeping my virginity for the past 38 years,' Tu told *Shanghai Daily*. 'But many young people have failed to do so. I saw on the TV news or websites that some are living tragic lives because they don't treasure their virginity.'... According to the *Shanghai Daily*, the social stigma can be such that some teenaged Chinese girls resort to buying fake hymens in a bid to 'restore' their virginity – at least cosmetically.

Why is female virginity so important to the men in some cultures and societies? We first search for answers from an evolutionary perspective. In ancient times, when the technology of DNA tests was unavailable, the requirement that the bride be a virgin ensured that the gene of the groom was passed to the next generation. Thus, to the extent that people valued the survival of their genes, there was real value to an unmarried young woman in the marriage market if she was a virgin. This argument is vividly illustrated by the birth controversy of Qin Shi Huang, the first Emperor of China, which is described by Wikipedia as follows:[30]

> According to the Records of the Grand Historian, written by Sima Qian during the next dynasty and avowedly hostile to Qin Shi Huang, the first emperor was not the actual son of King Zhuangxiang of Qin. By the time Lü Buwei introduced the dancing girl Zhao Ji ... to the future King Zhuangxiang of Qin, she was allegedly Lü Buwei's concubine and had already become pregnant by him. According to translations of the Annals of Lü Buwei the woman gave birth to the future emperor in the city of Handan in 259 BC, the first month of the 48th year of King Zhaoxiang of Qin. The idea that the emperor was an illegitimate child added to the negative view of him for most of the next 2000 years after his death.

In most ancient culture and societies, female virginity was considered important, and various virginity tests were implemented. Two main tests are still conducted. One involves directly inspecting whether a female's hymen has been broken. The other involves observing the woman's vaginal bleeding after the first time she has had intercourse, which stems from the assumption that if the hymen is 'intact', blood will surely result from the tearing of the hymen. (In the 1980s, when female virginity was still very important in China, there was a popular joke: the riddle of 'the wedding night'. The hint for the riddle was a famous American movie, and the answer is *First Blood*, a 1982 action thriller film directed by Ted Kotcheff and starring Sylvester Stallone.)

In modern societies, the material value of a bride's virginity before marriage, as measured by its assurance that the child the bride will carry will be her husband's, no longer exists to a large extent. For example, a DNA test can be conducted if a father is uncertain whether his child carries his gene. However, female virginity may continue to be of paramount importance in modern societies. From a husband's perspective, whether his wife is a virgin may matter greatly to his vanity of possessions.

Chapter 2 explained that possession is an important feature of vanity (i.e. 'vanity via possession'). For example, consider a man who drives a BMW in a poor country. This man will most likely feel happy and proud to possess the BMW, even if he works nearby and does not have many opportunities to drive it. However, if the BMW is owned by his friend or a relative, and if everyone knows this piece of information, then he will obtain much less happiness from driving it, even if his opportunities to drive it remain the same.

Consider Van Gogh's paintings. According to Wikipedia, two of Van Gogh's paintings, *Portrait of Dr. Gachet* and *Irises*, sold for more than US$200 million (modern equivalent). Why are some people willing to pay such a high price for a painting when it can be viewed free of charge on the Internet? Also, it is not that expensive to visit the Van Gogh Museum in Amsterdam, where hundreds of the artist's paintings are on display. Yet it is the feeling of possessing Van Gogh's paintings and experiencing that rare opportunity that makes people willing to pay such astronomical prices.

In these examples, the vanity a person obtains from driving a BMW or owning Van Gogh's paintings depends critically on the value the society places on these commodities. If the society rates a BMW or Van Gogh's paintings as being of high value, then the owner obtains a value of vanity from possessing them. By the same logic, if a society highly rates the value of female virginity, then a husband cares greatly whether his bride is a virgin.

In summary, the value to her husband of a woman's premarital virginity is manifested in two ways. First, it better ensures that the children the woman gives birth to carry her husband's genes. Second, the possession of his wife's virginity represents a man's honour, dignity and pride, all of which are defined as belonging to his vanity. The exact value of this vanity of possessions depends on the culture of the society, which can be haphazard and arbitrary. If many people thought that Van Gogh's *Starry Night* was worth $1 million, then its market price would be $1 million. If they thought the painting was worth $100 million, its market price would likewise reflect that. The logic is essentially the same for female virginity.

To the best of my knowledge, no empirical evidence or real-world stories show how the price of female virginity is determined or varies with demand factors. However, the famous story of 'tulip mania' in the economics and finance field may prove useful for our understanding. Wikipedia provides the following description:[31]

Tulip mania ... was a period in the Dutch Golden Age during which contract prices for bulbs of the recently introduced tulip reached extraordinarily high levels and then suddenly collapsed ...

The tulip was different from every other flower known to Europe at that time, with a saturated, intense petal color that no other plant exhibited. The appearance of the non pareil tulip as a status symbol at this time coincides with the rise of the newly independent country's trade fortunes. No longer the Spanish Netherlands, its economic resources could now be channeled into commerce and the country embarked on its Golden Age. Amsterdam merchants were at the centre of the lucrative East Indies trade, where a single voyage could yield profits of 400%. The new merchant class displayed and validated its success, primarily by erecting grand estates surrounded by flower gardens, and the plant that had pride of place was the sensational tulip. As a result, the flower rapidly became a coveted luxury item, and a profusion of varieties followed ...

The tulip was itself a conspirator in the supply-squeeze that fueled the speculation, in that it is grown from a bulb and that cannot be produced quickly. Normally it takes 7–12 years to grow a flowering bulb from seed; and while bulbs can produce both seeds and two or three bud clones, or offsets annually, the 'mother bulb' lasts only a few years ...

The point of this story is that tulips were rare bulbs that were hard to reproduce, meaning they were scarce in supply. Depending on people's 'beliefs', which might have fluctuated significantly due to random factors, the value of tulips varied considerably. The article continues:

The beautiful effects of the virus made the flamboyant and extravagant plants highly coveted, and because they were rare and desirable, they were expensive. Given that, it is not surprising growers named their new varieties with exalted titles. Many early forms were prefixed Admirael ('admiral'), often combined with the growers' names: Admirael van der Eijck, for example, was perhaps the most highly regarded of about fifty so named ...

According to Mackay, the growing popularity of tulips in the early 17th century caught the attention of the entire nation; 'the population, even to its lowest dregs, embarked in the tulip trade'. By 1635, a sale of 40 bulbs for 100,000 florins (also known as Dutch guilders) was recorded. By way of comparison, a ton of butter cost around 100 florins, a skilled laborer might earn 150 florins a year, and 'eight fat swine' cost 240 florins ... However ... In February 1637 ... the demand for tulips collapsed, and prices plummeted ...

This article shows that, if other people value tulips highly, possessing them substantially enhances the social status of the owners. However, if other people ignored the status role of tulips in social gatherings, the possession of tulips would matter little to the owners' vanity.

The logic of 'tulip mania' is the same as the logic surrounding the value that people put on female virginity. Men would not care whether their wives were virgins before marriage if other men did not care. The men care because other people care. In fact, the men would care even if the information were completely private. In the belief that all people care about it, a man might feel inferior if his wife were not a virgin before marriage. Thus, in an abstract sense, the 'mania of female virginity' is just like 'tulip mania', and the magnitude of fluctuation of the value placed on female virginity may be much greater than that of tulips. The exact value placed on female virginity depends on how the culture of the society values it.

## 6.2  THE MARKET FOR FEMALE VIRGINITY

This section begins with a question based on a hypothetical scenario. A penniless, slum-dwelling man visits a large shopping mall in downtown Bombay, India. Visitors to the mall that day are offered the chance to take part in a free lottery. The poor man wins the lottery's top prize: a brand-new Porsche. What will he do with the car? A consensus may be reached that he should sell it to purchase necessities that would improve his life. I believe very few readers would suggest that the man continue to live in absolute poverty and enjoy driving the Porsche (assuming he could learn the necessary driving skills quickly).

Allow me to ask a much more sensitive question. Consider a poor household in ancient times, comprising two parents with five children. The members of the household are so poor that they are near starvation. The eldest child of the family, a daughter, has recently come of age and is a virgin. The richest man in the village sees the daughter of the family, and makes her parents the following offer. If their daughter sleeps with him for one night, he will be willing to give them a sum of money equal to 20 years' worth of income. Should the parents accept the offer?

To answer this question, recall Cheung's (1972, p. 641) remark from Chapter 4: 'Just as dogs were raised to hunt for their masters before they were pets, so in early traditional China, children were raised as a source of income and a store of wealth.' Indeed, when people are very poor, survival is their everyday goal. Under such circumstances, children are often effectively 'sold' by their parents as assets in the marriage market. In fact, it is not rare for some poor parents to sell their children into slavery and prostitution, particularly during famines. In this case, if female virginity can be sold for a large sum of money, some poor households may have a sufficient incentive to do so.

In the preceding section, it was stated that a husband may value his wife's premarital virginity due to his vanity of possessions. The exact value of female virginity is often culture specific. When a culture assigns a large value of vanity to female virginity, a man may want to possess not only his wife's virginity but also the virginity of other women. Thus a market for female virginity may exist (for women other than one's own wife).

As in any market, the price of female virginity depends on its supply and demand. On the supply side, the number of female virgins simply depends on the population of a community and the proportion of female children, which can be considered more or less fixed. Thus the price of female virginity may depend mainly on its demand. There are two important demand factors. The first is income inequality. It has been widely observed that richer people have a greater demand for luxuries. A man usually has a great desire to marry a woman who is a virgin. However, his desire to 'consume' the virginity of a woman who will not be his wife is considerably weaker. Thus the man is willing to pay for the price of another woman's virginity only if the price is sufficiently low relative to his income. In a society in which female virginity can be bought and sold, the poor households are always the 'producers' and 'suppliers' of female virginity. Thus, when a large proportion of households are poor, the price of female virginity tends to be low. Moreover, if a large proportion of the households live in absolute poverty and are close to starvation, they have a significant incentive to exchange female virginity for food. In such societies, the price of female virginity is low for rich people, and hence the demand to have sex with female virgins tends to be large.

The cultural factor may also greatly affect the demand for purchasing female virginity, as it determines the magnitude of vanity for possessing a girl's virginity. If a man does not want a woman to have his children, then possessing her virginity does not yield him any material benefit. In this case, the possession of female virginity is purely a function of vanity. Thus the desire to purchase female virginity depends crucially on the magnitude of vanity a man can obtain from consuming it. If the culture of a society places a high value on female virginity, then the rich people in that society have a substantial desire to purchase it, which increases its price in the market equilibrium.

However, in some circumstances, the market for female virginity will not operate even when the demand for it is high. For example, if every man places an extremely high value on his wife's virginity, a woman who sells her virginity to a rich man will not be able to find a husband. Further, the parents of a household may feel that the loss of dignity they experienced from selling their daughter's virginity is much more significant compared with the money they received from selling it. In these scenarios, even very poor parents are unlikely to sell their daughter's virginity. Facing such situations, in a society with little social justice, some rich men may take the virginity of daughters from poor households by force. For example, in Europe there existed a custom of Droit du seigneur, a French term that can be translated as 'lord's right' or the 'law of the first night'.[32] In medieval times, the lord of an estate had the right to take the virginity of his serfs' maiden daughters on their wedding nights. The custom is portrayed in the Hollywood blockbuster *Braveheart*, a historical drama directed by and starring Mel Gibson. Such a custom provided medieval lords with the privilege of obtaining additional vanity through possessing the virginity of females other than their wives.

Let us now discuss the empirical evidence for the female virginity market. The following two articles show that some parents have incentives to sell their daughter's virginity. The first article describes a virginity transaction in India:[33]

> In a shocking revelation by a leading newspaper from Europe, a 13 year old virgin girl called Suli near the town of Bharatpur of Rajasthan is up for sale on a highway. The highest bidder is expected to fetch the family Rs.20,000 ... She belongs to the Bedia community that is well known for its caste-based prostitution. The normal going rate for a night starts from Rs.100 rate, however virgins are valued 'commodities' and a pretty face can fetch as much as Rs.40,000 ($1000). Suli is likely to fetch about $500 and is awaiting the highest bidder ... Suli not knowing what to expect is resigned to the fact that she will go with whoever pays the maximum money for her. The poor child probably does not even know what a sexual encounter may entail with an adult. She will probably suffer in silence and accept this as her fate in obedience to her seniors in the family. The sale goes on in other families too in the hamlet of 60 odd huts that are located near the new highway. Another family with five girls have four prostitutes and are ready to sell the youngest 13 year old called Nita, a virgin for at least Rs.40,000. At present someone has offered Rs.25,000. They will wait and they are in no hurry. If a foreigner is lured then their dollars are more welcome as they generally are willing to pay a higher price for the unblemished flower ...

The second story describes an event in the USA:[34]

> A Utah mom pleaded guilty to sending sexually explicit messages about her 13-year-old daughter to a man who she hoped would pay $10,000 for sex with the virgin teen, The Associated Press reports. The woman, 33, promised the would-be john that the girl would perform oral sex and other sexual acts in

exchange for the money, according to *The Salt Lake Tribune*. The mother, whose name is being withheld to protect the daughter's identity, also sent lewd photos of the adolescent to another man ... The mom faces 30 years behind bars. Prosecutors dropped two first-degree sex abuse charges against her, which carried possible life sentences, because she agreed to plead guilty to sexual exploitation of a minor.

In contemporary times, most women cannot be forced by their parents to sell their virginity, as their parents would be committing a serious crime. As illustrated by the preceding article, the Utah mother was seriously penalized by the state. However, particularly in developing countries, some women choose to sell their virginity due to the lure of material gains.

Two Chinese reports provide examples. The first is a statement released by Chinese police on 28 May 2012 that caught national attention.[35] It reveals that at least 20 female middle-school students were selling their virginity in Yongkang City of Zhejiang Province, and that the police arrested six persons. At the time of writing (October 2013), the event was still under police investigation. The second report makes the following statement:[36]

A teenage girl in China has offered up her virginity in exchange for an iPhone 4 ... The girl posted a photo of herself on the website alongside some personal information, and offered to sell her virginity to anyone who buys her the new Apple smartphone.

While the selling of female virginity is currently rare in developed countries, it continues to happen occasionally. A report entitled 'Teen reveals aftermath of selling her virginity online' reveals the following:[37]

Alina Percea, 18, sold her virginity online for around $13,000. Now she tells what it was like going through with a deal made virtually. Alina Percea, 18, needed to pay for a computing degree. So, perhaps in an attempt to prove how significant computing is in modern life, she auctioned her virginity on a German Web site. However, unlike Natalie Dylan, the American who claims to have secured bids of $3.7 million for the privilege of deflowering her (although no deeds seem either to have been signed or done), Alina did not attract offers in quite the same region. The best bid she managed to secure came in at £8,800, or just over $13,000. The bidder, a 45-year-old Italian man, came through at the last minute by doubling the leading price ...

Another report in 2012 entitled 'Brazilian woman sells virginity for $780,000' reveals the following:[38]

A 20-year-old Brazilian woman has sold her virginity for $780,000 in an online auction to a Japanese man known simply as Natsu. Catarina Migliorini's virginity auction was organized by Virgins Wanted, the project of Australian filmmaker Justin Sisely ... The auction had been live since Sept. 17, but until Wednesday – the last day of bidding – the highest bid for Migliorini had been $150,000. Natsu beat out five other high rollers who all bid in excess of $600,000 for the chance to bed the virgin. Under the rules of the auction, Migliorini will be examined by a gynecologist and will 'provide the winning bidder with medical evidence of her virginity.' ... The winning bidders must submit to a medical examination and a police check, and cannot be intoxicated during their time with the virgins. No kissing or fellatio is allowed, and although the virgins and the winners are to agree about the length and duration of the sex, 'the minimum consummation time is one hour,' the rules state ...

On the same website, a poll asking the following question was also conducted: 'Should someone be allowed to sell their virginity?' The results from anonymous voters were as follows.

- Yes, 65 percent (6861 votes)
- No, 28 percent (2958 votes)
- Maybe, 6 percent (669 votes)

This ballot indicates that many people are not against the market transaction of female virginity. However, it is against the morality of most people, who might not vote in the first place.

In summary, when the income gap between the rich and poor is large in a particular society, a market for female virginity may exist in which rich men purchase poor women's virginity and do not marry the poor women or have children with them. The market for female virginity is rare in the contemporary world, and most people feel that it is morally repulsive. However, it might not be rare under circumstances of extremely unequal income distribution and it may exist even today. It provides a vivid example about the role of 'vanity' in male–female relationships and shows that some people choose to pay a large sum of money for this complete vanity.

## 6.3 FEMALE VIRGINITY, ACQUAINTANCE RAPE AND THE SECLUSION OF WOMEN

Acquaintance rape is not rare. It poses a challenge to economists, who assume that people are rational. In the case of acquaintance rape, the rapist will be easily caught. Meanwhile, the penalty for rape is often very severe. Then, why do some people engage in acquaintance rape? How to design effective policies to prevent it? To answer these questions, consider the following report entitled 'Morocco outraged over suicide of girl who was forced to marry her rapist', published by the Associated Press on 14 March 2012:[39]

> The case of a 16-year-old girl who killed herself after she was forced to marry her rapist has spurred outrage among Morocco's internet activists and calls for changes to the country's laws. An online petition, a Facebook page and countless tweets expressed horror over the suicide of Amina Filali, who swallowed rat poison on Saturday to protest her marriage to the man who raped her a year earlier. Article 475 of the Moroccan penal code allows for the 'kidnapper' of a minor to marry his victim to escape prosecution, and it has been used to justify a traditional practice of making a rapist marry his victim to preserve the honour of the woman's family ... Abdelaziz Nouaydi, who runs the Adala Assocation for legal reform, said a judge can recommend marriage only in the case of agreement by the victim and both families ... he ... admitted that the family of the victim sometimes agrees out of fear that she won't be able to find a husband if it is known she was raped ... In many societies, the loss of a woman's virginity outside of wedlock is a huge stain of honour on the family. In many parts of the Middle East, there is a tradition whereby a rapist can escape prosecution if he marries his victim, thereby restoring her honour.

This article also features an interview with the girl's father, and continues as follows:

> According to the father's interview, the girl was accosted on the street and raped when she was 15, but it was two months before she told her parents. He said the court pushed the marriage, even though the perpetrator initially refused. He only consented when faced with prosecution. The penalty for rape is between five and 10 years in prison, but rises to 10 to 20 in the case of a minor. Filali said Amina complained to her mother that her husband was beating her repeatedly during the five months of marriage but that her mother counseled patience ...

This is not an isolated tragedy. Reports about honour killings in some Muslim countries have also been published, and offer details such as the following:[40]

In many Muslim societies, women are often held responsible and stigmatized for the violence against them. Rape continues to remain a taboo subject and in some cases women will face discrimination instead of the recognition and vital assistance they need after being abused. Some rape victims are murdered by relatives because the violation of a woman's chastity is viewed as an attack to their family's honour. Almost 50 percent of women in a study of female deaths in Alexandria, Egypt were killed by a relative after being raped. In a number of countries a rapist can go free under the penal code if he proposes to marry the victim. The United Nations Population Fund (UNFPA) estimates that the annual worldwide number of honour killing victims may be as high as 5,000 women. Even female relatives frequently support honour attacks as they too believe women are responsible for embodying a family's honour. As a result, rape victims remain silent and refrain from seeking help because they are afraid of repercussions and lack of justice. At the same time, there are other women who take their own lives, in what is known as 'honour suicides,' due to mounting family pressure and fear.

Rape is a major traumatic event for its victims. Its harm can go far beyond the physical. The psychological trauma that results from being raped often leads to lasting and devastating effects on victims.[41] In most countries, the penalty for rapists is rightly very severe. Thus there is a question that is not sufficiently addressed: why do some men engage in rape when they know they cannot escape? In particular, why does date rape (acquaintance rape) often take place?

Complete answers to these questions are beyond the scope of this book. This chapter attempts to provide an answer that is usually ignored, and addresses the issue from the perspective of female virginity.

In the following analysis, I consider a society in which the rule of law is well established, reflected in two aspects. First, if a man commits rape, he will most likely be caught and punished if the victim reports the event to the police. Second, the penalty for a rapist is very severe, with prison sentences reaching as long as 30 years. In this society, no man would commit rape if he believed his potential victim would report it to the police. One may be tempted to conclude that rape would never occur in such a society.

However, this conclusion can be totally wrong. In some circumstances, a rape victim will never report the case to police. Why? The key to the answer is female virginity, and the details of analysis are given as follows.

Let us consider three scenarios in which female virginity is not important, moderately important and extremely important for a woman from a marriage perspective. We consider the decisions made by a rape victim, who we assume was a virgin at the time of the rape, in the different scenarios. For now, we consider that a rape victim makes the decision only whether to report the rape to police. For the sake of presentation clarity, we use a numerical example, shown in Table 6.1.

*Table 6.1   A numerical example*

|  | Female virginity is not important | Female virginity is moderately important | Female virginity is extremely important |
|---|---|---|---|
| The victim's utility if she reports the rape | −10 | −300 | −900 |
| The victim's utility if she does not report the rape | −100 | −200 | −400 |

Recall that 'utility' refers to the happiness/unhappiness indices in economics. The victim's utility is always negative in all cases, since rape brings her misery. However, the degree of misery depends on the degree of importance of female virginity in the society. If female virginity is extremely important in the society, then a rape victim not only suffers the psychological trauma of the sexual violence but also faces a much worse marital prospect resulting from the loss of virginity. Thus, in this example, it is assumed that if the victim does not report the case to the police, her utility decreases from '−100' to '−200' to '−400' when the degree of importance of female virginity increases from 'not important' to 'moderately important' to 'extremely important'. However, if the victim reports the case to the police, then the rape may be known to many people, which would exacerbate the shame brought on her and her family if female virginity is important in the society. Therefore, in this example, it is assumed that if the victim reports the case to the police, her utility will become '−300' if female virginity is moderately important, and '−900' if female virginity is extremely important.

In this example, a rape victim will report the case to police only in the first scenario, where female virginity is not important. In this case, she will wish to see the rapist undergo a public trial and be severely punished, which will substantially lessen her pain and other psychological trauma resulting from the tragic event. However, even in a case where female virginity is moderately important, reporting the rape to the authorities will reveal to the public that the woman is no longer a virgin, which may bring shame (i.e. negative vanity) to her parents and future husband. In this case, although the woman suffers from a major psychological trauma from the rape, the social culture will introduce additional misery to her and her loved ones if she does not keep the information private. In a case where female virginity is extremely important, the woman's first or even only thought after the tragic event will be to not leak the information. Thus this analysis presents an important lesson for policy-makers and law enforcers: no matter how efficient the legal system is at catching rapists and how severe their penalty is, many women will continue to be raped if the rape cannot be prevented in the first place.

This reasoning may provide an explanation for the 'seclusion of women' culture observed in many parts of the world that exists even today. The following statement describes the culture in India:[42]

> A particularly interesting aspect of Indian family life is purdah (from the Hindi parda, literally, curtain), or the veiling and seclusion of women. In much of northern and central India, particularly in rural areas, Hindu and Muslim women follow complex rules of veiling the body and avoidance of public appearance ... Rules of Hindu and Muslim purdah differ in certain key ways, but female modesty and decorum as well as concepts of family honour are essential to the various forms of purdah. In most areas, purdah restrictions are stronger for women of high-status families.

Even worse, in societies where female virginity is extremely important, a man may use rape as a strategy to force an attractive woman to marry him. If a woman is raped in such a society, she usually does not report the case to police. As such, she faces a painful choice over whether to accept the rapist's proposal to marry him. If she does not marry the rapist, her future husband will consider her a 'damaged product'. In a society where female virginity is extremely important, the woman may not be able to find a husband, and even if she does, the husband may be of 'low quality' in various ways. In this case, she may make a decision that Westerners would find shocking: she may marry the rapist. In fact, in the 1970s and 1980s, such stories were often heard in China, and the 'raw rice is cooked' idiom was ascribed to the situation. The following two true stories provide vivid illustrations.

During China's 'cultural revolution' between 1966 and 1976, the majority of urban secondary-school graduates, over 17 million in total, were sent to rural areas.[43] There were several underlying reasons for this mass rustication movement. For example, it was Mao Zedong's belief that young urban intellectuals needed to receive 're-education' from poor peasants in China. Further, during the period, China's rural areas were better able to employ large labour forces than were cities.

Life for those urban secondary-school graduates was generally difficult. They worked hard, ate simple food merely to stay alive and usually lived in peasants' homes, which served as uncomfortable environments. Phoenix TV recently produced a series of programmes documenting the lives of some of these 'young urban intellectuals', most of whom went back to the cities after 1976.

One of these intellectuals, a woman originally from Beijing, stayed in the poor rural village of Shanxi, where she continues to live today. The TV programme goes something as follows: 'One day, a rumour spread among the villagers that a son of the household where the woman lived "entered into her room". The local police arrived quickly but found only the woman in the room.' Then the TV programme shows the woman, who was pointing at her husband and saying, 'He escaped.'

Then the woman told Phoenix TV that the police immediately interviewed her privately and told her:

> If you say he raped you, we will execute him immediately. Rape is a crime in China. However, if he raped you, it would be much more serious than a criminal offense. It would be a ruin of Chairman Mao's Great Strategy of the re-education of young urban intellectuals.

The woman said nothing. She ultimately married the man, and has stayed in the village ever since.

I must emphasize that there is no mention at all in the film of whether the woman was raped by her husband. Its main message is that, in that environment, a man would face the death penalty if he were accused of rape and did not have a clear alibi. However, rape sometimes occurs even in an environment where rapists face an extremely harsh penalty.[44] In each case, the criminals firmly expect that the victims will not report the rape to the authorities, and in some circumstances believe that their victims will choose to marry them.

In the 1980s, some began to doubt the obsession with female virginity. One Chinese newspaper challenged its existence by publishing a story about a village in Henan Province. A beautiful woman in the village was raped, and the rapist was quickly arrested and sentenced to prison. (Indeed, at the time, a rapist could rarely escape severe punishment as long as the woman reported the case to the authorities.) After six years in prison, the rapist was freed, quickly got married and began to live an ordinary life. However, the girl remained single, as no one in the village would marry her.

Similar stories discourage many rape victims from reporting cases of rape to police. In response, some rapists have taken the risk of trying to rape women whom they intended to marry. They were not concerned about the dire consequences of being arrested, as they believe that their victims would not report them. Moreover, the rape itself was not their only purpose. They continued to harass the victims, threatening to reveal the details of the rapes to their future husbands if they refused to marry them.

The above analysis has an important policy implication. Due to the tremendous heterogeneity of the importance of female virginity in different societies, the optimal criminal procedure of prosecuting a rape suspect should differ across countries. For example, a country where female virginity is not an issue may be very transparent in the legal procedure of a rape trial, where the suspect is often given the right of confronting the rape victim in open court. However, if a country that places a traditional value on female virginity tries to copy this legal procedure, then the rape victims of the country will not resort to the legal authority at all. Consequently, potential criminals will not be deterred by any severe punishment for rape officially stated since they predict that rape victims will not report them in the first place. In this case, sexual crimes may often occur. Therefore, in the countries where female virginity is valued highly, the protection of women's privacy must be given high priority in criminal trials, which is a necessary condition for the police to get the collaboration of rape victims in prosecuting rape suspects. This would not only substantially reduce the misery of rape victims, but also effectively deter the criminal acts of potential rapists.

Moreover, the obsession with female virginity is often an important source of gender inequality in cohabitation and marriage. In societies where female virginity is highly valued, once a woman loses her virginity to a man, she is considered a 'damaged product' by other men. Knowing this, the woman finds it difficult to leave her partner/spouse even if she is beaten frequently. This reasoning may provide an explanation for the social custom observed in many traditional societies that a wife must defer to her husband. For example, Broude (1994, p. 61) states:

> Wives are expected to exhibit one or another kind of deference behavior towards husbands in a number of cultures of the world ... a traditional Ganda wife of Uganda was required to wash her husband's feet every night. A rural Ukrainian wife always walks behind her spouse in public and always enters the house after him. Japanese husbands are the first to be served at a meal and the first to take a bath. They also have a special seat near the fire. Among the

Chuckchee of Siberia, the choicest food is given to the husband. And a traditional Rajput wife in India crouches on the floor with her sari over her face when her husband is present ...

# 7.   Sexual liberation

Chapter 6 discussed the importance of female virginity. A bride's virginity introduces a great deal of vanity of possession to her groom. However, premarital sex is currently widespread in most developed countries, and value is rarely placed on female virginity. Thus the following question must be addressed: why has sexual revolution swept across the world, particularly to developed countries? This chapter aims to provide answers to this question and some other related questions.

## 7.1   PREMARITAL SEX: WHAT ARE THE PRECONDITIONS?

This section tries to discover the preconditions for widespread premarital sex, and arrives at three conclusions. First, children are no longer the property of their parents. Second, the cost of engaging in sexual activities solely for pleasure is sufficiently low. Third, economic development has reached a level where most people are no longer concerned about survival issues. I address each of these three points in detail.

First, if parents make decisions about their children's marriages, they will tend to maximize their children's value in the marriage market. Female virginity is often an important determinant of this market value. Thus, to ensure that a girl's virginity is not sold (explicitly or implicitly) by her parents, particularly for a poor household, children cannot be considered the property of their parents by either law or social custom. As discussed in Chapter 4, children in ancient China were essentially the property of their parents, and parents usually tried to explore opportunities to seek pecuniary benefits in the marriage market for their children. In such a case, if a female virgin was 'sold' in the marriage market at a much higher bride price than a non-virgin, parents and particularly poor parents had a strong incentive to maintain their daughter's virginity, such as by restraining her activities outside the home.

A comprehensive study of why children are or are not their parents' property in different circumstances is beyond the scope of this book. I provide only some simple discussions. The relative economic power between parents and children may be the most important determinant of whether children are their parents' property. In an ancient agricultural society, if the parents owned land and their children had to depend on the land for survival, then the parents were able to control their children and make decisions about their marriages. In modern times, most young people do not work for firms controlled by their parents, implying that their parents cannot easily control their marriage decisions by economic means. Moreover, along with economic development, legal and social development may prevent parents from controlling their children's dating and marriage decisions. Therefore, in the contemporary world, particularly in developed countries, children are usually not their parents' property in the marriage market, and can make their own decisions about romance and marriage.

Second, for sexual liberation to take place, the cost of having sex solely for pleasure must be sufficiently low. In most traditional societies, non-marital sex is a taboo for women, and the main purpose of marriage is procreation. However, the purpose of premarital sex is pleasure only. Thus the cost and effectiveness of birth control is crucial in the decision to engage in premarital sex. If there is no effective way to prevent pregnancy, then premarital sex often results in unwanted births. As such, the women who engage in premarital sex usually have to raise the unwanted children alone, as the men often dodge such responsibilities. In this case, the negative consequences for women are not only the loss of their virginity, but also the liability for raising unwanted children, which substantially reduces the value of those women in the marriage market. Thus a necessary condition for widespread premarital sex is that an effective way of preventing unwanted births must be available. Moreover, another necessary condition is that, for ordinary people, the cost of birth control must be sufficiently low.

One may argue that people can engage in birth control through abortion. However, abortions often lead to serious damage to the health of the women involved. Even with the most modern medical technologies, the health costs associated with abortion can be very high. One US report provides a long list of the negative consequences of abortion:[45] it is the fifth leading cause of maternal death in the USA; it increases the risk of breast, cervical, ovarian and liver cancer; it may result in serious complications and infections; and it substantially increases the risk of premature birth in subsequent pregnancies.

The introduction of the 'pill' was an important ingredient in the sexual revolution experienced in the USA. Wikipedia offers the following observation:[46]

'The pill' provided many women a more affordable way to avoid pregnancy ... As part of the woman's quiet sexual revolution, pills gave women control over their future ... This was due in part to fears over illegitimate pregnancy and childbirth, and social (particularly religious) qualms about contraception, which was often seen to be 'messy' and unchristian. Modernization and secularization helped to change these attitudes ... The pill divorced contraception from the act of intercourse itself, making it more socially acceptable ... It was often said that with the invention of the pill, the women who took it had immediately been given a new freedom – the freedom to use their bodies as they saw fit, without having to worry about the burden of unwanted pregnancy.

The third precondition for sexual revolution is that a woman does not have to depend on a man for her survival and that of her children. For most people, and particularly young people, romance and sex are the major sources of happiness after basic survival needs are met. However, for most of human history, many people have struggled to obtain more resources, such as food, clothing and shelter for their own survival and that of their children. Meanwhile, women have clearly been the weaker sex, and they and their children have had to depend on men to satisfy their basic survival needs. However, this picture has drastically changed in recent decades. The struggle largely came to an end with the continuous economic development and technological progress achieved in developed countries, and women's economic dependence on men has been substantially reduced.

For example, Table 7.1 is taken from DeLong (2005) and presents estimates of the average income per person from ancient times to the present. It shows that economic growth, as measured by average income,

*Table 7.1   Indicators of economic growth*

| Year | GDP per person (in 2000 US dollars) |
|------|-------------------------------------|
| 5000 BC | 130 |
| 1000 BC | 160 |
| 1 AD | 135 |
| 1000 AD | 165 |
| 1500 AD | 175 |
| 1800 AD | 250 |
| 1900 AD | 850 |
| 1950 AD | 2030 |
| 1975 AD | 4640 |
| 2000 AD | 8175 |

was slow before 1800. After the Industrial Revolution, a secular increase in average income enormously enhanced the average living standard. The most important and obvious aspect of this enhancement is that most people are now no longer tortured by hunger or a lack of other basic living materials. Indeed, whereas in ancient times most people worked on farms to produce food, only a small fraction of the labour forces in developed countries today work in the agricultural sector.

Parallel to this phenomenal economic growth are major social development and demographical transitions. A key component of the demographic transitions is that a typical woman now has far fewer children than before. She therefore takes on far less of an economic burden in raising her children, meaning that her economic dependence on her husband for basic needs is much lower than before. Meanwhile, a social development has manifested itself, based on the substantial increase in society's and government's concern for the poor and the resultant large increase in social welfare expenditures. In developed countries, if a woman and her children are in poverty, the woman can obtain sufficient help from the government to ensure the survival of her family members.

When people's basic needs are satisfied, sex and romance become life priorities for a significant proportion of the population, both women and men. In particular, a woman may be willing to sacrifice her virginity for the pleasure of having a sex life when she meets a satisfactory partner. In situations where only a fraction of women engage in premarital sex, men still value female virginity in marriage. In this case, holding other things constant, a woman who loses her virginity may face worse prospects of finding a desirable husband. For example, she may have to marry a worse-looking man. However, some women may find it worthwhile to engage in premarital sex. The joy of sex in a premarital relationship may outweigh the decrease in the 'quality' of future marital partners.

## 7.2 FROM VIRGINITY TO SEXUAL LIBERATION: WHAT HAPPENED?

The previous section discussed the preconditions for sexual liberation. However, the satisfaction of these preconditions does not imply that a sexual revolution will necessarily occur. Indeed, human sexual desires can usually be restrained, and restraining sexual desires may not make people feel less happy. For example, we usually have no sexual desires at all when we focus on other activities (work or play) or even when watching an interesting television programme. In fact, many people feel happy without a sexual life. For example, in the early years at Oxford and Cambridge Universities, the teachers were not allowed to get married or have a sex life by other means.[47] However, many intellectuals competed for teaching positions at these two universities. Indeed, it appears that sexual desires can largely be inhibited when we do not have such thoughts, and this inhibition does not appear to result in misery.

Nevertheless, for the past half-century or so, a sexual revolution has spread quickly in many countries of the world, particularly in developed countries. As illustrated by popular movies, sex is currently an important aspect of a modern culture. In fact, many people consider a rich and colourful sex life the most important aspect of a happy life. Thus it is interesting to investigate the underlying forces of the social transition from a culture that emphasizes virginity to a culture of sexual promiscuity. This section suggests the following three factors. First, a significant delay in women's first marriage, associated with the demographical transition, induces sexual liberation. Second, much of the media has belittled premarital female virginity and glorified sexual promiscuity, which has considerably changed the culture in that men now obtain a great deal of vanity from sexual promiscuity and little vanity from having a virgin bride. Third, many women compete for 'high-quality' men in dating and romance, which can purely suit the women's vanity in the pre-marital period rather than be necessary from a marriage perspective. These points are elaborated as follows.

First, as is carefully described and explained in later chapters of this book, a demographic transition occurred in developed countries before expanding to most countries of the world. Two key components of this demographic transition were a substantial reduction of the fertility rate and a significant increase in the age at which women married for the first time. The preceding section shows that a substantial reduction in the fertility rate is a precondition for sexual liberation. Let us now consider the effect of the age at which a woman gets married for the first time on her decision to have premarital sex. When virginity is valued in the marriage market, the cost to a woman of engaging in premarital sex is that she will face worse prospects in finding a desirable husband. For example, she may have to marry a worse-looking man. However, there is a clear benefit to premarital sex: the woman can enjoy sex earlier. Moreover, the greater her age when she gets married, the greater the benefit of premarital sex. For example, if a woman gets married at the age of 16, premarital sex presents very little benefit. However, if she get marries at the age of 35, the benefit of premarital sex is considerable.

The age at which a woman marries for the first time has increased substantially in all the countries that have experienced sexual revolutions.

Table 7.2 shows the secular increase in marriage age that has taken place in the USA, for both men and women.[48]

*Table 7.2   Age of first marriage in the USA*

| Year | Males | Females |
| --- | --- | --- |
| 1950 | 22.8 | 20.3 |
| 1960 | 22.8 | 20.3 |
| 1970 | 23.2 | 20.8 |
| 1980 | 24.7 | 22.0 |
| 1990 | 26.1 | 23.9 |
| 2000 | 26.8 | 25.1 |
| 2010 | 28.2 | 26.1 |

This trend is shared by almost every developed country. In fact, in most of them, the average age at which a woman gets married for the first time appears to be higher than in the USA. Table 7.3 provides the relevant information for a number of European countries in 2008.[49]

There may be an intrinsic interactive relationship between marriage age and sexual revolutions. Simply put, people, particularly men, delay marriage to enjoy more sexual partners before they commit to one person. This delay in turn induces more women to find engaging in premarital sex worthwhile. The joy of sex in premarital relationships is more likely to outweigh the decrease in their future marital partner prospects as their marriage age increases.

Thus, in the contemporary world, if a man has a strong desire to have a virgin bride, he must often marry a woman who is far below the average first marriage age. For example, for the honour of the royal family, Prince Charles was advised by Lord Mountbatten to marry a virgin. This was an important reason for Charles choosing Diana as his bride. When Charles and Diana's engagement was officially announced on 24 February 1981, Charles was 32 and Diana was only 19.

The second important factor contributing to sexual revolutions is the media. Of course, promoting sexual liberation may not be the media's intention. However, in most developed countries with capitalist systems, the media industries (e.g. newspapers and television) are very competitive. Because sex is often a hot topic for audiences, it is widely covered in the media. Consequently, the media has played an important role in promoting sexual liberation. It can substantially influence people's sexual

*Vanity economics*

*Table 7.3   Age of first marriage in European countries*

| Country | Males | Females |
|---|---|---|
| Austria | 31.7 | 28.9 |
| Belgium | 30.7 | 28.5 |
| Denmark | 34.8 | 32.4 |
| Finland | 32.5 | 30.2 |
| France | 31.6 | 29.6 |
| Germany | 33.0 | 30.0 |
| Greece | 31.8 | 28.9 |
| Iceland | 34.3 | 32.1 |
| Ireland | 32.1 | 30.4 |
| Italy | 32.8 | 29.7 |
| Netherlands | 30.7 | 28.3 |
| Norway | 33.4 | 31.1 |
| Spain | 32.0 | 29.8 |
| Sweden | 35.1 | 32.5 |
| Switzerland | 31.4 | 29.1 |
| UK | 30.7 | 28.5 |

desires and behaviour in at least two ways. First, it stimulates sexual desires directly. Second, it makes people feel that sex is an important aspect of social status.

For example, pornography can enormously change a person's sexual appetite. Some people are so addicted to it that they need to seek help from psychologists. One may argue that pornography can be censored. However, sex has permeated many 'normal' forms of media such as television, which may significantly affect people's taste in sex. One article entitled 'Media May Prompt Teen Sex' elaborates as follows.[50]

Teens who see and hear a lot about sex in the media may be more than twice as likely to have early sexual intercourse as those who are rarely exposed to sexual content. A new study shows that 12- to 14-year-olds exposed to the most sexual content in movies, music, magazines, and on television were 2.2 times more likely to have had sexual intercourse when re-interviewed two years later than their peers who had a lighter sexual media diet ... Researchers measured each teen's sexual media diet by weighting the frequency of exposure to sexual content in four major types of media: TV, movies, music, and magazines. The teens were divided into five equal-sized groups ranging from the lowest exposure to the highest exposure. The results showed that exposure to sexual content at ages 12–14 increased the risk of early teen sex among white teenagers even after taking into account other factors known to reduce the likelihood of teen sex, such as parental disapproval of teen sex and getting good grades. In fact, each increase in grouping of sexual content media exposure increased the risk of teen sex by 30 percent. Researchers found that white teens with the highest level of sexual content exposure were 120 percent or 2.2 times more likely to have initiated sexual intercourse than those with the lowest levels of exposure to sexual content in the media...

The media often portrays men who 'get the girls' as winners in life, and those without active sex lives are often labelled 'pathetic losers'. The lyrics of recent song 'I Just Had Sex' serve as an illustration:[51]

> I just had sex, and it felt so good ... I just had sex. And I'll never go back to the not having sex ways of the past ... I just had sex, and my dreams came true. So if you've had sex in the last 30 minutes, then you're qualified to sing with me ...

Indeed, it appears that sex has become an important aspect of social status and self-esteem. In this modern cultural environment, both women and men are clearly motivated to lose their virginity and have an active sex life as early as possible, which would not only satisfy their sexual desires but also enhance their social status and self-esteem. For example, in an influential textbook, Masters et al. (1995, pp. 231–2) state:

> Much of the sexual behavior in early and mid-adolescence is motivated by expectations about gender-appropriate behavior and the related desire for peer acceptance rather than by actual sexual desire ... Teenagers 'prove' their masculinity or femininity in part by being seen going through the right heterosexual rituals or talking as though they have. A 16-year-old boy who's never had a girlfriend, who doesn't talk about the great centrefold in last month's *Playboy*, and who isn't seen wrapped around a female body in some starry-eyed 'close dancing' at a class party may be suspect. Similarly, a 16-year-old girl who doesn't date may be socially ostracized as an 'undesirable'; this negative labeling may be even stronger if she doesn't dress in a manner that is 'in' for girls at her high school or if she seems too aggressive in her nonsexual conduct.

In the early 1990s, when I was a graduate student at Brown University, I remember reading a textbook on human sexuality that quoted a teenage girl as saying, 'My sister lied that she was a virgin. Now I am lying I am not a virgin.'

One important question remains to be answered. How did a culture that prized female virginity transition to a culture of sexual promiscuity? Such a transition obviously did not occur overnight. When female virginity is held in esteem, the initial few women who engage in premarital sexual activity are looked down on by most of the men in the society. Who are these pioneering women of sexual liberation? While the long delay of marriage induces women to have premarital sex, the age at which a woman gets married is, after all, a choice. A woman may tell a man that she wishes to be married before having sex. However, she may not insist on it. Why?

The answers to these questions are precisely the third point of this section. Many women compete for 'high-quality' men in dating and romance, which could purely suit the women's vanity rather than their marriage prospects. For example, Masters et al. (1995, p. 239) state:

> Boys and girls also have different motivations for becoming sexually experi-enced. For teenage boys, sex is first and foremost a badge of manhood: becoming sexually experienced is part of the process of achieving maturity, acquiring social status, and regarding themselves as grown up. While teenage girls certainly also see sex as a marker of personal and social maturity (and thus desirable as a way of leaving childhood behind), girls are more likely than boys to view intercourse as a way of obtaining and solidifying love and commitment … . Teenage boys don't think about love and intimacy in the same romanticized way girls do: mirroring the practice of past decades, a boy is still more likely to give a girl a line in order to convince her to have sex, and one of the most common lines still in use is, 'If you loved me, you would'.

Consider the following hypothetical scenario of a high-school class. John is the most attractive boy in the class. He is tall, handsome, intelligent and the best football player. All the girls in the class liken him to Prince Charming and would love to go out with him. One day he asks out Jennifer, who considers it a dream come true. All the other girls in the class envy Jennifer, who holds John's hand in public with extreme pride and happiness. One day, Jennifer goes to John's home at a time when his parents are at work. John asks Jennifer to have sex with him. Jennifer knows that, if she says no, they will break up, and that, if she says yes, she will be John's girlfriend for some time. They are only in high school, and hence Jennifer knows that the chance that John will ultimately marry her is very slim. In such a scenario, the girl's answer depends on a comparison between a cost and a benefit. The cost is her decreased value in the marriage market that stems from the loss of her virginity to the boy. The benefit is the glory (or vanity) she obtains from holding the boy's hand in front of her classmates. Jennifer may also enjoy having sex with John. However, if we consider her to be a girl who does not care much for sex, this benefit is much smaller than the benefit of the vanity she would obtain from holding John's hand in public. Thus, if the benefit of the vanity Jennifer would obtain from having the best-quality boy-friend is greater than her concern for losing her virginity, she will definitely say yes. In Chapter 4, the competitive forces in the marriage market are considered. For example, even in contemporary India, dowries often account for 50 per cent of household wealth. The competitive forces in the 'dating market' can be equally strong. In the preceding example, Jennifer's virginity is the 'dowry' she must pay for the privilege of having John as her boyfriend. In other words, Jennifer would essentially trade her virginity for vanity.

From this hypothetical story, we can draw the general conclusion that, when the importance of female virginity decreases to a certain level, the girls who care most about vanity may choose to engage in premarital sex for the benefit of having a 'high-quality' boyfriend to show off in public. As a result of those girls' deviation from the social norm, the importance of premarital female virginity is undermined.[52] Consequently, it induces more girls to engage in premarital sex.

By a similar logic, we can also explain that cohabitation may stem from the competition for 'high-quality' men in the marriage market. Again, consider a hypothetical story. Michael is considered a very attractive, rich bachelor. He is dating two girls, named Carole and Karen. He is facing a difficult choice about whom to marry, as Carole and Karen are equally attractive. The women know that Michael dates both of them, and both consider him a rare opportunity. One day, Michael asks Carole to move in with him. They live in a conservative society, and Carole and Karen are still virgins. Carole knows that if she lives with Michael for some time and they do not get married, she will gain a bad reputation that will seriously hurt her prospects of getting married to another man. However, after thinking over Michael's proposal for a week, Carole agrees for the following reasons. Doing so automatically removes Karen from the competition. In fact, her cohabitation with Michael breaks Karen's heart. Carole predicts that if she moves in with Michael, there is an 80 per cent chance that he will ask her to marry him. If she says no, the chance will fall to 50 per cent or even lower.

Although this story is hypothetical, it is commonplace. Widespread cohabitation exists even in societies where female virginity is valued. By essentially the same logic, we may also explain why some women accept unprotected sex simply because their boyfriends do not like to use condoms, which may result in unwanted pregnancy during cohabitation and subsequently out-of-wedlock births. Moreover, the competition for 'high-quality' men, which manifests a fear of losing current boyfriends, may induce women to do something that is very harmful to them.

The following is a true story that shocked Hong Kong.[53] From 2001 to 2008, Gillian Chung was one of the most popular entertainment stars in the region. She developed a very successful career portraying 'squeaky-clean' characters. In 2008, naked photos and a sex video involving her and secret boyfriend Edison Chen, also a popular entertainment star in Hong Kong, were released online. The photos and video were stolen from Chen's computer when he sent it in for repair. Chung apologized to the public for being 'naive and silly'. In a later interview, she was asked why she had agreed to have the video/photos taken in the first place. Chung replied that she agreed because she was afraid of losing Chen if she said no.

## 7.3   THE AGE OF SEXUAL REVOLUTION: WHY GET MARRIED? WHO GETS MARRIED?

This section begins with a story about famous NBA star Wilt Chamberlain, whom Wikipedia describes as follows:[54]

> In 1991, Chamberlain wrote his second autobiography, *A View from Above*. There, the lifelong bachelor claimed he had sex with 20,000 women. For this to be true, he would have had to have had sex with 1.37 women per day from the age of 15 up until the year of the autobiography's publishing, a rate of over nine women a week ... Chamberlain defended himself: 'I was just doing what was natural – chasing good-looking ladies, whoever they were and wherever they were available' and pointed out he never started a relationship with a married woman.

From an evolutionary perspective, a male may want to have multiple female sexual partners to produce more offspring and thereby increase his genetic fitness.[55] This argument clearly also applies to humans. Although nowadays most sexual activities are not suited for procreation, the taste for a variety of sexual partners may be naturally hardwired into the minds of men, who may consider marriage a bad deal from the perspective of sexual enjoyment. In a modern culture, it also appears that sex is an important aspect of social status and self-esteem or vanity. Those who do not have an active sex life are often labelled 'pathetic losers'. Also, a man often 'counts numbers' when it comes to the women he has sex with. This kind of culture is clearly an important reason behind Wilt Chamberlain boasting of his 20 000 sexual partners.

A natural question thus arises: in the age of sexual liberation, why are men willing to get married? While a man could have sex with other women after getting married, his wife and commitment to the marriage constrain him from engaging in extramarital affairs. The cultures of the USA and many other developed countries are strongly influenced by Christianity. In these cultures, committing adultery is a disgrace. However, if a man stays single, he will never commit adultery (by its very definition) no matter how promiscuous he is. By a similar logic, in the above quotation, Wilt Chamberlain emphasized that he never had a relationship with a married woman.

This section answers the preceding question in several steps. For ease of exposition, we divide men roughly into two types: 'desirable' and 'undesirable'. A desirable man is tall, handsome and rich, all characteristics desired by women. In contrast, an undesirable man may be short, ugly and poor. The first argument that this section makes is that, even at the age of sexual liberation, it may still be hard for an undesirable man to find a sexual partner. If he is lucky enough to do so, he may have a strong incentive to marry her. (For simplicity's sake, prostitution is not considered in this chapter, but is carefully discussed in Chapter 8.)

Sexual liberation does not mean that a man and woman mate randomly. Instead, for premarital sex to take place, a man and woman must first fall in love. However, 'falling in love' is difficult and costly for a significant proportion of the population for the following reason. In the modern world, the media shapes our mentality to make everyone believe that only 'desirable' men and women are lovable. By this standard, most men and women have 'deficiencies'. Thus an 'undesirable' man and woman must overcome significant psychological obstacles to accept and fall in love with each other. In other words, it can be difficult and costly for a significant proportion of the population to have sexual relationships. Once such a relationship is established, it makes sense for the people involved to maintain it, which induces them to get married.

One may ask whether only 'undesirable' men want to get married. This is not the case. Although a man may want to have multiple sexual partners from an evolutionary perspective, the same is not true of women, for whom having multiple sexual partners does not increase their 'fitness' *per se*. Therefore marriage is attractive to a woman when she finds a desirable man. This explains why it is usually the woman who pushes, forces and often begs the man to get married during a cohabitating relationship.

Let us now consider a scenario in which a 'desirable' man and woman are dating. If the man insists on not getting married, the desirable woman is tempted to marry another man. If the desirable man keeps missing opportunities to marry a desirable woman, his advancing age will make him increasingly less desirable, meaning that his potential marital partner will be increasingly less desirable according to the theory of assortative mating. Thus, to ensure he will marry a desirable woman, a desirable man will not delay marriage indefinitely.

The main benefits of marriage stem from the vanity of possessing a spouse, children and family, which confers on an individual social status and self-esteem. The vanity of possessions is first manifested in the vanity of possessing a spouse, followed by the vanity of possessing children and family. Thus, even a man with a tendency to be sexual promiscuous may be induced to get married. Some men may be willing to trade promiscuity for vanity.[56]

Because the 'quality' of one's spouse is their most important indicator of self-esteem and social status, people are usually extremely choosy when it comes to mate selection. If an individual has a 'desirable' spouse, they may be the envy of their peers, and hence achieve a great level of happiness from possessing the spouse. However, if an individual has a 'low-quality' spouse, they may be ridiculed as being 'pathetic' or a 'loser' by their peers, and hence may experience a great deal of unhappiness. In contrast, if an individual does not have a spouse, their peers may not ridicule them because it is always possible that they will obtain a 'high-quality' spouse. By this reasoning, we may predict that 'desirable' men and women are more likely to get married, and tend to marry earlier than 'undesirable' men and women.

Furthermore, there are other benefits to marriage, suggested in the economics and sociology literature.[57] Both sociologists and economists argue that, when a household is formed, it is efficient to have a division of labour within the family. It usually takes the form of the husband working in the marketplace and the wife spending more time and effort looking after the children and doing household chores. Such a division of labour is more efficient when the couple has more children, the gender earnings gap between men and women is higher, and the economy is less developed so that material consumption is a greater concern.

Once a couple has a child, the household's activities fundamentally change. A woman must often endure much pain and fatigue during pregnancy. The amount of time and effort required to take care of and educate a child is enormous. An infant must be fed frequently. The mother usually wants to feed her infant with her own milk, which is healthier for the infant than animal milk. The side effect is that the mother must be at home frequently, usually four to five times a day during working hours, which seriously disrupts her work. Hence the usual decision is to engage in division of labour, as mentioned earlier.

The second major economic benefit of marriage is the sharing of the consumption goods in a household. Such items include televisions, refrigerators, computers, cars and, perhaps most importantly, a house/apartment. These household goods can be enjoyed by one household member without hurting the consumption of the spouse. For this reason, economists consider these as a household's public goods (Public goods are those goods that are neither excludable nor rivalled: 'consumption rivalry' occurs when one person's use of the good reduces the benefits available to others.) Moreover, marriage allows a man and woman to pool their incomes, enabling them to purchase more luxurious residences, cars and other status-enhancing material goods. Their joint possession of such goods further increases their happiness through the channel of vanity.

One may argue that there may be some kind of 'crowding-out effect' in the use of household goods. For example, if a woman drives a car to work, her spouse cannot use it if they work at different locations. This may be true to a certain extent. However, in many cases, vanity is the main purpose of a major household good. Housing is such an example. Further, in big cities such as Hong Kong, where public transportation is convenient, many people seldom drive their cars. In Hong Kong, if a person owns a luxurious car, it is mainly to show off their social status. In this case, whether one person or a couple owns a luxurious car makes no difference.

In an abstract sense, the economics literature considers children a 'public good' for their parents. Indeed, the most important 'public goods' for a couple are usually their children. In a later chapter, I discuss in detail how children add enormously to the vanity of their parents. A man and a woman must get married to share the presence of their children.

However, many people are not married, which implies that marriage has a cost. What are the negative aspects of marriage? First, when two people live together continuously for a period of time, they usually experience some conflicts. For those who are not good at dealing with interpersonal conflicts, marriage may result in a great deal of mental suffering. They may choose not to get married to achieve the peace of mind they value.

Moreover, in contrast to the commodities market, the marriage market has a unique feature that may significantly delay marriage for many people. This unique feature is the emotion associated with the process of finding a marital partner. If a person shops for an apple, computer or car, there is no emotion at all in the purchasing process, and it takes little time to settle the purchase. However, for many people, the participation in the marriage market itself may be associated with a loss of dignity.

Let me illustrate this point with a story. In 2011, an influential woman in China made a provocative statement that a woman's best gift to her future husband is her virginity. This statement fostered much debate among the Chinese on the Internet and other media. In particular, Phoenix TV organized a debate on the issue.[58] During the debate, a woman argued that the statement was absurd because it essentially treated women as objects. However, every participant (man or woman) in the marriage market is treated as an object by other participants and their family members and friends. They are carefully scrutinized according to important aspects such as height, income and education, and unimportant aspects such as accent, hand size and anything else one may possibly imagine. In particular, as long as a person participates in the marriage market, they will have to face the cruel reality that every single deficiency they have will be highlighted and discussed by their potential marital partners and their family members and friends. Such 'naked' scrutiny is particularly blatant in meetings whose purpose is clearly for singles to mingle, such as 'speed-dating' events. This explains why most people, particularly 'high-quality' singles, are reluctant to participate in speed dating or Internet dating.

Indeed, dating can be an unpleasant or even painful experience for many people. The following lyrics to a song entitled 'The Rose' serve as an illustration.

> Some say love it is a river that drowns the tender reed; some say love it is a razor that leaves your soul to bleed; some say love it is a hunger, an endless aching need. I say love it is a flower, and you it's only seed. It's the heart afraid of breaking that never learns to dance. It's the dream afraid of waking that never takes the chance. It's the one who won't be taken who cannot seem to give. And the soul afraid of dying that never learns to live. When the night has been too lonely and the road has been too long. And you think that love is only for the lucky and the strong. Just remember in the winter far beneath the bitter snows lies the seed that with the sun's love, in the spring, becomes the rose.

Thus, despite the benefits of marriage, many people choose to delay it or stay single. A cost–benefit analysis for this decision may centre on vanity. If one is single, the most awkward occasions may involve the most important days for family gatherings. In China, this is exemplified by Chinese New Year.[59] Facing embarrassment, some women choose the strategy of 'renting boyfriends' with whom they can spend the New Year. In fact, this business has become so popular in recent years that it is advertised by large e-company taobao.com, China's eBay counterpart.[60]

A recent BBC News report describes a story of a Chinese lady in Beijing.[61] While she has a good job and enjoys her life, she has one problem: she is 38 and still single. One important reason for her to work in Beijing is that it is far from the city where her parents live. Her parents are ashamed that she remains unmarried, and they do not take her to their social gatherings.

Finally, sexual liberation changed the pronounced social custom of marriage proposal. In traditional societies, men proposed marriage to women by lowering themselves to one knee. In the contemporary world, it is often the women who beg their boyfriends to marry them if they are in a cohabitation relationship. This has happened to many people I know. For example, I have a close friend who has lived with her current husband for several years before their marriage. While she had long wished to marry him, he became angry whenever she mentioned the idea. Thus she needed to work out careful strategies to urge her boyfriend to marry her without irritating him. He finally agreed. I attended their wedding. She cried throughout the wedding, and many of the attendees also cried, as they all knew the true reason for her tears.

# 8.  Prostitution and commercial sex

## 8.1  THE DEMAND FACTORS

Prostitution and commercial sex have existed throughout human history. Wikipedia makes the following observation.[62]

> Ancient Greek men believed that refined prostitution was necessary for pleasure and different classes of prostitutes were available. Hetaera, educated and intelligent companions, were for intellectual as well as physical pleasure. Peripatetic prostitutes solicited business on the streets, whereas temple or consecrated prostitutes charged a higher price. In Corinth, a port city, on the Aegean Sea, the temple held a thousand consecrated prostitutes.

This section discusses the demand factors for commercial sex. Why do some men visit prostitutes? The most obvious reasons are their sex drives and desire for a variety for sexual partners. Moreover, as discussed in Chapter 7, such motivations are reinforced by a culture that promotes sexual promiscuity. Even in the age of sexual liberation, many men find that the most effective way to maximize their number of sexual partners is to have sex with prostitutes.[63]

As for any other commodity, the demand for commercial sex is determined by income and prices. When the income inequality between the rich and poor is high, the prices of commercial sex are often low for the rich. Consequently, the demand for prostitution tends to be high. For example, in the 1990s, there was a huge disparity in per capita income between Hong Kong and Mainland China.[64] The spirit of capitalism was introduced into the country[65] and the degree of economic integration between Hong Kong and Mainland China was high.[66] Moreover, China experienced a sudden dramatic degeneration of traditional morality after 1990. All these factors created an environment that led many Chinese women to become prostitutes. As a result of the aforementioned large income inequality, Hong Kong residents, even those from the low-income class, find it cheap and easy to engage in sexual affairs in Mainland China. One survey conducted by the Chinese University of Hong Kong in 1997 interviewed a random sample of 1200 Hong Kong men who crossed the Hong Kong/Chinese Mainland border over the course of one day, and

18.3 per cent of the interviewees admitted to having a sexual affair while in China.[67]

Moreover, when income inequality between the rich and poor is high, commercial sex often takes various forms. For example, in the 1990s, many Hong Kong men had one wife in Hong Kong and another in Mainland China simultaneously. They found that having two wives could further enhance their vanity of possession. The problem was so serious that it even attracted the attention of the Western media.[68] For example, on 21 June 1999, the *Wall Street Journal* published an article entitled 'It's Doubtful China Meant One Country, Two Sets of Families – A Mainland Village Prospers as Hong Kong Men Keep House with No. 2 Wife'. In particular, it states:

> The cross-border sex industry has flourished on the Mainland side of the high economic wall that separates Hong Kong and China. But this is 'concubine village,' as its many visitors from Hong Kong have dubbed it. It has a curious veneer of domesticity over its hard core. Money is at the root of it all. The former British colony has returned to Chinese sovereignty, but it retains many of its former institutions and remains a bastion of capitalism. Economic disparities with China are still huge. Hong Kong men find that even modest salaries can cover a flat and a mistress for weekend getaways or longer when business takes them north. Some end up maintaining a family on each side of the border. The women gain material comfort and maybe their only chance of escape to a better life across the border. That hope has grown with a recent legal ruling that could affect thousands of illegitimate children in China. 'All the girls want Hong Kong boyfriends,' says S. Kwan, a middle-aged business-man. He boasts about his romance with a 20-year-old who he says is 'prettier than Gong Li,' the star of the Oscar-nominated film 'Farewell, My Concubine.' The businessmen says he rented an apartment for $120 a month for his consort, and the $240 or so he gives her every month is about a tenth of what a Hong Kong mistress demands.[69]

If we infer men's sexual tastes from an evolutionary perspective, then the 'No. 2 wife' problem is puzzling. First, to maximize the chance that his genes will survive, a male should try to have sex with as many females as possible. Thus a man should gain more sexual satisfaction from a large number of prostitutes rather than from a single 'No. 2 wife'. Second, as indicated in the preceding article, most Hong Kong men who keep a 'No. 2 wife' in Shenzhen visit these women at weekends only. Thus they need to pay these women for the time they spend waiting for the men to return to China, even when no sexual services are being provided. The solution to this puzzle lies in the central theme of this book: vanity. If a man has a 'No. 2 wife', he harbours a strong sense of possession that offers him much more vanity compared with that obtained from having sex with prostitutes.

With China's continuous development, cross-border sexual affairs between Hong Kong and China have been declining. However, this has become increasingly widespread within China. One *New York Times* report in 2011 observes the following:[70]

> Jian, a 42-year-old property developer in the booming southern metropolis of Shenzhen, had acquired just about everything men of his socioeconomic ilk covet: a Mercedes-Benz, a sprawling antique jade collection and a lavishly appointed duplex for his wife and daughter. It was only natural then, he said, that two years ago he took up another costly pastime: a beguiling 20-year-old art major whose affections run him about $6,100 a month. Jian, who asked that his full name be withheld lest it endanger his 20-year marriage, cavorts with his young coed in a secret apartment he owns, a price he willingly pays for the modern equivalent of a concubine. 'Keeping a mistress is just like playing golf,' he said. 'Both are expensive hobbies'.

Moreover, there is one form of commercial sex that is directly related to the fantasy (i.e. an extreme form of vanity) created by the media: having sex with female stars in the entertainment industry.

For example, Hong Kong supermodel Xiong Dailin told the local media that she received an invitation to have meals with an unidentified rich man who offered her HK$3 million for three days of her time.[71] Further, one anonymous man who was reportedly in his fifties put a nearly naked photo of a female Hong Kong star on the Internet, claiming to have had sex with the woman and paid her HK$1 million to spend one night with him.[72] The photo was taken from behind the woman's back, which implies that he took it secretly.

Why are wealthy Hong Kong men willing to pay prices 1000 times higher to sleep with a female star rather than a prostitute? Vanity may be the only answer. Sleeping with a female star gives them a sense of triumph, a sense of success that cannot be achieved by ordinary people in Hong Kong. In fact, with the opening up of China, many ordinary prostitutes are as good-looking as many female stars. However, the stars are often in high demand because they represent a 'famous brand'. At this point, we may recall the example that a man bought an Louis Vuitton handbag at a price 60 times higher than that of a bag without a brand, despite realizing that there was no difference in quality between the two bags.

Why did the rich man secretly take the photo of the female star? He did so for the 'bragging right' it afforded him in front of his friends and acquaintances. This bragging right had a multiplier effect on the vanity he obtained from sleeping with the female star. Moreover, his act of putting the photo in the Internet allowed many more people to find out about it, making the multiplier effect much larger.

Such reports have also been made in India. One article entitled 'The Bollywood Actress As Prostitute' offers the following details.[73]

> In India, there's long been a myth of the 'Bollywood Brothel' – the idea that all actresses are available for a price. The arrest of several Tollywood film stars has brought the idea back into circulation. In the past year, 3 minor actresses have been busted for prostitution. It seems, at first glance, like an odd throwback to the days when the stage was a marginal profession and respectable women didn't pursue it. But, as XX's Amana Fontanella-Khan writes, it's still very much a complicated issue in India. Demand for sex with actresses is very high in India ... In addition, many a prostitute will pass herself off as an actress – with some pimps going so far as to make fake film ads to add to the womens' cachet and acting price ...

Another article, entitled 'The Myth of the Bollywood Actress Turned Hooker', offers a further example.[74]

> After two Indian actresses were arrested for prostitution last month, an old story has made new rounds: actresses are available for the right price. It starts with demand. Men love the Bollywood actresses ... If that's not enough, pimps have connections in the film industry. They buy ad space and create advertisements for fake films to glorify an 'actress' in the lead role. The movie never gets made, of course, but the sex worker's rate goes up a whole lot of rupees.

These stories ultimately indicate that vanity matters greatly in prostitution.

Finally, there is an example of Thailand, a country with a reputation for sex tourism. To cater to the demands of those who prefer stable long-term relationships with some emotional attachment, the country facilitates 'wife-rental' businesses. One report states the following (with a modification of its grammatical error):[75]

> In Thailand 'rented wife' is a very common phenomenon, a lot of foreigners to Thailand will find local black girl as Tenants wife, also known as the 'Black Pearl'. They not only provided a wife's 'basic' responsibility, but also served as tour guides. Foreigners provided money, shelter ... The time limits of a 'rented wife' varied, ranging from as short as a few days to several months long or even a lifetime.

## 8.2  PROSTITUTION: THE SUPPLY FACTORS

This section begins with an example that has nothing to do with prostitution at the superficial level. The following is a sensational story that unfolded in China and was then reported by the media of other countries. On 3 June 2011, a Sky News article entitled 'A Chinese teenager has sold his kidney to buy an iPad and iPhone' reported the following:[76]

> Xiao Zheng, from the country's south-eastern Anhui province, is believed to have met a broker on the internet who said he could help him sell his kidney for £1,825 (Yuan 20,000). He is said to have left a message for the middleman saying: 'I want to buy an iPad 2.' Zheng then travelled to Chenzhou in central Hunan province, where he had his right kidney removed in a hospital. His mother told reporters she was devastated by the news. She said: 'When my son came home he had a laptop computer and an Apple phone. Where did all that money come from? Only when he could bear it no longer did he tell us. He said, "Mum, I sold my kidney." When I heard it I felt like the sky was crashing down on our family.'

In English, a prostitute is sometimes described as a woman who sells her body. In Chinese and Japanese, a sex worker is often described as a woman who sells her flesh. In the preceding example, the young man indeed sold his flesh and a part of his body at a low price.

Many studies on prostitution and commercial sex have been conducted. This book adds one important yet largely neglected element into the literature: vanity. In modern times, commercial sex may to a large extent stem from envy and the vanity of possessing material goods. This is in contrast to ancient times, in which women were usually forced into prostitution due to hunger and absolute poverty. In fact, a large proportion of sex workers are considered 'high-quality' candidates in the marriage market in terms of looks and education. For example, in Moldova, a majority of students (about 70 per cent) reportedly 'think that work in the sex industry abroad is a good way to earn money' (UNICEF, 2002, p. 27).

A woman will choose to be a sex worker only if the benefit is greater than the cost. There are often two factors that induce women to become prostitutes. First, it provides more money compared with other occupations. Second, the increased income substantially increases one's happiness. Whether a prostitute can earn substantially more than her peers in other occupations depends on her potential patrons' willingness to pay. This condition is more likely to be satisfied if her patrons are rich. Thus, holding other things constant, prostitution tends to be more rampant in a society with higher income inequality. By the same logic, in a world in which a large income disparity exists across countries, some women in poor countries have strong incentives to work in rich countries if they choose to be sex workers.

Under what conditions does an increased income substantially increase one's happiness? Absolute poverty is one answer. If a person is on the verge of starvation, she will do almost anything to earn money to save her life. However, in most countries today, hunger or absolute poverty are not the main reasons inducing women to become prostitutes. Another answer is drug addiction. A drug addict usually cannot control her urge to take drugs, which are typically expensive. As drug addicts are often unproductive in other occupations, a woman's addiction may induce her to become a prostitute. However, this answer explains the behaviour of only a small proportion of prostitutes, most of whom are not addicted to drugs.

This book suggests that the main answer to the question is vanity. The vanity of possessing more material goods is often strong in a modern consumerist society. Stark and Fan (2011a) show that this urge can be considerably reinforced by interpersonal comparisons or envy. For example, a person can feel particularly miserable because they lack a fashionable item such as an iPhone if many of their peers have them.

To understand why, we need briefly to review some of the game-theory concepts developed by John Nash. He became famous all over the world not so much because he received 1994 Nobel Prize in Economics as because of the 2001 Oscars-winning biographical drama film, *A Beautiful Mind*, which is based on Nash's real-life stories.

Nash was a first-rate mathematician. For example, he was a strong contender for the Fields Medal, although he narrowly missed getting it. (The Fields Medal is the most prestigious award in mathematics.) However, possibly to his own surprise, Nash's contribution to economics is greater, and possibly much greater, than his contribution to mathematics. Nash made two important contributions in this field. The first is the non-cooperative game theory, described below. The other is the bargaining theory, which will be described in later chapters.

Now I briefly describe non-cooperative game theory. (The movie, *A Beautiful Mind*, described a little bit about it, but unfortunately it misses the main point, and can be misleading.) A crucial concept of game theory is the Nash equilibrium, which was, of course, developed by John Nash. There are two key components in a Nash equilibrium: strategy and belief. A Nash equilibrium exists if no player has the incentive to deviate from their strategy given the belief that the other players will not deviate

(Nash, 1950a). As this definition is fairly abstract, some examples are necessary to improve understanding.

The 'prisoner's dilemma' is a famous example of the Nash equilibrium concept. Two criminal suspects ('A' and 'B') are caught by the police. The police know that they have committed a serious crime, but have little evidence to prove it in court. The two suspects could be sentenced to 10 years in prison if sufficient evidence exists to prove that they committed the crime. A confession would be sufficient evidence. However, given the little evidence obtained, the court can send each criminal to prison for only one year. The police concoct the following strategy to induce the two suspects to confess. The suspects are separated into two different rooms, and the police visit each of them, offering the following deal: if one testifies in court for the prosecution of the other and the other does not, the one who testifies will go free and the other will be sentenced to prison for 10 years. If both choose to testify, each will receive an eight-year sentence. The prisoner's dilemma is summarized in Table 8.1.

*Table 8.1　An example of the 'prisoner's dilemma'*

| A/B | Loyal | Betray |
| --- | --- | --- |
| Loyal | $(-1, -1)$ | $(-10, 0)$ |
| Betray | $(0, -10)$ | $(-8, -8)$ |

What should the two suspects do? The conceptual framework of the Nash equilibrium provides a useful way of answering this question. In this example, the only Nash equilibrium is that both of the suspects betray their partners, consequently sentencing themselves to prison for eight years. In particular, note that (Loyal, Loyal) is not a Nash equilibrium. If one prisoner believes the other is 'loyal', then it is in his interest to confess to ensure his own freedom.

Although this example illustrates the concept, it is so simple that it does not necessarily require the Nash equilibrium to arrive at the correct answer. The following example illustrates the usefulness of the Nash equilibrium in a more complicated scenario. It is also a famous example of game-theory teaching known as 'the battle of the sexes'. A man and woman are deciding between two evening events: a boxing match and a ballet recital. The man would prefer the former and the woman the latter. However, as they are in love, the most important outcome is that they be together. Table 8.2 illustrates the game.

*Table 8.2 An example of 'the battle of the sexes'*

| Man/Woman | Boxing | Ballet |
|---|---|---|
| Boxing | (2, 1) | (–1, –1) |
| Ballet | (–5, –5) | (1, 2) |

This simple example assumes that in 'playing the game' the man and woman cannot communicate. It nicely illustrates the two crucial components of the Nash equilibrium concept: strategy and belief. First, in the belief that a dating couple will watch the boxing match, they will choose to watch boxing. In other words, the belief is a self-fulfilling prophecy. Second, in the belief that a dating couple will watch the ballet recital, they will choose to watch ballet, marking another self-fulfilling prophecy. In other words, there are two Nash equilibria in this example: (Boxing, Boxing) and (Ballet, Ballet).

Stark and Fan (2011a) show that envy may result in a competition among women that induces them to become prostitutes, and that this competition makes everyone worse off. We present the idea in an analytical framework of the Nash equilibrium. Our main ideas can be illustrated by the following examples. Consider two women named Jennifer and Karen, respectively. To highlight the essentials, we assume that the women are identical in all respects. Their sources of happiness or unhappiness are income and vanity from consumption. They can choose one of two occupations: secretary or prostitute. While prostitution is a very unpleasant job, it offers a higher income than the job of a secretary.[77] I now use the numerical example in Table 8.3 to illustrate the main point.

*Table 8.3 Example 1*

| Jennifer/Karen | Secretary | Prostitute |
|---|---|---|
| Secretary | 5, 5 | 1, 6 |
| Prostitute | 6, 1 | 3, 3 |

This example presents the following intuition. If both Jennifer and Karen take regular jobs (secretary), they both receive ordinary pay and are happy with it. Specifically, this example assumes that the happiness index (or utility) is 5 for both Jennifer and Karen. However, if Jennifer works as a secretary but Karen works as a prostitute, Karen's income may be much higher than Jennifer's. As a result, Karen can purchase many fancy items (such as an iPhone) that Jennifer cannot afford. In a culture of consumerism, this interpersonal comparison gives Karen a sense of superiority over Jennifer, who is made to feel miserable. In this case, Karen's happiness index is 6 while Jennifer's utility is 1.

The story would be essentially the same (with opposite results) if Karen worked as a secretary and Jennifer as a prostitute. In this case, Karen's happiness index is 1 while Jennifer's utility is 6. The worst case is that both of them work as prostitutes. In this case, they work in a degraded occupation, which brings mental suffering that cannot be fully compensated by the higher earnings. Also, since they earn the same amount of income, neither of them can show off to the other. Thus the utility is 3 for both Jennifer and Karen.

However, it is not hard to see that the only equilibrium outcome is that both Jennifer and Karen work as prostitutes. In particular, note that it is not an equilibrium outcome that both of them work as a secretary. For example, if Jennifer sees that Karen works as a secretary, then Jennifer will be induced to work as a prostitute, which will increase her happiness index from '5' to '6'. On the other hand, if both of them work as prostitutes, then neither of them will have any incentive to make a change. In this case, if either of them switches to work as a secretary, her utility will decrease from '3' to '1'. Thus they are essentially caught in a 'prisoner's dilemma'. Their incomes are higher than before, but they are less happy because prostitution is a lousy job.

We now modify this example slightly by assuming that if one woman works as a prostitute while the other does not, their happiness (or utility) indexes are (4, 1) rather than (6, 1). In other words, in this modified example, a person feels equally miserable if she has less consumption goods than others. However, the example is modified in that if one has more consumption goods than others, she is not so happy about it as the last example (4 < 6). The game table is thus modified as shown in Table 8.4.

*Table 8.4   Example 2*

| Jennifer/Karen | Secretary | Prostitute |
|---|---|---|
| Secretary | 5, 5 | 1, 4 |
| Prostitute | 4, 1 | 3, 3 |

In this modified example, there are now two equilibria: (1) both of the women work as secretaries; and (2) both of the women work as prostitutes. First, in the belief that the other chooses to be a secretary, both Jennifer and Karen will choose to be secretaries. In other words, this belief is a self-fulfilling prophecy. Second, in the belief that the other chooses to be a prostitute, both Jennifer and Karen will choose to be prostitutes, indicating another self-fulfilling prophecy. In this example, the culture of the society matters greatly in the women's strategic choices. If the culture led people to believe that they cared only about money, the women would indeed work as prostitutes, which would in turn reinforce the belief of the culture. In economics, this is known as 'coordination failure'. It is a 'coordination failure' in this example because both Jennifer and Karen are happier in the equilibrium of working as secretaries than in the equilibrium of working as prostitutes. However, once the bad equilibrium of working as prostitutes is reached, they will get stuck in it. Note that the reality is far more complicated than this example, in that there are a large number of women rather than two women. It is obviously very difficult for a large number of women to make the right coordination.

The preceding theoretical analysis is empirically supported by a CNN report entitled 'Girls sell sex in Hong Kong to earn shopping money'.[78]

> She doesn't want to be identified, except by her nickname 'Sze,' and she has a secret past. Her father doesn't know what she did as a 16-year-old, and she hopes he never finds out … 'My first customer was an ordinary man in his 40s. We skipped the dinner part and went straight to the guest house for sex,' Sze recalled. 'Actually, I was a bit scared, but I knew this was the only way I could get money. This customer wasn't bad, though. We just had sex, he paid, and then he left. I thought this was easy money, and that's why I continued doing this kind of thing.' … Sze said she (worked as a prostitute) because many of her classmates at an all-girls school were doing it. She says she became jealous when she saw the designer clothes, bags and cosmetics they bought with the money they earned through compensated dating. Sze wanted the same for herself, so her classmates introduced her to Internet chat forums where she met male customers.

Let us now discuss the cost of being a prostitute. From a woman's perspective, choosing the occupation of prostitution has a 'fixed cost' and a 'variable cost'. The fixed cost stems from the stigma of being a prostitute. Even if no one in her social circles (neighbours, friends, casual acquaintances) were to find out, a woman may still carry emotional scars inflicted by her history as a prostitute. The variable cost increases with the number of customers. For example, the more men a woman has sex with, the more likely she is to catch sexually transmitted diseases (STDs). However, in most developed countries where condoms are carefully used in the sex industry, STDs are not a major threat to sex workers. Thus the variable cost tends to be low. In contrast, a woman's revenue from prostitution is strongly related to her number of customers. Thus one would find being a prostitute worthwhile only if the demand for prostitution were sufficiently strong, namely, if there were a large number of potential customers.

This reasoning also suggests that both the quality and quantity of prostitutes depend a great deal on government regulations. If a government could effectively reduce the number of customers by increasing the cost of visiting a prostitute, more women would find the revenue from prostitution to be smaller than the fixed cost. 'Higher-quality' women are usually more likely to exit the sex market because they tend to have better alternatives. Moreover, if fewer women became prostitutes and the quality of prostitutes decreased, fewer men would look to prostitutes for sex. Thus a government could effectively reduce or even eliminate prostitution if it were determined to do so. This provides an explanation for why prostitution thrives in some places of the world and hardly exists in others.

## 8.3 'COMPENSATED DATING'

In their best-selling book, *SuperFreakonomics*, Levitt and Dubner (2009) tell the story of a prostitute in Chicago named Alice. After receiving $200 from her first customer, Alice had the following reflection (p. 50): 'I'd been giving it away for years, and the fact that someone was going to give me even a penny – well, that was shocking.' Levitt and Dubner (2009) continue: 'She was immediately tempted to take up prostitution full-time, but she was worried her family and friends would find out. So she eased into it, booking mainly out-of-town liaisons.'

In the era of sexual liberation, men and women in the dating market usually interact purely for sexual pleasure and romance. In a 'pure' dating relationship, a man and woman use each other's bodies to satisfy their sexual and vanity needs. If we consider this relationship as a kind of mutual exchange, it can be described in economics terms as 'barter'. In 'barter', some goods and/or services are directly exchanged for other goods and/or services without the involvement of money. As analysed earlier, a man and woman involved in such a trade should have a similar attractiveness, for example in terms of their looks, age and height. For such a 'barter' to take place, a condition must be satisfied: the 'double coincidence of wants', a term coined by William Stanley Jevons.

For example, Wikipedia has the following description:[79]

> The coincidence of wants problem (often 'double coincidence of wants') is an important category of transaction costs that impose severe limitations on economies lacking money and thus dominated by barter or other in-kind transactions. The problem is caused by the improbability of the wants, needs or events that cause or motivate a transaction occurring at the same time and the same place. One example is the bar musician who is 'paid' with liquor or food, items which his landlord will not accept as rent payment, when the musician would rather have a month's shelter. If, instead, the musician's landlord were to throw a party and desire music for it, hiring the musician to play it by offering the month's rent in exchange, a double coincidence of wants would exist.

In the case of bartering for sex and romance, the double coincidence of wants mainly indicates that the man and woman involved have a similar level of attractiveness in terms of their looks. However, this is not enough. As discussed earlier, an ugly man and woman may prefer to be alone rather than date each other to avoid negative vanity. Dating may also be an unpleasant or even painful experience for many people, particularly those who lack social skills or good looks.

'Compensated dating' emerges against such a background. Wikipedia offers the following definition:[80]

> 'compensated dating' ... is a practice which originated in Japan where older men give money and/or luxury gifts to attractive women for their companionship and, possibly, for sexual favors. The female participants range from primarily school-aged girls to housewives.

Many participants argue that compensated dating is not prostitution, and some academic researchers concur.[81] In fact, as Levitt and Dubner (2009) describe, Alice effectively considered many of her customers as boyfriends, and she and one of them often behaved like romantic couples.

The practice of compensated dating has spread to many East Asian countries. As indicated by the direct interpretation of its name, compensated dating is a practice located between dating and prostitution. Thus one may argue that it is a modified form of dating. For example, the CNN report described in the previous section also interviewed a social worker in Hong Kong, and reported:

> 'Most girls who engage in compensated dating don't view themselves as prostitutes,' said social worker Chiu Tak-Choi. 'For the girls, they don't think

so because they think they can quit anytime. The girls – even though they post their details on the Internet – they think they can quit. Even if they encounter the guys, if he is not good-looking, she can quit and say "I don't do it." They think they have a lot of power to control whether they do it or not, so they think of it very differently from prostitution.'

In fact, compensated dating recently even found its way to the USA. For example, Wikipedia offers the following description:[82]

In a report by the Huffington Post in 2011 the arrangements involve females signing up for free at websites using their college email address as 'sugar baby' candidates. Male clients, referred to as 'sugar daddies', join such websites with paid subscriptions as proof of their financial means. The individuals would be matched online followed up by in person meetings at a public place, i.e. a coffee shop. The candidates may decide whether the other candidate is suitable, i.e. age, physique, personality etc. If the candidate is desirable the next date may involve sex. The Huffington Post reported compensation of about $500 per night. Ideal 'sugar babies' appear to be college students below the 'mid twenties'.

Compensated dating may improve the welfare of both the male buyers and female sellers of sex and romance. It allows male patrons to enjoy sex and romance with the kind of girls it would be impossible for them to find in the 'pure' romance/dating market. Moreover, if they desired to have sex with many girls and obtained vanity from doing so, compensated dating would be a convenient channel. Moreover, if the female participants had already lost their virginity to their boyfriends or previous boyfriends, they would have little to lose if the compensated dating were operating in a low-crime environment such as Japan. In fact, if they wanted to consume more material goods (driven by vanity), it would offer an easy way for them to obtain the cash needed for such purchases.

With some modifications, one economic theory could help us better understand the theoretical foundations of compensated dating. The principle of 'compensating wage differentials'[83] postulates that, in efficient labour markets, a higher wage is offered to compensate for jobs with 'bad' characteristics such as risk, dirtiness, low social status, unpleasantness or other undesirable attributes. Jobs with 'good' characteristics such as ease, cleanliness, pleasantness or other desirable attributes pay a lower wage.

The 'compensating wage differential' principle is one of the oldest insights in economics. In his classic book *The Wealth of Nations*, which established the foundations of modern economics, Adam Smith (1776, ch. 10) states that 'the wages of labour vary with the ease or hardship, the cleanliness or dirtiness, the honourableness or dishonourableness of the employment'. He assigns a particularly important role of honour or humiliation to the principle of a compensating wage differential:

> Honour makes a great part of the reward of all honourable professions. In point of pecuniary gain, all things considered, they are generally under-compensated ... The most detestable of all employment, that of public executioner, is, in proportion to the quantity of work done, better paid than any common trade whatever.

In the dating market, if a woman dated a man who had desirable height, handsomeness, intelligence and youth characteristics, she would be happy to have sex with him without receiving any money in return. As described in Chapter 7, such a romantic relationship can bring a woman a great deal of vanity (or honour) and sexual pleasure. However, if a woman were to date a man who had undesirable characteristics, she would be willing to have sex with him only if she received a sufficient amount of money to compensate for her unwillingness to do so, and the foregone opportunity of having sex with a man with more pleasant characteristics and its associated vanity. This financial compensation is the fee charged by a woman in the 'compensated dating' relationship.

Of course, there is another cost of 'compensated dating', which may be paid by the both parties to the relationship. This is the moral cost, and this cost is higher in a society with more religious influences. Therefore 'compensated dating' is common in Japan and some other East Asian countries, but is rare in the USA and European countries.

# 9. Extramarital affairs

## 9.1 WHY ARE EXTRAMARITAL AFFAIRS A CONCERN? WHY DO THEY OCCUR SO OFTEN?

Wikipedia describes the plot of *Indecent Proposal*, a 1993 Hollywood film starring Robert Redford, Demi Moore and Woody Harrelson, as follows:[84]

> High school sweethearts David (Woody Harrelson) and Diana Murphy (Demi Moore) are a married couple who travel to Las Vegas, hoping they can win enough money to finance David's fantasy real estate project. They place their money on red in roulette and lose. After gambling away all of their savings, they encounter billionaire John Gage (Robert Redford). Gage is attracted to Diana and offers David one million dollars to spend a night with her. After a difficult night, David and Diana decide to accept the offer, and a contract is signed the next day ... Although he had hoped to forget the whole incident, David grows increasingly insecure about his relationship with Diana ... Because of this tension on their relationship, David and Diana separate ...

This story illustrates that spousal fidelity is central to the quality of a marriage and hence marital stability. In *Indecent Proposal*, David and Diana receive an enormous amount of money in exchange for Diana spending one night with another man. From the perspective of 'pure' economics, this sounds like a 'dream deal': the revenue is astronomical and the cost is virtually zero. However, the deal courts disaster for David and Diana, who deeply regret their participation.

Why is extramarital sex so harmful to a marriage? This question can be answered in two ways. First, it can be understood from an evolutionary perspective. If a female has multiple sexual partners, a lack of effective contraception makes knowing the father of her offspring difficult. Effective contraception has been largely unavailable throughout evolutionary history. Thus a man is 'hardwired' by nature to be strongly averse to his wife's extramarital sex. In fact, a similar form of this aversion can be found in many animals with relatively well-developed intelligence. For example, the dominant male gorilla of a group of gorillas has the exclusive right to have sex with all the females in the group. He does not tolerate any other sexual relationships occurring within the group, even in cases where the number of females is large and he does not have enough energy to satisfy their sexual needs. From this reasoning, we can see that the value of a woman's fidelity after marriage is similar to that of her premarital virginity. It also explains why, in most cultures and societies, and particularly in traditional societies, a woman's infidelity is considered a much more serious breach of a marriage than a man's infidelity.

Second, the importance of spousal fidelity can be explained from the perspective of vanity. In most modern households, where the rights of men and women are relatively equal, neither the husband nor the wife accepts their spouse's extramarital affairs. Why? The answer is simply vanity – the vanity of possessing the spouse, and particularly the exclusive possession of the spouse's body during sexual intercourse. In Veblen's theory of conspicuous consumption, vanity is manifested in the possession of material goods such as delicate handbags and luxurious cars. In this book, a person's vanity is reflected in the possession of their spouse. An individual would feel that this sense of possession were seriously damaged or even ruined if their spouse engaged in an extramarital affair. In analogous terms, suppose a man possesses a luxurious car, say a Rolls-Royce. He seldom drives it, but possessing it fills him with pride. One day he is informed that another man has secretly taken the car for joy rides a number of times. Although the car is not damaged, the man is furious after hearing this piece of information. The knowledge that another man drove the Rolls-Royce damages his sense of possessing it and the associated vanity. In parallel to this analysis, consider a man who is married to a very attractive woman. He is proud of his wife, who is often praised by his friends. One day he discovers that his wife has had sex with another man. Although his wife promises that she will not engage in another extramarital affair, the man is furious. From that point on, he is no longer proud to have an attractive wife, or able to feel happy when his friends compliment him at social gatherings on being a 'lucky' guy.

These examples show why spousal fidelity is an essential ingredient of marital quality. However, extramarital affairs are common. They often occupy media headlines, exemplified by the extramarital affairs of Bill Clinton and Tiger Woods. On 19 February 2010, Woods openly apologized on television for engaging in extramarital affairs, making a very honest confession about his motivation: 'I felt that I had worked hard my entire life and deserved to enjoy all the temptations around me. I felt I was entitled. Thanks to money and fame, I didn't have to go far to find them.'[85]

Why do some people engage in extramarital affairs? The answer to this question is straightforward from an evolutionary perspective. To maximize his genetic fitness, a man is 'programmed' to have sex with multiple females. A male animal has no sexual desire for the same female after mating with her for a time sufficient to impregnate her. If ten days are sufficient for the female to become pregnant, sex on the eleventh day is purely a waste of resources for the male. Even worse, it presents a great risk: a fierce animal (such as a lion or tiger) may take the opportunity to attack during mating. Thus the loss of a male's sexual appetite for one female after a short mating period is simply an evolutionary advantage.

A recent newspaper article entitled 'New Love: A Short Shelf Life' offers the following vivid illustration:[86]

> In fairy tales, marriages last happily ever after. Science, however, tells us that wedded bliss has but a limited shelf life. American and European researchers tracked 1,761 people who got married and stayed married over the course of 15 years. The findings were clear: newlyweds enjoy a big happiness boost that lasts, on average, for just two years ... Familiarity may or may not breed contempt; but research suggests that it breeds indifference. Or, as Raymond Chandler wrote: 'The first kiss is magic. The second is intimate. The third is routine.'... Evolutionary biologists believe that sexual variety is adaptive, and that it evolved to prevent incest and inbreeding in ancestral environments. The idea is that when our spouse becomes as familiar to us as a sibling – when we've become family – we cease to be sexually attracted to each other ...

Marriage requires a husband to have sex with only his wife. As acknowledged by Tiger Woods, a man is often tempted to engage in extramarital affairs. Based on her extensive interviews with several hundred divorced husbands, wives and former mistresses, Eskapa (1984) reaches the conclusion that men have a strong tendency to seek extramarital sex regardless of whether they are happy with their marriages.

From an evolutionary perspective, women should have much less of an incentive to engage in extramarital affairs. A woman can become pregnant by one man only during an extensive period of ten months. In reality, it is indeed the case that women are less likely to engage in extramarital affairs, particularly when they are involved in happy marriages.

However, when their marriages are unhappy, women may also want to have extramarital affairs for at least one reason. While a woman may not want multiple sexual partners at a time, she may love to have sex. Her husband may lose sexual interest in her too quickly. As described earlier, since unprotected sex can almost surely get a woman pregnant within a short period, through evolutionary history a man may be 'hardwired' in such a way that he will lose his sexual appetite after that period. In fact, most animals have a 'mating season' that comprises only a small fraction of a year.

While after thousands of years of human civilization a man's sexual desire for his wife should be much longer than the period required to impregnate her, this desire does dwindle over time. Nevertheless, nature may 'programme' a woman in such a way that she experiences sexual desire as long as she is not pregnant. This tendency, in fact, also appears to be pro-evolution. Due to the current advanced technology of contraceptives, a woman may never become pregnant. Thus, if she finds that her husband has lost sexual interest in her, she may be tempted to look for another sexual partner.

To resolve the conflict between marriage vows and sexual desires, some couples choose an open marriage arrangement such as partner swapping that allows extramarital sexual relationships. However, most married people do not accept open marriage. Why? This book provides an explanation from a vanity economics perspective: an open marriage seriously damages the sense of possessing one's spouse, and this cost is usually much greater than the benefit of the increased sexual satisfaction achieved from an open marriage. In other words, most couples find that the loss of vanity of possessing one's spouse exclusively outweighs the benefit of achieving more hedonistic pleasure from having multiple sexual partners.

However, in some relationships in which the power dynamic between the husband and wife is highly uneven (such as those in ancient times), extramarital sexual activities are both open and common. When women depend on men economically, the men can have extramarital sex but the women must be absolutely loyal to their husbands. For example, Posner (1992, p. 40) writes,

> The social life of ancient Greek men was passed either with other men or with the high-class prostitutes … Apart from the duty of economic support, a husband's legal obligation to his wife was limited to having sexual intercourse with her a few times a month and not installing another woman in his house. Beyond that he was free to seek sexual pleasure anywhere he pleased …

This is also currently widespread in places where men have more economic power than women. For example, in Chapter 8, I cite a *Wall Street Journal* article about a residential area in Shenzhen, China where Hong Kong men kept house with their No. 2 wives. The article further states the following:

Other men are happy to have what is called a 'No. 2 wife' and child. The practice harks back to pre-Communist China, when polygamy was common and accepted. 'Many men like to have two families,' says Paulina Kwok, a social worker who staffs a telephone hot line in Hong Kong for domestic disputes. She notes the trophy factor. 'For these men to have a beautiful, young, sexy girl is a personal achievement.' ... The last thing many men want is their Mainland offspring showing up in Hong Kong, followed by mom. And keeping a second family under wraps has become harder as the stakes have risen. Yet many Hong Kong wives 'will tolerate a second wife for the sake of their children,' says Ms. Kwok, the social worker. Many wives fear divorce because of the stigma it carries and because their husbands are the bread-winners.

Indeed, in some relationships in which the power dynamic between the husband and wife is highly uneven, vanity induces the husband to engage in an extramarital affair, often in the form of taking a mistress. In China, Hong Kong and some other East Asian countries, these mistresses are often called the 'second wife'. Some CEOs in China often compare the beauty of their mistresses (usually their personal secretaries). Those who do not bring mistresses to social gatherings are often subjected to significant social pressure and treated as 'inferior' to others. Therefore, even a man without any interest in promiscuity may be tempted to have a mistress to secure a high social status among his peers.

## 9.2 STRATEGIC RESPONSES TO SPOUSES' EXTRAMARITAL AFFAIRS

Extramarital affairs are currently common.[87] Buss and Shackelford (1997) estimate that about 30–60 per cent of all married individuals in the USA will have extramarital sex at some point in their married lives. This section addresses the following interrelated questions. First, why do so many people tolerate their spouses' extramarital affairs? Second, what are a woman's best strategies in dealing with her spouse's infidelity?

Both women and men encounter extramarital affairs. However, in most societies women are more often the victims of spousal betrayal. Thus, in the theoretical expositions developed in this section, the discussions and analyses focus only on cases in which the husband of a household has an incentive to engage in an extramarital affair and the wife attempts to prevent it.[88]

I recently saw a television drama on the lives of an emperor and his numerous wives in ancient China. On the show, the emperor's wives felt helpless when he decided to have more wives. They could do nothing to punish him for inviting more women into his palace. In modern times, women are endowed with many more rights, and they usually exercise effective measures to prevent spousal infidelity or at least reduce the level and frequency of their husbands' extramarital activities.

The most drastic measure a wife may take is divorce. In fact, this is often a woman's first emotional response when she discovers that her husband has cheated on her. If a divorce occurs, the husband is often separated from his children, which he is likely to find very painful. Divorce also necessarily results in a split of the couple's wealth, which can be very costly, particularly when much of the assets suit the purpose of conspicuous consumption – vanity.

For example, the major function of a large, beautiful home is to show off the economic status of the household. No one will feel crowded if the house is sufficiently large, regardless of whether a man lives there alone or with a family, which is usually the case in many developed countries. However, when a couple divorce, a big house may have to be sold so that the husband and wife can divide its value. Consequently, the husband must buy another much smaller house, and therefore suffer a decrease in economic status.

In some big cities such as Hong Kong, where public transportation is very convenient, even a luxury car is purchased mainly for the purpose of showing off the owner's social status to friends and colleagues. Luxury cars are often used only for family leisure activities at weekends and public holidays or for attending social gatherings. They are rarely used for transportation to work. If a divorce occurs, only one person can possess the car. For example, if the wife gets the car in the divorce settlement, the husband is no longer able to possess it and thus the vanity it offers.

However, if a woman chooses to divorce her husband in reaction to his extramarital affairs, she is typically suffering significantly, perhaps more so than her husband. The financial cost clearly applies at least equally to both a wife and a husband. Moreover, in comparison with men, women often find divorce costly in terms of future remarriage. It is usually much more difficult for a divorced woman to find a new partner for the following reasons.

First, many if not most men seek youth and beauty in a partner in the marriage market. Youth itself is an important component of beauty for women. By this criterion, a divorced woman may find it difficult to compete with younger women in the market. However, age is usually not a serious problem for men who are seeking marital partners. For example, George Clooney, who was born in 1961, is still considered one of the sexiest unmarried men in the world. The 'double standard of premarital virginity' persists in some cultures, resulting in a major stigma for divorced women in the marriage market. In contrast, very few women are concerned about whether their potential husbands are virgins, and a divorce record often has little effect on a man's attractiveness in the marriage market unless he is known to have a history of being physically abusive. Moreover, after a divorce, it is usually the women who take care of the children. As a result, women often have little time and energy to enter into a romantic relationship.

Due to these obstacles, a woman may face the serious possibility that she will not be able to marry again if she divorces. A divorced woman often expects that she will not have a sexual/romantic partner again, particularly when she is left to take care of her children alone. Thus divorce is usually the last option a woman considers when she calms down and thinks rationally after discovering her husband's extramarital affair.[89] We can analyse the scenarios in which a wife may or may not choose divorce in response to her husband's extramarital affair according to game theory.

I analyse the strategic interactions between a husband and wife in this situation using a simple example. Consider a scenario in which the husband has an intention to engage in an extramarital affair. The affair can be at either a high or low level. For example, a low-level extramarital affair can take the form of a one-night stand with a stranger the man meets at a bar or with a prostitute. A high-level extramarital affair (EA) is a husband's lengthy relationship with a woman with whom he has some emotional attachment. Thus the husband's 'strategies' can be summarized as follows:

- no extramarital affair (no EA),
- low-level extramarital affair (low EA),
- high-level extramarital affair (high EA).

For simplicity's sake, in this example we assume that the wife never engages in an extramarital affair. In response to her husband's choice, she chooses one of two strategies: divorce or not divorce. The happiness indexes (or utility) of the husband and wife are given in Table 9.1.

Using the knowledge of game theory introduced earlier, we know that, in this example, there are two Nash equilibria if they 'move' together: (Low EA, Not divorce) and (High EA, Divorce). In the first equilibrium, the husband believes that his wife will not react with divorce if he engages in a low-level extramarital affair. Note that in the case that the husband engages in a low-level extramarital affair, the wife's happiness index (or utility) will be 5 if she does not divorce and her utility will

*Table 9.1  An example of the divorce/EA game*

| Husband/wife | Divorce | Not divorce |
|---|---|---|
| No EA | (–10, –20) | (0, 10) |
| Low EA | (0, –10) | (10, 5) |
| High EA | (5, 0) | (8, –10) |

Note that the numbers in parentheses are the happiness indexes of the husband and wife, respectively.

be –10 if she chooses to divorce. Therefore, in this case, the wife will choose not to divorce, which means that in this example the husband's above belief is indeed self-fulfilling.

In the second equilibrium, if the wife believes that her husband is having a high-level extramarital affair, she will choose divorce. In this case, the wife's utility will be 0 if she chooses to divorce and her utility will be –10 if she does not divorce. Therefore, in this case, the wife will choose to divorce, which means that this belief is also self-fulfilling.

However, in practice, the husband can usually make the first move in choosing to have an extramarital affair. When he does so, obviously he will choose a low-level extramarital affair, which results in the only Nash equilibrium in which his wife will tolerate his extramarital affair, namely (Low EA, Not divorce). It is because the husband will be better off in the equilibrium (Low EA, Not divorce) than in the other equilibrium (High EA, Divorce) in which divorce will occur.

In equilibrium, the husband engages in a low-level extramarital affair, and his wife tolerates it. Thus, in this example, the husband need not hide his low-level extramarital affair. In fact, he must only make sure that his wife does not mistake his low-level extramarital affair for a high-level extramarital affair.

Does this theoretical analysis have any bearing on reality? The answer is yes. 'Forgive and forget' is often an important piece of advice to take when dealing with low-level extramarital affairs. In fact, several popular songs are based on young couples' games of 'forgive and forget'. The lyrics to Abba's 'Mamma Mia' provide an example:

> I've been cheated by you since I don't know when. So I made up my mind, it must come to an end. Look at me now, will I ever learn? I don't know how but I suddenly lose control. There's a fire within my soul. Just one look and I can hear a bell ring. One more look and I forget everything, o-o-o-oh. Mamma mia, here I go again ...

In many East Asian countries today, lots of women accept their husbands' extramarital affairs as long as they are not told about them. At first sight, this bottom line appears to be meaningless. If a woman knows nothing about her husband's extramarital affair, she will naturally not feel anything about it. However, there are two deeper meanings to this acceptance.

First, not knowing about an extramarital affair means that it does not become the wife's public humiliation. If an affair is revealed to any individual within the couple's social circles, the wife is usually informed of it. Thus the bottom line described earlier is essentially equivalent to no one in the couple's social circles knowing about the affair, including friends and colleagues. If a man's extramarital affair is so conspicuous that even his neighbours know of it, then his wife will suffer from a large loss of vanity and hence feel very unhappy about it. Consequently, she may feel that she would be happier choosing a divorce, which at least serves as a signal to her neighbours that she cares about her dignity.

Second, a husband is usually able to conceal an extramarital affair if he is having it only for sexual pleasure and is not emotionally involved. For example, in a serious extramarital affair with substantial emotional involvement, the 'third person' is usually not satisfied that the romantic affair is being kept secret. Indeed, once a woman is physically and emotionally involved with a married man, she will not accept that she is inferior to his wife, and the secret status of their relationship is such an indicator of her inferiority. The third person often has a strong incentive to inform the wife of her affair with her husband. Thus a wife's declaration that her husband can have sex with another woman, as long as she has no knowledge of it, is actually a practical way of making sure that any affair her husband has is purely about sex.

This argument is consistent with the following online comment:[90]

> One of the first things I learned about Japan was that their regard for sexual behavior is quite different from that of Westerners. I was told, and this was a notion that was reinforced as the years went by, that sexual acts were regarded as a biological necessity, much like the need to urinate or eat. This was offered as an explanation as to why some Japanese women would tell their husbands or boyfriends that they understood if they strayed, but they simply never wanted to know about it. Cheating is tolerated to a greater extent because it is seen as a release, not as a threat to relationships.

In fact, one report states that, in Japan, if a married man is going to be out of town, his wife will make sure to put enough condoms into his suitcase and remind him to practise safe sex.[91]

Moreover, underlying the statement 'you can have sex with others, but don't let me know about it' is an implicit strategy that the wife will not spend any resources to try to discover her husband's extramarital affairs. If a wife hired a private agent to follow her husband, it would be very difficult for him to hide anything. However, when a wife takes no action to investigate the matter, her husband is often able to keep his affairs a secret.

Of course, not all women tolerate their husbands' low-level extramarital affairs, particularly in societies that are strongly influenced by Christianity. Christian groups consider adultery to be highly immoral. Thus a Christian wife may not only be seriously hurt emotionally but also totally lose trust in her husband's character and integrity if she discovers he is having an extramarital affair. Further, if women are sufficiently financially independent, the threat of divorce is often credible enough. For example, if a woman is a housewife and her earning potential in the marketplace is very low, she will starve without the financial support of her husband, who will simply not believe that she will leave him, no matter what he does to her. By this logic, the greater a woman's earning or potential earning power in the marketplace, the less her financial concern after a divorce, and hence the more likely she will be to choose divorce in response to her husband's betrayal.

Moreover, a woman often has many measures other than divorce to punish her husband. In modern societies in which women's rights are well protected, a wife can refuse to have sex with her husband. This measure is usually costless to the wife when she discovers that her husband is having an extramarital affair. Indeed, when a woman knows that her husband has recently had sex with another woman, the prospect of having sex with him often disgusts her, and this feeling often lasts for a considerable time. This measure can be effective against a husband, particularly if his underlying motivation for extramarital sex is a strong desire for sex with a variety of women.

In addition, if a woman learns that her husband is cheating on her, she may renege on their household labour distribution agreement and demand that he devote more time and effort to domestic work such as raising the children. Because the division of labour between wife and husband enhances economic efficiency and the wife can choose whether to cooperate with her husband in the allocation of work, she has some bargaining power at home,[92] including the power to control her husband's extramarital affairs.

I use game theory to show that certain measures can effectively prevent a man from engaging in an extramarital affair if his wife is committed to punishing him for any transgression. To understand the reasoning here, the 'supergame' concept must be introduced.

The game theory examined thus far describes a 'one-shot game' in which the players interact only once. A supergame is an infinite sequence of identical one-shot games. The supergame theory guides us to understand a strategic equilibrium in which people interact repeatedly. To simplify the point, let us again look at the example of the prisoner's dilemma introduced in Chapter 8. This example is described again in Table 9.2.

*Table 9.2   An example of the 'prisoner's dilemma'*

| A/B | Loyal | Betray |
| --- | --- | --- |
| Loyal | $(-1, -1)$ | $(-10, 0)$ |
| Betray | $(0, -10)$ | $(-8, -8)$ |

In Chapter 8, it is explained that if the two criminals interact only once, then the only Nash equilibrium is that both of the suspects betray their partners, and consequently each is sentenced to prison for eight years. We can modify the assumption by assuming that the criminals interact repeatedly for possibly endless periods. Thus their cooperation benefits them not only in the current period, but also in future periods. From Table 9.2, we can see that, in the current period, the benefit of cooperation is

$$-1 - (-8) = 7$$

As there is a certain probability that the criminals will cease to interact with each other in any period, there is a time discount rate. For example, if the probability that the criminals will interact in the next period is only 90 per cent, then the time discount rate cannot exceed 0.9. In our example, the time discount rate is assumed to be 0.8. The mathematical formula that can be used to calculate the total benefits in the current period and in all future periods is[93]

(the benefit of cooperation in each period)/(1 − the time discount rate)

We call this 'Formula A'.

In this example, based on 'Formula A', the total benefits of cooperation are then

$$7/(1 - 0.8) = 35$$

Thus, the total benefits of future cooperation (excluding this period) are

$$35 - 7 = 28$$

But, if either criminal cheats by choosing to 'betray' while his partner chooses be 'loyal', his gain in the current period is

$$0 - (-1) = 1$$

However, if one criminal betrays, there will be never cooperation in the future. In this example, both suspects will choose 'loyal' because the cost of betrayal is much greater than its benefit, that is, 1 is less than 28.

Returning to the first example in this chapter, we modify two assumptions. First, the husband and wife interact repeatedly for possibly endless periods, and the time discount rate is 0.8. (This is clearly a realistic assumption, as husbands and wives live together for long periods.) Second, the wife can take an action that reduces her husband's happiness by 12 and her own happiness by 10. This action may be her refusal to have sex with her husband for half a year if he engages in any kind of extramarital affair.

We consider the scenario in which a wife's husband engages in a low-level extramarital affair. Under these assumptions, if the wife does not take action to punish her husband, her gain is 10. However, without any penalty, her husband will continue to engage in low-level extramarital affairs in the future. If the wife takes action to punish her husband and her husband does not engage in any kind of extramarital affairs in the future, based on 'Formula A', her gains in all periods (current and future) are

$$5/(1 - 0.8) = 25$$

Therefore, her gains in future periods are

$$25 - 5 = 20$$

Because 20 is greater than 10, the wife's benefit of punishing her husband is greater than the cost. Thus the wife will punish her husband as long as he engages in any kind of extramarital affair.

Let us now consider the husband's decision. From Table 9.1, we can see that, in each period, the benefit for the husband to engage in a low-level extramarital affair is 10 (0 −(−10)). But that the cost is now assumed to be 12, which is greater than the benefit (10). Thus the husband will choose not to engage in an extramarital affair. In this example, the outcome in equilibrium is that the husband never engages in an extramarital affair. The penalty remains a threat, but never happens in equilibrium. In other words, in this 'supergame', in the equilibrium of the strategic interactions of a couple, the husband never engages in an extramarital affair.

It should be noted that the wife is able to completely maintain her husband's marital fidelity under several conditions. First, she is willing to sacrifice herself by punishing her husband. In this example, the self-sacrificing action is that the wife chooses not to have sex with her husband for a certain period. Second, in relation to the first point, the legal system must protect women's rights so that the wife can take such a measure. In some societies, because women's rights are weak, their husbands may resort to rape or other physical abuse when they refuse to have sex. In this case, a wife cannot stop her husband from having extramarital sex if he has such an opportunity. Third, the wife must be strongly concerned about her husband's extramarital affairs at any level, which is more likely to be the case in Christian countries. In cultures where men having casual sex is not treated as a big deal, the wives are unwilling to sacrifice their own pleasure to punish their husbands. This explains why women are more tolerant of their husbands' casual sex in East Asian countries.

# 10. Homosexuality

Although the exact figure is hard to obtain, a non-negligible proportion of people are homosexuals. Most sociology research appears to indicate that, in Western countries today, 1 per cent to 3 per cent of the population is homosexual.[94] Moreover, homosexuality appears to be a hot topic of discussion in the media, as illustrated by the frenzy caused by the statement Barack Obama made in support of gay marriage during his 2012 US presidential election campaign.

## 10.1 SEXUAL PLEASURE VERSUS 'SURVIVAL OF THE GENE': A PRINCIPAL–AGENT PROBLEM

This chapter tries to answer the following long-standing question: why are some people homosexuals? From an evolutionary perspective, homosexuality is perplexing, as homosexual activities cannot lead to procreation. Thus the first task of this chapter is to make sense of homosexuality in the context of evolution. It proposes that homosexuality may be a product of intelligence in the evolutionary process.

The principle of evolution is the survival of the gene (Darwin, 1859; Dawkins, 2006). However, such a goal is not achieved by the 'gene' itself. Instead, it is directly achieved by its host – a living being (or an organism) such as a human. The gene induces a living being to achieve its goal of survival through a number of biological desires, particularly for food and sex. While desire for food guarantees that an organism has enough of an incentive to acquire sufficient nutrition to stay alive, sexual desire induces a living being to overcome obstacles and difficulties to find a mate and give birth to offspring so that the gene will survive after the death of the living being's body.

The relationship between the gene and its host (an organism) belongs to the 'principal–agent problem' in economics. This problem often arises in a two-party relationship, such as that of an employer and a worker, a client and a lawyer, an insurance company and an insured person, or a group of shareholders and a firm manager. In such a relationship, the principal delegates to the agent an action that influences the principal's welfare.

- In the relationship between an employer and a worker, the employer is the principal and the worker is the agent, and the latter affects the former through the agent's production output.
- In the relationship between a client and a lawyer, the client is the principal and the lawyer is the agent, and the latter affects the former through a court's judgment for the client.
- In the relationship between an insurance company and an insured person (e.g. car insurance), the insurance company is the principal and the insured person is the agent, and the latter affects the former through the care they take while driving.
- In the relationship between a group of shareholders and a firm manager, the group of shareholders is the principal and the firm manager is the agent, and the latter affects the former through the agent's carefulness and restraint in risk taking and the expected investor profits.

The principal–agent problem arises when the agent takes an action that maximizes their own interest at the expense of the principal. Consider the following examples.

- A worker is paid a fixed salary, chooses to take it easy and has little incentive to work hard.
- A lawyer is paid according to the number of hours worked, does not work enough and causes a client to lose a case in court.
- A person has their car completely insured and takes little care of it.
- A fund manager takes too high a risk: if they win the gamble, they will receive a large bonus; if they lose, the shareholder bears the loss, resulting in a government bailout.

Such a principal–agent problem may also exist in the relationship between a gene and its host (organism). The problem may not be serious when the organism's intelligence level is low. For example, some types of male spider are often eaten by their female partners after mating. This culmination increases the probability of the survival of the gene at the expense of the male spiders' welfare. However, the male spiders' instinctive mating behaviour forces them into it, as they are 'hardwired' by their genes and have a low level of intelligence. (If male spiders had a higher level of intelligence, they would learn from the mating results of other spiders and would probably refuse to mate.)

However, the principal–agent problem tends to become more serious as an organism's intelligence develops. This problem can be particularly pronounced in humans, the organisms with the highest level of intelligence. For example, most human sexual activity is currently practised for the purpose of pleasure rather than procreation. From the perspective of the 'fitness of the gene', any sexual activity that is not conducive to procreation is a waste of resources and energy. However, the survival of the gene is far from the only concern of a modern human being.

Intelligence is often considered an output of evolution. A more intelligent living being is more likely to survive, particularly in a changing environment (e.g. Itzkoff, 1983; Lynch and Granger, 2008). However, from a genetics perspective, an unintended consequence is that the principal–agent problem between genes and humans becomes more serious in relation to sexual behaviour when intelligence develops. For example, oral and anal sex were long ago discovered by human beings to satisfy sexual desires. However, neither oral nor anal sex can result in procreation. Two persons can clearly perform both types of sex regardless of their genders. Thus it is not a surprise that homosexual activities occur among some fraction of the human population.

Moreover, oral sex, anal sex or other non-vaginal sexual activities eliminate the risk of unwanted pregnancy, which is often very costly. Homosexual activity is an obviously effective alternative to ensuring that vaginal sex never takes place. This reasoning may incidentally provide an explanation for the common sexual relationship between men and young boys in ancient Greece. As Chapter 11 elaborates, overpopulation often resulted in famines, massive killings and other disasters in ancient times. This may be an important reason why, in almost all traditional societies regardless of the culture, premarital sex was a taboo for males and females. Therefore homosexual activity might have emerged as a way to satisfy people's sexual desires and control population growth at the same time.

## 10.2  VANITY AND HOMOSEXUALITY

The proportion of homosexuals in a human population may vary drastically in different societies and at different times. There may be some genetic differences across individuals that influence a stronger sexual preference towards the same sex. However, because the millions of years of evolution have produced only a few thousand years of civilization, it is reasonable to assume that humans are rather homogeneous in their homosexual tendencies, which means that the proportions of homosexuals in different societies and at different times should be the same.

Thus the question remains: why do some individuals choose to be gay or lesbian? There are many answers to this question, which are complicated, controversial and beyond the scope of this book. This chapter aims only to offer a new answer in line with the central theme of this book: vanity. Let me put it clearly at the outset that the discussion in this section is only one dimension in the study of homosexuality. It attempts only to add to the vast literature on this topic, and it absolutely does not make any moral judgement.

When a society is strongly against homosexuality, even those who are strongly homosexual hide their sexual preference. A person's happiness and misery often stem from many sources, one being their degree of sexual satisfaction. However, for many people, the degree of sexual satisfaction may be far less important than other considerations, such as their earnings and social status. For example, human sexual desires can be controlled to a large extent. Indeed, most people do not exhibit strong sexual desires during an eight-hour workday. Thus, in a society where homosexual behaviour introduces a major stigma, homosexuals are hardly observed.

When a society is not strongly against homosexuality, those who are strongly homosexual will 'come out of the closet'. By revealing their true sexual orientation, a homosexual person has an easier time finding a partner, and one who is more desirable. Further, when a homosexual person hides their true sexual orientation, they experience a sense of shame and stigma. Thus, in relation to the main theme of this book, 'coming out' itself provides a homosexual person with an open identity and hence a sense of dignity and pride, which this book defines as belonging to the general category of vanity.

As societies develop further, homosexuality is becoming increasingly accepted. The theory of this book suggests that some of those who are weakly homosexual in the sense that they slightly prefer to be 'straight' may choose to be gay or lesbian. Where does this prediction come from? The answer again rests on vanity. Due to their concern for vanity, under the condition that the person has no strong sexual orientation preference, they may choose to be a homosexual if their looks are preferred by the same sex over the opposite sex.

For example, if a man is regarded as 'physically unattractive' by the mainstream culture, he is likely to be rejected if he pursues females. He may often be humiliated and insulted by both men and women in his pursuit of a female sexual partner. In this case, if the man chose to be 'straight', it is likely that he would feel inferior and defeated. According to the theory posited in this book, the man would experience a great deal of negative vanity. However, if the man chooses to be gay, 'physical unattractiveness' determined by the mainstream culture may be much less emphasized in the gay community. Consequently, he may find himself welcomed and respected by a homosexual partner. Therefore, even if he slightly prefers women to men sexually, he may choose to be gay. Consequently, although the degree of his sexual satisfaction decreases, he will experience greater dignity and self-esteem in life.

This reasoning also incidentally explains why Westerners insult males by using the word 'faggot', a term that appears particularly in competitive fights over 'manhood'. By calling his opponent a 'faggot' or simply 'gay', a man is indirectly saying that his opponent lacks desirable male characteristics such as muscularity. In other words, the 'faggot' insult may stem from a man's desire to show off his enhanced 'masculine' traits, or from the competition for male vanity.

This chapter provides an analysis of homosexuality from a new angle, which aims to better understand this phenomenon. But it should be emphasized that it does not offer any 'normative' or moral judgement. As noted in Chapter 2, this book is not a framework for morality.

PART III


Vanity economics and population theory

Agro-economics and population trends

# 11. Classical population theory

This chapter introduces a new topic: children. I demonstrate in the following chapters (but not this chapter) that vanity plays a key role in many important decisions related to children in modern societies, such as whether to have children, how many to have and how much to invest in their education.

Before studying the 'vanity theories of population', however, this chapter presents the classical population theory, in which vanity plays no role. The theory posits that, for most of human history, as with other animals, fertility has not really been a choice but simply a by-product of sex. As simple as it is, this theory is surprisingly powerful in explaining population and economic growth in ancient times. It also provides a comparison benchmark for modern fertility theories. Therefore this classical theory is still often taught in population and development economics courses today.

The classical population theory was developed by Thomas Malthus (1798). Malthus's theory has three important components. First, humans have only two desires: food and sex. Second, there is a subsistence level to food consumption. If a person consumes below the subsistence level, they will die. However, once they obtain enough food to consume at the subsistence level, their only remaining desire is sex. Third, as a population increases, the wage rate decreases.

These assumptions appear to be overly simplified in the contemporary world. But they made a great deal of sense in ancient times. For most of human history, people lived on farms and had simple consumption styles. In contrast to the consumerism in modern societies, the purpose of consumption was to have enough food to stay alive. This point is vividly illustrated by the 'pond of wine and woods of meat' folktale that describes the luxurious life of King Zhou in ancient China.

Also, one may argue that it is absurd to assume that, once people obtain enough food to consume at the subsistence level, their only remaining desire is sex. However, the essence of this assumption is that a person's sexual desire dominates their desire for food as long as they are not hungry. The previous chapters discussed many aspects of human sexuality. Indeed, humans and other animals have a great deal in common in this area, and sexual drive is an important reason for the continuation of both human and animal species. Life expectancy in ancient times was much shorter than it is today. Because younger people have a greater sexual urge, people's sexual desires were stronger on average than they are currently.

In fact, in some developing countries where effective contraceptive methods are not accessible to many people, sexual desire remains an important reason for having too many children. In their influential textbook on development economics, Gillis et al. (1996, p. 205) make the following statement:

> Why, then, do people have children? Is it because they are moved by Malthus' 'passion between the sexes' and do not know how to prevent the resulting births? … [as] was stated by a Latin American doctor at an international conference a few years ago. 'People don't really want children,' he said. 'They want sex and don't know how to avoid the births that result.' This viewpoint captures the element of spontaneity that is inevitably present in the reproductive process.

Malthus argues that, due to 'the passion between the sexes', populations tend to grow rapidly when there is enough food. This appears to be a reasonable argument for human behaviour in ancient times, when the technology of birth control was rudimentary and often ineffective.

An insight of Malthus is that, as a result of population growth, the wage rate decreases. This statement is consistent with economists' observed evidence from human history. In fact, Malthus is one of the classical economists who developed the theory of 'the law of diminishing returns'. This economics proposition states that, holding other inputs constant, the extra output generated by an additional unit of one input, known as the marginal product of the input, will ultimately become increasingly smaller.

The most important inputs in ancient times were labour and land. In this context, the law of diminishing returns implies that the marginal product of labour tends to decrease and will eventually diminish as the labour supply increases, holding land supply constant. The marginal product of labour is defined as the (additional) output produced by one additional unit of labour. The implication of the law of diminishing returns is fairly intuitive. On a given piece of land, the first worker is very productive. As more workers begin farming the same piece of land, the working environment becomes increasingly crowded, which reduces labour productivity.

Suppose that the law of diminishing returns holds. An important proposition in economics is that, in an economy with a competitive labour market, the wage rate is determined by the marginal product of labour. Mankiw (2013) provides the basic logic of this proposition, which with some modifications can be stated as follows. Consider a scenario in which a landowner hires peasants to work on a given piece of land. If the marginal product of labour is higher than the wage rate, from the perspective of the landowner, the net profit generated by the last peasant hired is positive. The landowner would thus like to hire more peasants as long as the marginal product of labour continues to be higher than the wage rate. However, this scenario cannot last for long, as the marginal product of labour becomes increasingly small as more peasants are hired due to the law of diminishing returns. When the marginal product of labour is equal to the wage rate, the landowner will stop hiring more peasants. Otherwise, the marginal product of labour will continue to decrease, which implies that the landowner will suffer a net loss if more peasants are hired. Thus, in equilibrium, the marginal product of labour is equal to the wage rate in a competitive labour market.

The best example of the law of diminishing returns is the 'Black Death' (i.e. the bubonic plague), which spread across Europe in 1348. This epidemic reduced the population of Europe by about one-third within a few years. However, any person who survived the epidemic enjoyed an economic fortune: the real wage rate doubled after the disaster (Mankiw, 2013).

Based on this proposition, Malthus argues that if wages are above the subsistence level, people will tend to marry younger and have more children. However, this increase in fertility leads to an increase in the labour supply over time, ultimately resulting in the wage rate falling back to the subsistence level. Thus, in the world depicted by Malthus, the only stable equilibrium is that the wage rate remains precisely at the level of subsistence.

Let me again summarize the three key ingredients of Malthus's population theory. First, an individual obtains happiness from only two sources: food and sex. Second, there is a minimal level of food consumption that sustains life, and everyone is content to consume at the subsistence level. The resultant passion for sex then automatically leads to rapid population growth. Third, the law of diminishing returns exists in agricultural production, and limits the speed of the growth in food supplies along with a population expansion.

The last point can be illustrated by the numerical example shown in Table 11.1.

*Table 11.1   A numerical example*

|              | Year 1 | Year 2 | Year 3 | Year 4 | Year 5 | Year 6 |
|--------------|--------|--------|--------|--------|--------|--------|
| Food         | 12     | 14     | 16     | 18     | 20     | 22     |
| Population   | 4      | 8      | 16     | 32     | 64     | 128    |

In this example, if the subsistence level of food per person is equal to 1, then famines and rising deaths will ensue from Year 4.

According to Malthus, population growth is limited primarily by two types of measures. The first type comprises 'positive checks', which are the measures taken to increase the death rate. This type includes war, famine and epidemics. The second type comprises 'preventive checks' that aim to reduce the birth rate, such as by instituting a later marriage age.

At this point, one may wonder whether this population problem also applies to animals. Indeed, all the key ingredients of Malthus's population theory exist for all animals. Animals desire food and sex and have a subsistence constraint of food consumption. When they have enough food to eat, they will have sex and produce more animals. When there are more animals of the same species, each animal will have less food to share. It is fortunate that almost all animals have natural enemies.

The following real example illustrates the importance of natural enemies to the survival of a species. In the 1950s, the new Chinese Communist government in a region realized that deer produced high economic value, with deer meat being nutritious and deer horn a valuable medicinal ingredient. The government also noted that many deer were being killed by wolves. They decided to kill the wolves in the region, and did so within a short period. To the government's great surprise and disappointment, all the deer died off within a few years of the wolf extermination.

What went wrong? After careful investigations, the government found the root of the problem: without the natural enemy of wolves, there were more and more deer. The large number of deer ate all the leaves and grasses within a short period of time. Consequently, almost all deer died: they had no more food since it takes time for leaves and grasses to grow again. In other words, the wolves were preventing the deer from exhausting their own food supply and hence starving to death. Although wolves are the natural enemies of deer, the deer would die off to a greater extent without them.

The logic underlying this story explains why human murders were so frequent in ancient times. Consider the scenario where a famine occurs. If a war breaks out and many people are killed, a fraction of the population will survive by consuming at a level above subsistence. On the other hand, if people are so 'civilized' that wars are not fought, everyone may consume below the subsistence level in this famine and consequently all the people may starve.

Malthus's population theory has two main implications. First, people always consume at the subsistence level, which means that the economic growth rate remains at zero. Second, rich families have more children. These implications are consistent with the observed evidence taken from most of human history. For example, in England, the real wage rate remained the same in 1800 as it was in 1300; in China, it remained the same in the eighteenth century as it was in the first century.[95] In addition, Ashraf and Galor (2011) show that, during AD 1–1500, technological superiority and higher land productivity increased population density but had insignificant effects on average income. These findings are in strong support of the classical population theory developed by Malthus.

Moreover, it is commonly observed that rich families had more children in ancient times. Indeed, without religious and legal restrictions, a richer man often had more wives. For example, Moulay Ismail, the Emperor of Morocco in the early eighteenth century, had more than 1000 children (Wright, 1994). The most drastic example is Genghis Khan, who, along with his children and grandchildren, conquered most of the world in the thirteenth century. Some researchers argue that about 1 in 200 men in the world today carry the genes of Genghis Khan.[96]

Despite the simplicity of its assumptions, Malthus's population theory yields interesting theoretical predictions that effectively explain the observed evidence taken from historical times. Although it is an old theory, it is still taught in modern economics courses.

# 12. Gary Becker, vanity economics and modern population theory

The classical population theory developed by Malthus provides a good explanation for fertility behaviour throughout human history until about 200 years ago. However, this classical theory cannot be employed to explain fertility behaviour in modern societies for at least two reasons.

First, most people today completely separate having sex from having children. In other words, children are no longer the by-products of 'the passion for sex'. For example, newspapers and magazines sometimes report the announcement of a celebrity couple who have cohabited for many years that they are getting married for the purpose of having children. Also, some couples arrive at pre-marriage agreements that they will not have children after marriage.

Second, in contrast to the implication of the classical population theory, we have witnessed a clear negative correlation between the level of fertility and the level of income for the past century. This is in fact one of the most robust empirical findings in demography and economics. Fertility rates are low in rich countries and high in poor countries, and in a given country poorer households tend to have more children than richer households. Such a negative correlation between fertility and income sharply contradicts the implications of Malthus's population theory.

This chapter focuses on Gary Becker's modern theories on child quantity and quality. Moreover, it shows that vanity economics can help us better understand the underlying assumptions of Becker's theories.

## 12.1 THE FIRST MODERN THEORY OF FERTILITY

The modern theory of fertility starts with Becker's contributions in the 1960s. In one study, Becker (1960) puts forward the modern theory of fertility by making an assumption that is in sharp contrast with Malthus's theory. He assumes that, in making decisions on fertility, people achieve happiness directly according to the number of children they have. Thus Becker's theory completely separates 'the passion for sex' from fertility.

Moreover, Becker assumes that, as a first-order approximation, contraceptive technology is advanced enough to allow a couple to effectively control the number of children they choose to have regardless of the degree of their sexual activity. Further, in contrast to Malthus's theory, Becker considers that an individual achieves more happiness when they consume more material goods. This modification is clearly necessary in the era of consumerism.

As the starting point of his pioneering research, Becker considers a simple formulation in which an individual obtains happiness from two sources: the number of children they have and material consumption. A question immediately arises: why does a couple achieve more happiness when they have more children? The answers to this question are surprisingly complicated.

First, some people want children because children are lovely. In modern societies, whether Eastern or Western, an increasing number of couples are obtaining a great deal of pleasure from children. This trend appears to be closely related to economic and social development, and is much more pronounced in modern times than it was in ancient times. In ancient times, when a city was conquered, the invaders often did not hesitate to kill all the people in the city, and had no mercy at all for children and infants. In modern times, many people find children and particularly infants adorable.

However, taking care of children is an extremely time-consuming job. It requires much effort, as the caretaker must pay attention to the child at all times. A moment's lack of attention may result in an irreversible tragedy: the child may fall off a balcony window or put a finger into an electric outlet. Moreover, it is a dirty job: a little child is prone to urinating and defecating. Even after a child is old enough to know how to use a toilet, they may still not know how to clean themselves, putting the responsibility for the dirty job on the caretaker (usually the parents). Thus the admiration of most people for infants may not provide them with enough of an incentive to take care of children.

The second common answer to why people choose to procreate is that they want to 'live forever' through their children, grandchildren and so on. From an evolutionary perspective, many people are concerned about the extension of their family lines or the survival of their genes. This concern may be even greater for those who do not have strong religious beliefs. Having a large number of children and grandchildren may considerably mitigate the fear of death. For example, in Chinese culture, when an elderly person is going to die, all their children and grandchildren are required to visit at all costs. (Such a practice is not strongly adhered to in Western cultures, as a priest can serve as a substitute and provide psychological comfort to a dying (religious) person.)

Indeed, even animals do not treat their offspring purely as the by-product of their sexual activities. For example, they (particularly female animals) often make significant sacrifices and even risk their own lives to protect their offspring after giving birth. To the extent that animals act conscientiously, they also desire to ensure the survival of their offspring.

However, concern for the survival of the gene may be weak in modern societies. For example, some people may think that the survival of the gene does not really represent an extension of life. Indeed, when a person is alive, they do not require others to live for them. When individuals are dead, they do not feel anything, including whether others are living for them.

In addition, the theory of DNA teaches us that every human has 23 pairs of chromosomes, with one member of each pair being inherited from the mother and the other from the father. Thus an individual's DNA (the gene) comes from their parents, who in turn obtained their DNA from the individual's grandparents, who obtained theirs from the individual's great-grandparents and so on. By this reasoning, a person may think that their DNA is not really their own, and instead ultimately traces back to Adam and Eve from a religious standpoint. In this case, how much is an individual's incentive to have children for genetic extension? The incentive will be trivial, particularly when one considers that now there are seven billion people doing the work for Adam and Eve. On the other hand, if one is not religious and accepts evolution, then one infers that all human DNA originates from the few hundred people 'out of Africa', and even primates. In other words, a person may think that their DNA is not really their 'property' to transmit to future generations. Thus this consideration may also discourage people from having children if genetic extension is the main concern.

In general, the idea that children are the extension of one's life is weaker in Western countries, in which many people practise Christianity. Christians believe that every individual is essentially created by God. In churches, Christians refer in prayer to God as the 'Father'. Therefore they tend to have a much weaker belief that children represent an extension of their lives through the passing on of genes.

This explains why child adoption is much more common in Western countries. For example, in China, the single-child policy has led some parents to abandon their infant girls. Many of these have been adopted by people from the USA and other Western countries. However, very few have been adopted by Chinese or other Asian families. Different degrees of religious beliefs may serve as the main explanation for this.

In conclusion, when the intelligence and knowledge levels in a society are relatively low, individuals' consciousness that their children are extensions of their life becomes stronger as human intelligence develops. As human intelligence further develops, this consciousness becomes increasingly weaker. This argument is presented graphically in Figure 12.1.

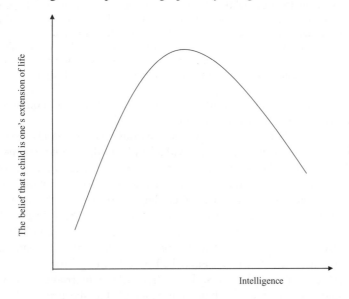

*Figure 12.1    Inverted U-shaped curve between intelligence and the consciousness that children are one's extensions of life*

The following further elaborates on this argument. When intelligence is underdeveloped, one's offspring are simply a by-product of sex. For example, rather than consciously wanting to produce offspring, animals simply want to have sex. However, even animals have the instinct to feed and protect their babies, which implies that their instinct to reproduce goes beyond sexual desire.

When intelligence is underdeveloped, females usually have a much closer relationship with their offspring than males. This is consistent with our observations of most animals, and is easy to understand from an evolutionary perspective. Even if an animal has a low intelligence level, a female will recognize that her baby is closely related to her when she observes it coming out of her body. However, a male animal will not be sure whether a baby carries his gene, even with the perfect knowledge that he had sex with its mother. After all, the mother might have also had sexual intercourse with other male animals.

Humans experience a similar problem. The early stages of human history are characterized by matrilineality, which is a system in which an individual belongs to their mother's lineage. For example, Wikipedia provides the following description:[97]

> In Greek mythology, while the royal function was a male privilege, power devolution often came through women, and the future king inherited power through marrying the queen heiress. This is illustrated in the Homeric myths where all the noblest men in Greece vie for the hand of Helen (and the throne of Sparta), as well as the Oedipian cycle where Oedipus weds the recently widowed queen at the same time he assumes the Theban kingship.

A small number of matrilineal societies persist in the contemporary world. The Mosuo of China is such an example.

In more recent human history, most cultures and societies have been patrilineal in the sense that an individual links to the previous generation mainly on their father's side. Patrilineal societies emerged and developed for two main reasons. First, humans became increasingly intelligent, and at some stage of development men began to realize the connection between their ejaculated sperm and the resultant new-born infants. Thus, if a female was having sex exclusively with a certain man, the infants she gave birth to were considered as 'belonging to' that man. Second, private ownership was increasingly established either through the stipulation of the state and/or social norms. In particular, the marriage system was developed. In a marriage, a man (the husband) has the right to have sex exclusively with a woman (the wife).

In a patrilineal society, people derive family names from their father rather than their mother. While this practice highlights the dominance of men in such a society, it may also benefit the women. A mother always knows that she is a mother. Thus, allowing her child to take on its father's family name reassures the father that the child is his, inducing him to exercise more responsibility and protection over his family.

However, in the modern world many people no longer believe that they can extend their lives by having children and grandchildren. They may reason as follows. 'If I am alive, I don't need anyone to live for me. If I die, I will become ashes, dust and water. Who can live for ashes, dust and water?' Thus the desire of 'living forever' is no longer a main reason for having children. This is reflected in the unpopularity of sperm donation. In most countries, a man is usually paid to donate his sperm, a practice that is clearly against the argument that most modern people desire to maximize the survival of their genes. Otherwise, every man would compete to donate his sperm, which would cost him nothing. Meanwhile, every man would compete to offer awards to those women who will accept his sperm to conceive a child.

What is the motivation for modern people to have children? This book argues that it is vanity – the vanity of possessing one's own children and hence forming a 'complete' family. If everyone believes that a society assigns a social status to couples with children, then, similar to the analysis in some of the previous chapters (e.g. the analysis of the value of female virginity), we can show that this belief is self-fulfilling. In such a belief, couples that do not have children have a low social status. Consequently, people may have a strong incentive to have children. Thus, in an abstract sense, having children is equivalent to possessing material goods (e.g. a luxury car) to demonstrate social status. Moreover, in most societies, the social status gained from having children is much greater than that gained from having luxurious consumption goods such as cars or houses. This is particularly true in more traditional societies.

The tradition that a child adopts the family name from its father rather than from its mother may also be related to vanity. With this additional vanity, the father is induced to care more for his offspring and sacrifice more for his family. Consequently, such a practice may also benefit the mother.

Moreover, for many people, banishing boredom may be another important reason to have children. It is often said that life is like a journey. However, it is not well realized that this journey can be overly long if one has little to do. In other words, life can be very boring.

Having children may be an effective way of banishing boredom. Indeed, it is often said that one can relive one's childhood by having a child, which not only banishes boredom but also generates much happiness. Thus banishing boredom and the expectation of obtaining pleasure from children may also be important reasons for people to start a family.

This reasoning provides a justification for Becker's argument that having children makes people happier. In fact, Becker argues that, in an abstract sense, the happiness that children bring to a family is essentially the same as the happiness that durable goods bring to a household. He also assumes that, the more children a couple has, the happier the couple is.

Given this set-up, what are the implications of Becker's theory? A proposition of the standard economic theory is that, as incomes rise, the quantity of a commodity demanded tends to increase. In economics, such a commodity is called a 'normal good'. In the unusual case that the quantity of a commodity demanded decreases with income, the commodity is called an 'inferior good'. Becker's key insight is that he treats children as a commodity when analysing a couple's rational fertility choices and consumption of material goods.

Suppose that children are considered a 'normal good' for parents. As such, the preceding theory implies that, when incomes rise, people tend to have more children. This implication is consistent with Malthus's population theory. In contrast, Becker's theory implies that people consume more materials such as food when they become richer. These implications are consistent with many empirical observations made up to recent times. Even today, a greeting often used during Chinese New Year, 'Ding-Cai-Liang-Wang', refers to prosperity in terms of both wealth and offspring.

## 12.2 THE 'QUALITY' OF CHILDREN

The previous section introduced the first modern theory of fertility developed by Becker. This theory argues that parents achieve happiness directly from having children. The more children they have, the happier they are. Yet the question is: how do we reconcile this theory with the often-observed negative correlation between fertility and income? Given its simple set-up, the reconciliation obviously entails the assumption that children are considered an 'inferior good' for parents. However, this assumption is intuitively very unsatisfactory, as children are usually highly treasured by their parents. For example, many children in China are currently spoiled as 'little princesses' and 'little kings'. How could parents possibly consider them 'inferior goods'?

This unsatisfactory implication led Becker and his co-author Arthur Lewis to develop a new theory known as the theory of the interaction between the quantity and quality of children. In this theory, Becker and Lewis (1973) add one more dimension to Becker's earlier framework: parents also achieve happiness from the 'quality' of each of their children. A child's quality may include characteristics that are desirable to its parents, such as high educational attainment, social–economic status, health and intelligence.

One question immediately arises: why do parents care about the quality of their children? In his *Treatise on the Family*, Becker (1991) suggests an answer from an evolutionary perspective: a more healthy, wealthy and better-educated individual is in a better position in the marriage market. However, in a well-known review of Becker's book,

Arthur (1982) comments that such an answer may not be fully satisfactory. It is commonly observed that individuals with lower educational attainment, lower income and lower social status, namely individuals of lower 'quality', tend to have more children.

One may argue that some aspects of quality such as height and physical appearance matter greatly to one's attractiveness to the opposite sex. However, while a better-looking child is more likely to lose its virginity earlier and have more sexual partners, there is no evidence that she/he will have more children. Thus an explanation from the evolutionary perspective seems insufficient.

Moreover, Arthur (1982, p. 396) states:

> A fundamental problem remains. What exactly is child 'quality' and why should parents be so interested in it? Not wanting to narrow the definition to schooling, Becker defines 'child quality' (p. 95) as 'the expenditure on each child.' But then how does expenditure have a price? And surely if, as Becker says, modernization causes family members to look more to the outside and become more individualistic, then they should take less interest in their children. Becker's escape (p. 95) from this inconsistency appears to be that parental interest in child quality is biologically built in: 'A reduction in the number of children born to the couple can increase the representation of their children in the next generation if this enables the couple to invest sufficiently more in the education, training, and "attractiveness" of each child to increase markedly their probability of survival to reproductive ages and the reproduction of each survivor.' 'High-quality' children, in other words, make better marriages, and this has biological advantages. Becker may be right. But if positive assortative mating (like-marrying-like) is indeed the case, and if the lower orders à la Becker tend to have more, but 'lower quality' children, then upper-crust genes would do better to belong to less educated bodies, unless survival differences were strong indeed. The question is empirical. Even if the 'snobbish gene' does exist, it fails to explain why the motto of many traditional societies remains: Ask not what you can do for your children, ask what your children can do for you. The underlying drive for child 'quality' is a mystery in the entire thesis.

In response to this criticism, some economists suggest an alternative explanation for why parents are concerned about the 'quality' of their children: vanity. For example, Pollak (1988) argues that a 'high-quality' child who becomes a doctor gives cause to its parents to brag about their child's profession. This book strongly agrees with this explanation. Indeed, if having children itself is a type of vanity for parents, the quality of their children naturally also feeds into their vanity. I provide a useful analogy as follows. In the early 1980s, a family in China was envied by its neighbours if it possessed a television, usually a simple black-and-white model. The country developed economically, and an increasing amount of households adopted televisions in the mid-1980s, whereupon families had to have a colour television to secure a high social status. Such a transition from the sheer possession of goods (e.g. televisions) to the possession of better-quality goods applies to most durable goods. By this logic, we can understand why the 'quality' of children matters to their parents.

Indeed, for most families, the quality of their children is much more important than the quality of consumption goods such as televisions and cars. Children are often considered 'representations' of their parents. If a child's quality is high, it signals to others that its parents have good genes, which substantially increases the parents' vanity and happiness.

There is another important reason why the quality of children matters greatly to their parents: children can fulfil their parents' 'dreams'. When people are young, they are usually full of ambitions. For example, many migrants to the USA are attracted by the American Dream. However, life is full of uncertainties and the workplace is competitive, and although most people crave success and the fulfilment of their dreams, only a fraction are ultimately 'successful'.

At a certain stage in life, many people may become aware that the chance that they will be 'successful' in achieving their ambitions is very slim. In this case, they may have a strong desire for their children to be successful in achieving these goals. In modern societies where food and material consumption goods are abundant, the goals that most people set for themselves are vain in nature. Thus people often find their children to be good substitutes in dream realization. I refer to the process of an individual living vicariously through another individual to achieve certain vain goals as 'vanity through affiliation'. Further, I refer to the latter individual as the former's 'vanity affiliate'.

Akerlof (1997, p. 1010) states: 'I shall let individuals occupy different locations in social space. Social interaction ... will increase with proximity in this space.' The shorter the 'social distance' between an individual and their vanity affiliate, the happier the individual is when their affiliate achieves certain goals. The shortest social distance between most people and their vanity affiliate is that between parents and their children. Thus parents often have a strong incentive to have 'higher-quality' children who are more likely to achieve the goals that fulfil their parents' dreams.

When the quality of children is taken into account, parents may want to limit the size of their family by reducing their number of children. More children means reductions in the expenditure on and average parental attention paid to each child, which may reduce the children's quality. Thus many parents may spend more on improving the quality of their children rather than increasing their quantity as their incomes rise.[98]

Such a trade-off between the quality and quantity of children was realized even in ancient times. For example, one practice of the royal family of the Ottoman Empire might have related to the concern for this quality/quantity trade-off. Burbank and Cooper (2010, p. 135) offer the following observation:

> Another tweaking of Islamic rules further constrained the sultan's sex life. Once a sultan's consort gave birth to a potential heir, she was not allowed to share the sultan's bed again but would accompany her child, a prince and a candidate for both sultanate and murder, out to the provinces, where the boy would be given a governorship. Competition to become the next sultan took place on a somewhat level playing field – no son would be born of a wife, and each had a different slave mother.

When a mother had only one son, she would devote all of her energy to caring for and educating him, which was most beneficial to the education of the next king of the Ottoman Empire.

# 13. The cost of children in population theory

## 13.1 THE COST OF CHILDREN AND FERTILITY

Chapter 12 introduced and further extended the modern theory of fertility put forward by Becker. One of Becker's insights is to treat children as a 'durable consumption good' from their parents' perspective in the economic analysis of fertility. The chapter analysed people's changing fertility patterns as their incomes rise. In terms of microeconomic theory, the 'pure income effect' on fertility was examined in that chapter. To further understand people's decisions on fertility, we must consider another factor: the 'price effect', which is related to the 'cost of children'. Microeconomic theory posits that the demand for a commodity is determined by both household income and the price/cost of the commodity. Thus the demand for a certain number of children, like the demand for any durable good, should be determined by both the cost of children and the parents' income levels.

Substantial evidence indicates that the cost of children tends to increase significantly with economic development. We can apply the 'law of demand' to explain fertility changes across space and time. The law of demand indicates that, holding other things constant, the quantity demanded of a certain commodity decreases when the price of the commodity increases. This is an established law in economic theory that has proved to hold in most circumstances. Thus, as children are usually more expensive in high-income countries than in poor countries, the application of the law of demand provides another explanation for the observed negative correlation between fertility and the level of economic development.

## 13.2 THE COST OF EDUCATION

In most developed countries, governments provide free public education, particularly for primary and middle schools. However, many parents continue to complain about high education costs. Why? There are at least two major reasons. First, many parents look for high-quality kinder-gartens for their children that are usually not free. Second, private schools are expensive, and many parents choose not to send their children to free public schools. I elaborate these two points as follows.

According to some education research, about 50 per cent of a child's cognitive development occurs by the age of three or four,[99] and 80 per cent of its potential intelligence is developed by age eight.[100] Of course, one theoretical possibility is that a child's intelligence is mainly deter-mined genetically, according to the inheritance of parental intelligence and other random factors. However, no evidence rules out the importance of early education. In fact, some economists argue that almost all of a child's early conditioning environment is created by the child's parents, and it is in these early years that the child's basic traits, including cognitive and non-cognitive development, are largely shaped and will greatly affect its future academic performance.[101]

In developed countries, free public education is available to almost every citizen. However, kindergarten expenditures are usually paid by parents, which may significantly influence their children's human capital formation. The teachers in a high-quality kindergarten often receive valuable professional training. Meanwhile, a kindergarten provides an environment in which a child interacts with other children. Such an environment, which usually does not exist at home, helps children to develop valuable social skills through interpersonal interactions. Heck-man et al. (2013) examine the mechanisms of the influential Perry Preschool programme, an early childhood education programme that boosted adult outcomes. The programme, which was carried out from 1962 to 1967, provided high-quality preschool education to three- and four-year-old African-American children from poor families. Heckman et al. (2013) arrive at two important findings. First, the programme had little lasting effect on the IQs of its participants. Second, the programme substantially increased its participants' non-cognitive traits, in turn explaining a sizeable portion of later-life effects on education, employ-ment, earnings and crime. Thus, if parents' teaching can increase their children's IQs or cognitive skills, then the findings of Heckman et al. (2013) suggest a complementary effect between parental and kindergar-ten inputs in early childhood education.[102]

In a series of papers, Heckman and his co-authors investigate the effects of early childhood education on human capital.[103] In particular, these studies show that there is a dynamic complementary effect of educational investments in an individual's whole period of education. For example, if an individual's education receives little investment during early childhood, then the investment in their education when they are in

middle school will be ineffective. Thus, to the extent that poor households cannot invest much in their children's early education, the children
tend to experience poor educational outcomes that in turn suggest that
they will receive low earnings in the labour market.

In sum, a kindergarten education may be very important in determining
a child's educational attainment. Thus many parents spend considerable
amounts of money on their children's early education.

The second reason for the high cost of education is that many parents
send their children to private schools. For example, in the USA, many
public high schools are of low quality according to the 'peer-effects'
measurement.[104] For example, disruptive behaviour in classrooms may
distract students from their studies. It has also been observed that many
children are often strongly influenced by the social behaviour of their
peers.[105] If the peers' focus of attention is on 'street culture' in terms of
extravagance in consumption, playing video/computer games, promiscuous sex, drugs or school violence, a considerable amount of the students'
attention will be diverted from their studies to the pursuit of these other
activities. In such cases, the teachers must spend a great deal of effort
maintaining order in their classrooms and hence have less energy to
teach. Thus many parents in the USA send their children to private
schools, which usually charge high tuition fees.

## 13.3  PARENTAL VANITY AND THE COST OF CHILDREN

In Hong Kong, a well-known advertisement created by Hang Seng Bank
in 2006 stated that the cost of raising a child in Hong Kong was
HK$4 million (US$510 000) at the time, an amount that would be higher
today due to recent inflations. This advertisement was influential partly
because it featured Hong Kong celebrity Lai-Shan Lee, who won the
only Olympic gold medal for Hong Kong in the sporting event of
professional windsurfing in 1996.

The expensiveness of educational institutions may also largely be
caused by the vanity of the parents. For example, in Hong Kong, the
government fully funds the schools in the primary, secondary and tertiary
education systems. Thus the education expenditures on the part of the
students and parents are very small. However, many parents who have
ambitious dreams for their children can find various ways of substantially
increasing educational expenditures. Many people in Hong Kong send
their children to very expensive kindergartens that provide extravagant
facilities and hire native English speakers as teachers. Moreover, that

their children are attending famous kindergartens often becomes a status symbol for the parents, further motivating them to send their children to very expensive kindergartens based on their 'brand names'.

When the children grow older, they are sent to attend summer camps in English-speaking countries. While primary and secondary education is completely free for government schools in Hong Kong, some parents send their children to expensive international schools to learn better English and particularly better English speaking skills. While the tuition fees of local universities in Hong Kong are low, some parents send their children to US or UK universities that charge much higher fees. Many elite universities look at several aspects of their applicants' qualifications, such as their extracurricular activities. In response, parents enrol their children in numerous extracurricular activities such as piano and violin classes to improve their chances of getting into higher-ranked US or UK universities.

Spending money on children's education in this way should yield real returns for the children. For example, in non-English-speaking countries, English proficiency is a major aspect of human capital and educational attainment. A child is more efficient at learning a foreign language at preschool age.[106] Thus it is highly beneficial for a child to have a good teacher who speaks native English. However, spending more money does not always necessarily yield positive education returns. For example, at Hong Kong universities, some academic staff members enjoy so-called 'education allowances' for sending their children to attend international schools in Hong Kong. (This fringe benefit was given to academic staff members who were recruited before 1997, and aimed to encourage 'expatriates' to teach in Hong Kong universities.) However, many academic staff members gave up these education allowances and sent their children to local schools based on the following rationale: in Hong Kong, most people speak Cantonese, a dialect of Chinese. However, possibly because Hong Kong was a British colony before 1997, many people still have the mind-set that speaking English is superior. Children who attend an international school are made to speak English as their first language. As a result, they develop a 'superiority complex' that makes them difficult to get along with and hence will eventually hurt their chances at success when they join the labour market. Thus the real value in spending so much money on children's education is hard to assess.

Moreover, the expenditure on a child's education itself sometimes becomes a matter of parents' conspicuous consumption. For example, if the social norm dictates that parents who send their children to international schools have a higher social status, then many parents will not send their children to local schools even if they think their children would be better off there. In addition, suppose that a social norm emerges that those parents who enrol their children in extracurricular activities attain a higher social status. In that case, some parents will hire tutors to teach their children to play the piano, even if they think such extracurricular activities are virtually useless.

Thus vanity induces people to spend more on their children's education so that their children can stand out among their peers in terms of academic achievement. While many people complain that children are expensive to raise, this expensiveness may largely stem from parental competition, not only in terms of increasing expenditures on the 'quality' of children but also by the 'conspicuous display' of spending money on children's education.

The following report illustrates the potential high cost of getting into an elite US university today:[107]

> How much would you pay to get your child into an Ivy League university? For Gerard and Lily Chow, it seems the sky was the limit. In 2007, the Hong Kong couple enlisted Harvard-lecturer-turned-admissions-consultant Mark Zimny to steer their two sons through elite U.S. boarding schools into a top-ranked university –preferably Harvard. For a monthly $4000 fee per child, their 'total education management' package included extensive admissions counseling, arranging homestays, private tutoring, and extra-curricular activities, whereby Zimny and his team functioned as 'parents away from parents' for their sons. The Chows later switched to a retainer of $1 million per child ...

High educational expenditure is an important reason for the observed demographic transition. In ancient times, educational expenditures were generally low. Nowadays, particularly in developed countries, the expenditure on children's education often accounts for a major fraction of household income. Therefore the demand for children decreases as the cost (or price) of children increases.

## 13.4   URBANIZATION, HOUSING PRICE AND THE COST OF CHILDREN

The cost of housing is another factor that explains why fertility rates vary across time and space. Before the Industrial Revolution, most people lived in rural areas comprising large open spaces. At the time, people faced severe consumption constraints, mainly in relation to food. However, living space was generally not a serious problem. The past 200 years have witnessed a secular economic development. Parallel to this economic development is a continuous urbanization. Indeed, as David Ricardo (1817) points out, economic take-offs are often fuelled by large-scale rural-to-urban migrations.[108] In the contemporary world, peasants are drawn to working in cities not only by the higher wage rates in urban areas, but also the colourful urban lifestyles. For example, many development economists emphasize that rural migrants are mainly induced by the 'city lights' to work and live in cities. Further, many people are attracted by the 'sex and vanity' of city life, such as that reflected in the television series *Sex and the City*, that is not available in rural areas.

In the modern age of consumerism, the varieties of goods and services available to consumers are ever expanding. However, consumers can enjoy these goods and services only if they live in a city. Thus increasing amounts of people crowd into cities, which are ultimately limited by their geographical size, resulting in ever-increasing housing prices. Every child requires a certain minimum living space, and the cost of raising one is very high in a large city simply by virtue of the involved housing cost.

Moreover, as technology progresses and the economy develops, a typical household purchases an increasing number of durable goods, some of which not only make life more comfortable and convenient but also may constitute conspicuous consumption. However, if a household's living space is small, having too many children may make finding enough room for the goods impossible. Even if a household manages to put a big, luxurious, durable item in a corner, the item will not reflect the conspicuous nature it is supposed to confer on the household. Thus high housing prices may strongly discourage a household from having a large number of children.[109] Also, the high cost of educating a child induces parents to limit their family size so they can afford a decent apartment when housing prices are high.

This reasoning explains why fertility in rural areas is often significantly higher than that in urban areas of the same country. In rural areas, there is usually a large expanse of land for each household. Thus, in developed countries and even many developing countries, every household in rural areas is usually able to afford a large house. In other words, the price of children is low in this important respect, which induces a rural household to have more children than an urban household.

# 14. Child labour, 'working daughters' and population theory

This chapter analyses several aspects of child labour, including its determinants and its effects on children's education, child welfare and fertility. There are two main reasons for this endeavour. First, child labour has commonly been observed throughout human history. Recall Cheung's (1972, p. 641) vivid description of the parent–child relationship in the traditional societies of China: 'Just as dogs were raised to hunt for their masters before they were pets, so in early traditional China children were raised as a source of income.' While Cheung's (1972) focus is on how parents tried to extract more money and resources through their children's marriages, the same logic clearly applies to child labour.

There is substantial empirical research documenting a large amount of information about child labour in both historical and contemporary times. For example, in 1861, 36.9 per cent of boys and 20.5 per cent of girls in the 10–14 age group in England and Wales were labourers (Basu, 1999). Child labour is still prevalent in many developing countries. According to an International Labour Organization estimation, about 200 million children under the age of 15 were working in 1995 (ILO, 1996). Further, in the 1980s, about 20 per cent of African children were working, with child workers constituting as much as 17 per cent of the workforce in some African countries (Fyfe, 1989).

Second, although child labour is rarely observed in rich countries today, its widespread existence in the past and in some poor countries provides economists with a 'natural experiment' to better understand parent–child and even sibling relationships within a family. Indeed, somewhat surprisingly, economists and sociologists find it extremely difficult to uncover the essential nature of parent–child relationships. 'Political correctness' and the concern for others' opinions about whether one is a good or bad parent make it almost impossible to elicit completely honest answers from parents through direct interviews and thereby to understand the full picture of these relationships. Thus child labour provides researchers with a rare opportunity to infer the true nature of these relationships through observing the behaviour of parents and children. This chapter finds that 'vanity economics' significantly helps us better understand child labour.

## 14.1   THE DETERMINANTS OF CHILD LABOUR

What are the main determinants of child labour? In the economics literature, Basu and Van (1998) provide the first formal theory to address this question. In particular, they put forward a 'luxury axiom' that states that a family will send its children to the labour market only if its income in the absence of child labour is below the subsistence level. While this luxury axiom reflects an ideology about how parents should treat their children, it often appears to be inconsistent with some observed evidence. For example, Bhalotra and Heady (2003) show that in rural Pakistan and Ghana in the 1990s, the children of households that possessed land and were relatively rich were more likely to work than those of land-poor households. As their finding appears to contradict the 'luxury axiom', Bhalotra and Heady (2003) refer to it as 'the wealth paradox'.

Beginning with Baland and Robinson (2000) and Hazan and Berdugo (2002), most economic theories of child labour are based on Becker's (1991) framework, in which parents care about their children's education and household consumption. The incentive to increase material consumption may stem from both a household's necessity and the parents' vanity. In a very poor society, a significant proportion of households may indeed face a binding constraint on survival, as emphasized by Malthus in the classical population theory. In this case, child labour is necessary to help lift a household out of absolute poverty. However, human desire does not stop when people no longer suffer from hunger and starvation. Indeed, human greed is universal and never satisfied, particularly in an environment of interpersonal comparisons, which is common in most cultures and societies. Thus, if child labour could contribute significantly to household wealth, parents might be tempted to send their children to work. Moreover, as discussed earlier, the 'quality' of children as measured by their educational attainment can be another important source of vanity for their parents.

These theories typically add that children's educational attainment is determined by how much time they spend studying, and analyse how parents allocate their children's time between studying and working. These theories essentially analyse a trade-off between household consumption and children's human capital in the study of child labour: child labour increases household consumption but reduces children's human capital.

In two studies (Fan 2004a, b), I add a dimension to the economics literature on child labour by considering that a child's human capital is determined by the financial resources placed into its education and time of study. (This assumption is supported by much evidence, which is summarized in the next section of this chapter.) With this new consideration, the effect of child labour on children's human capital becomes intriguing. While child labour reduces children's study time, it may substantially increase a household's income, leading to an increase in educational resources and hence a possible increase in the children's human capital. In most poor countries, education is expensive for the majority of households. To tackle this problem, parents may send their children to work to finance at least part of their educational expenditures. The details of this issue are addressed in the next section.

Further, in another study (Fan, 2011), I add to the analytical framework of Fan (2004a) that parents may directly care about their children's leisure. The more leisure time the children have for playing, the happier their parents are. This source of potential happiness may stem from people's altruism towards their children. It may also be a response to social or moral pressures, whether domestic or international. For example, if some parents in poor countries read on the Internet that the practice of child labour has been denounced, they may feel better when they ask their children to work less. This assumption is consistent with Basu and Van's (1998) key assumption, but it is not so radical.

The economic theory of child labour yields two important testable results. First, Hazan and Berdugo (2002) and Fan (2004a, 2011) all consistently demonstrate that the main determinant of child labour is the relative wage between child and adult labour. This result is intuitive. If the children's relative wage is higher, a family gives up more income if it allows its children to work less and spend more time studying or playing.

Second, somewhat surprisingly, Fan (2004a, 2011) shows that, holding the ratio between child and adult wage rates constant, child labour can be independent of parental income. How can this result make sense? The basic logic is as follows. As an adult's wage rate increases, the household's wealth increases, which induces the parents to try to increase the 'quality' of their children by reducing their working time and hence increasing the time they spend studying and playing. On the other hand, holding the relative wage between child and adult labour constant, a child's wage rate increases as the adult wage rises, which induces the parents to send their children to work in the marketplace more often. Fan (2004a, 2011) shows that these two opposite effects often offset each other exactly, which implies that a child's working time is independent of its parents' income.

In summary, this theoretical analysis implies that the main determinant of child labour is the relative wage between child and adult labour. Moreover, the relative productivity of child labour, namely the substitutability between child and adult labour, may matter much more than adults' absolute wage rate to children's labour market participation. The remainder of this section gathers some evidence that is strongly supportive of these theoretical predictions, and lists it in four categories.

First, while the Industrial Revolution greatly increased the average wage rates of adult workers in Britain, children's labour market participation rates also increased considerably when the Industrial Revolution began (e.g. Deane and Cole, 1967). A number of economic historians explain this by noting that the Industrial Revolution greatly increased the substitutability between child and adult labour (e.g. Nardinelli, 1990; Lavalette, 1998; Tuttle, 1999). In particular, based on her extensive empirical research, Tuttle (1999, pp. 75–6) concludes that,

> It was demand, not supply, which dramatically increased the employment of children and youths in certain leading industries during the British Industrial Revolution ... The Industrial Revolution in Great Britain had an impact on the demand for child labour because several new inventions in the textile industry and innovations in the production process of making cloth and extracting coal increased the productivity of children and youths. As children and youths became more productive, the demand for their services rose.

Meanwhile, Mantoux (1983, p. 410) states that, during the early Industrial Revolution, children were not only an adequate substitute for men, but were even preferable in some occupations in many respects, as 'for certain processes the small size of the children and the delicacy of touch made them the best aids to machines'. (Examples include the employment of children in mines and as chimney sweeps, both of which involved spaces that were too small for adults to crawl through.)

By a similar logic, further technological progress such as the mechanization of spinning and weaving in the later stages of the Industrial Revolution reduced the relative productivity of child labour and hence led to a reduction in children's labour market participation (Galbi, 1994; Grootaert and Kanbur, 1995).

Second, Levy (1985) examines the relationship between the change in child labour productivity (due to technological progress) and child labour in rural Egypt. Before the mechanization of Egypt's agricultural sector, the relative productivity of child labour was high in the production of cotton, which was Egypt's most important crop. Levy (1985) finds that the children's labour market participation rate was high during the period, and that child labour was a crucial part of Egypt's agricultural labour. In particular, Levy (1985, p. 778, 782) reports that 'cotton weeding and picking is better suited to children than tasks connected with cultivating rice, fruit, or vegetables ... it is commonly believed that child labor does not have good substitutes in cotton-related work'. However, Levy (1985) also finds that the mechanization of Egyptian agriculture, especially the expanded use of tractors and irrigation pumps, significantly reduced the relative productivity of children and particularly young children. Consequently, it contributed significantly to a decrease in child labour.

Third, in the contemporary world, India is a example of a large nation where child labour has been widespread. Much empirical research indicates that the relative productivity of child versus adult labour in India has been high. For example, Mehra-Kerpelman (1996) shows that a child's income sometimes accounts for 34–37 per cent of the total income of an Indian household. Further, Nangia (1987) conducted a survey in the Delhi region of India, comparing child wages relative to adult wages. Table 14.1 summarizes the survey results.

*Table 14.1    Child wages versus adult wages in India*

|  | Equal | 1/2 to equal | 1/2 to 1/3 | 1/3 to 1/4 | Less than 1/4 | Uncertain |
|---|---|---|---|---|---|---|
| Percentage | 39.5 | 19.1 | 7.0 | 3.7 | 6.1 | 24.7 |

Table 14.1 reports that about 40 per cent of child workers earn wages equal to adults and about 20 per cent earn 50–100 per cent of adult wages. Table 14.1 also shows that a small proportion of child workers earn significantly lower wages than adult workers. The large variation in earnings among child workers could be due to their large age variations. For example, a boy of 13 is physically much stronger and much more productive than a boy of seven. The variation could also be due to the apprenticeship system, which, according to some economists (e.g. Grootaert and Kanbur, 1995), can contribute to a process of socialization and know-how transference that ensures that child workers earn low wages in their early years of apprenticeship. These figures clearly suggest that the relative wage of child labour in the region is high, which helps explain why child labour in India has been serious and prevalent.

Fourth, based on their extensive study of the wages and child labour in Britain in the nineteenth century, Hunt (1973, 1986) and Nardinelli (1990) find that, despite the large regional variations in wages, the correlation between the general wages of adult males and the children's labour market participation rates is close to zero. In particular, Hunt (1973, p. 126) summarizes his findings as follows:

in the main, and for most of the periods, areas where men's wages were low were distinguished neither by high activity rates (i.e. children's labour market participation rates) nor high family earnings, while many other areas combined high wages for men with better than average opportunities for women and young people.

In short, the findings of Hunt (1973, 1986) and Nardinelli (1990) confirm the theoretical result that, holding the ratio between child and adult wage rates constant, child labour can be independent of parental income.

The aforementioned historical and contemporary evidence shows that child labour productivity and children's labour market participation are closely related. One question naturally arises: why do the relative productivity between child and adult labour differ significantly over time and space? To answer this question, consider an individual who possesses three production factors: endowed physical labour, endowed mental labour and acquired mental labour (i.e. education and training). In ancient times, because production technology was rudimentary, endowed physical labour was the most important factor of production. Hence, particularly in a hunting-oriented economy, the productivity of child labour is significantly lower than that of adult labour. At the beginning of the Industrial Revolution, machinery that was simple to operate was created as a great substitute for endowed physical labour in production. Consequently, physical labour became less important than endowed mental labour in production, and child labour productivity rose sharply.

As more progress is made in production technology, acquired mental labour such as formal education is becoming the most important production factor by far. Therefore, in the knowledge-based economies of developed countries, the productivity of a child, who often sacrifices schooling for work, becomes very low.

Nevertheless, the level of the world's economic development is uneven. Because production technology remains backward in many developing countries today, the relative productivity between child and adult labour in these regions is much higher than in developed countries. For example, Grootaert and Kanbur (1995, p. 196) point out that

Today's technology can have ambivalent effects on the demand for child work. Miniaturization and assembly-line production in the electronics and electrical appliance industries has again led to some demand for 'nimble fingers'. Not everywhere are robots the ultimate suppliers of this skill. In garment production, the advent of fairly cheap multi-function sewing machines has once again made possible home production, and much manufacturing relies on subcontracting arrangements, which can lead to girls' work at home.[110]

Finally, child labour for an individual household may exert a social effect, which in turn influences children's labour market participation for the whole society. Basu and Van (1998) consider the following scenario. In a poor economy, if none of the children work, then the adults' wages are high enough to support their families. However, if most of the children work, the adult income of a household may be driven below the subsistence level. In this case, all the parents must send their children to work, no matter how much they hate doing so.

Another social effect of child labour may stem from the interpersonal comparisons of household wealth. Neumark and Postlewaite (1998) show that the entry of some women into paid employment can spur other women's labour market participation. In particular, they find that a married woman is more likely to be in the workforce if her sister or sister-in-law has a paying job. They also find that women with non-working sisters are more likely to be employed if their husbands earn less than their sisters' husbands. By a similar logic, if most of the children work, a family may face the dilemma that its household income is much lower than its neighbours' if its children do not work. Consequently, interpersonal comparisons may induce a household to send its children to work as well.

## 14.2  CHILD LABOUR AND CHILDREN'S EDUCATION

In the previous section, it was noted that a child's human capital is determined by the financial resources available for its education and time for study. Indeed, where there is child labour, usually there is poverty. When people are very poor, financial resources matter greatly to their children's education. For example, Banerjee and Duflo (2007) show that, even in the contemporary world, many people live on US$1 per day (at purchasing power parity), and spend little on their children's education. In this case, the children's earnings would clearly help finance their education, such as by buying textbooks and basic educational materials. Further, a child's human capital includes its health, and a household's wealth is a very important factor in determining children's health. Thus, if a child's earnings substantially increase a household's wealth, they will in turn considerably increase the child's nutritional intake and hence improve its health.

The importance of financial resources for children's human capital in poor countries is consistently revealed in empirical studies. For example, Glewwe et al. (2009) and many empirical studies surveyed in their article demonstrate that educational expenditure plays a critical role in children's human capital accumulation in poor countries. In particular, some of the studies suggest that textbook provision should be given high priority in developing countries. Glewwe et al. (2001) find that better-nourished children perform significantly better in school. Horrell et al. (2001) show that, in ancient times a household's wealth was a very important factor determining children's health and human capital.[111] Indeed, the importance of financial resources for children's human capital formation in poor countries is emphasized by almost every development economics textbook (e.g. Todaro, 2000) and is easily noticeable when one pays a visit to very poor countries.

Considering that both educational expenditures and study time matter to children's human capital, I demonstrate that an increase in child labour may enhance human capital in poor countries (Fan 2004a, 2004b, 2011). When children's earnings are sufficiently high relative to those of adults, the positive effect of the increased financial resources on children's education may outweigh the negative effect of the reduced study time. Thus, in contrast to the conventional wisdom that child labour necessarily reduces children's human capital, the concern for children's human capital may precisely be an important reason why parents send their children to work. For example, a rise in child labour productivity may lead to an increase in both child labour and children's human capital.[112]

Moreover, a household often arranges for some of its children to work, as it allows other children in the family to receive better education. There may be a number of reasons for this arrangement. First, if a child works intensively for a long period every day, they may feel too exhausted to concentrate on their studies. Second, some children are more intelligent and able than others at studying. Third, in less-developed countries, a return to schooling may be higher for boys than girls, indicating a gender bias in favour of boys. For example, Parish and Willis (1993, p. 866) note that in traditional Chinese societies, 'one of the best things that can happen to a male, besides being born to rich, well-educated parents, is to have an older sister'.

Indeed, many empirical studies support this argument. In observing 21 Shanghai families, Lamson (1930) finds that all the child labourers were girls who all intended to help their brothers financially in schooling or obtaining apprenticeships. In the 1950s and 1960s, daughters usually performed most of the household chores in Hong Kong, such as cooking, washing clothes and hauling water from a distance. (At the time, there was a serious water shortage in Hong Kong, and most households had to obtain water from a distant location that centralized allocation.) If they had younger siblings, they were often the main caretakers, as their mothers had to work in factories. In Hong Kong in the 1960s and 1970s, a significant proportion of paid work was carried out at home. Most of the school-age girls helped their parents do the work, such as packing plastic flowers, assembling transistors, pressing metal eyelets and beading.[113]

Thus, in terms of contemporary child labour practice, it is seldom the case that every child of a household performs an equal share of the work. In most cases, some children work while others focus on their studies. This inequality is established by parents, implying that it is in their interest to make such an arrangement. The effect of this inequality on children's welfare was first addressed by Becker (1991, p. 190), although in a somewhat different context:

> Poorer families have a conflict between equity and efficiency and invest more in abler children only if efficiency outweighs equity ... The conflict between efficiency and equity is reduced when abler children are altruist and are concerned about the welfare of their siblings ... Poorer families then could also gain in the efficiency of investing more human capital in abler children without sacrificing the interest of other children, for the abler children would voluntarily transfer resources to the others when they become adults. Even if abler children were not altruistic, poorer families would invest more in them if they 'agreed' to look after their siblings, agreements that could be enforced by the legal system or by social norm.

This book offers a new explanation for why a child may be happy to accept the arrangement that it works while its siblings receive more education. Again, this argument rests on vanity. I posit that, if a child considered its brothers and sisters as 'vanity affiliates', then the child would be happy to see them stand out among their peers in terms of their education and career achievements. The degree of vanity affiliation depends greatly on the 'social distance' between an individual and their affiliate. Genetic connection is usually a major determinant of the social distance between two individuals. From this perspective, the social distance between an individual and their siblings is very short, implying that the vanity affiliation experienced from the siblings' education and career development achievements is very strong. This argument is empirically supported by Salaff's (1976, 1981) detailed studies on the 'working daughters of Hong Kong', which will be discussed and analysed in Section 14.4.

## 14.3 CHILD LABOUR AND FERTILITY

Because child labour reduces the cost of children, it increases the demand for children and therefore the fertility rate. In his famous *Treatise on the Family*, Becker observes that the 'price of children' tends to be low in underdeveloped economies and high in well-developed economies. Child labour is perhaps the most important reason for the relatively low cost of children in many developing countries. For example, Becker (1991) notes that children in rural India and Brazil often begin to contribute to farm work at the age of five or six and become important contributors to the family by age 12. Becker also refers to a vivid example of child labour provided by Adam Smith (1776, pp. 70–71) in terms of colonial America:

> Labor is there so well rewarded that a numerous family of children, instead of being a burthen is a source of opulence and prosperity to the parents. The labor of each child, before it can leave their house, is computed to be worth a hundred pounds clear gain to them.

The basic theoretical implication is that fertility tends to rise as the child labour wage rate increases. This implication is supported by several empirical studies. For example, based on US aggregate data, Rosenzweig (1977) finds that a reduction in the pecuniary returns from children within the agricultural sector, associated with capital-biased technological change, was a strong factor in the decline in farm birth rates between 1939 and 1960. Based on district-level data from the 1961 Census of India, Rosenzweig and Evenson (1977) report that a basic condition for Indian families' choice to have relatively large numbers of children in the late 1950s was the high return on the use of children as raw labour sources. Further, as labour and land are complementary inputs in agricultural production, Rosenzweig and Evenson (1977) suggest that a land redistribution programme aimed at promoting equality and unaccompanied by other changes would increase fertility and the incidence of child labour.

Levy (1985) finds that a major determinant of fertility in rural Egypt was child labour productivity. In particular, he concludes (p. 789):

> variations in labor contributions from children has an appreciable effect on farmers' attitudes toward fertility and actual family size ... cotton labor

> intensity is one of the basic conditions motivating Egyptian farmers to have relatively large families …

In fact, linking fertility to child labour helps explain why rural fertility has exceeded urban fertility. In rural areas, there are many jobs suitable for children, such as watching cows and other domestic animals, keeping birds away from crops, helping with the harvest, weeding and planting. In contrast, the jobs in urban areas require much more education and skills. Thus the productivity of child labour in rural areas is higher than that in urban areas, so the fertility is also higher. For example, Fyfe (1989, p. 24) notes: 'children in rural areas can make an early work contribution. This, in turn, can positively influence fertility as the family views children as more hands rather than more mouths …'.

Moreover, Fan (2004b) analyses the effects of child labour on the interaction between the quantity and quality of children. When children's earnings are sufficiently high relative to their cost, raising children is cheap but sending them to school is expensive. Thus parents may consider their quantity of children as a 'necessity' and the children's quality as a 'luxury' due to the 'price difference'.

Because people demand more luxuries and fewer necessities as they become richer, fertility decreases and children's educational attainment increases as parental incomes rise. Thus, when child labour is introduced, we can better understand why parents have fewer yet higher-quality children when incomes rise rather than the other way around, or rather than having more and higher-quality children at the same time.

This argument can also be restated in closer relationship to vanity. When people are very poor, having a family and children is not easy. In this case, the possession of children provides a source of vanity for the parents. However, when people become richer, most have the capacity to raise children, particularly because the cost of children is substantially reduced due to child labour. In this case, only the parents who have the type of children who stand out in terms of their educational achievement can gain vanity. Consequently, parents will focus more on the quality of their children.

## 14.4   'WORKING DAUGHTERS OF HONG KONG'

Section 14.2 discussed parents' unequal treatment of children. From the perspective of 'vanity affiliation', a new view was put forward that children may to a large extent or even fully agree to such an unequal arrangement, even when they are the one who is assigned to work rather than go to school. Salaff's (1976, 1981) study of the 'working daughters of Hong Kong' provides much evidence for this view. Most 'working daughters' were adults, and hence they are not 'child labour' according to the legal definition. However, the 'working daughters' willingly followed their parents' instructions, which implies that the underlying logic for the analysis of 'working daughters' is essentially the same as that of child labour.

Industrialization in Hong Kong took place in the 1960s and 1970s, generating a sudden large demand for labour. As was the case in the USA and other Western countries during the early stages of industrialization, unmarried young women accounted for a major part of the new labour force in Hong Kong's factories. Salaff conducted extensive and detailed interviews with unmarried, employed Hong Kong women in their early twenties. These women voluntarily sacrificed their self-interest by contributing most of their earnings to their parents before getting married, and sometimes by delaying their marriages.

As described by Salaff (1976, 1981) and also discussed in the previous section, most of these women were child labourers long before they formally participated in the labour market. They began to work in Hong Kong factories between the ages of 12 and 14, and gave most of the income they earned before marriage to their parents. They retained only a small amount of their earnings, an amount agreed by their parents in advance, for their own use. This amount usually increased when more of a girl's siblings joined the labour force.

In the 1970s, secondary education was free only to those who performed well at primary school, applying to about 25 per cent of the students. Attending secondary school was expensive for the remaining primary-school graduates. The working daughters' earnings substantially increased their households' wealth, enabling their younger siblings to receive more education. Salaff (1976, p. 446) refers to the example of an eldest sister in a family of five girls:

> still unmarried at age 29 she earmarked one-third of her factory earnings for the schooling of her youngest two sisters. All of her sisters had the opportunity to continue school past primary 6, and the youngest went further in their studies than the older ones. The eldest's economic assistance was to be continued until the next two working sisters could assume the entire burden themselves.

Salaff (1976) notes parents' strong gender bias in favour of boys. The people she interviewed stressed that boys were considered the 'future' of their families. Salaff (1976, p. 447) therefore concludes: 'The entry of daughters into the labor force at an early age is thus not only a response to the need for sheer survival, but also a recurrent solution to the family's desire for upward mobility through their sons' education.'

In the presence of such a strong gender bias, Salaff (1976) spots a puzzling fact: the girls in her study were willing to accept their roles. The following is a transcription of a conversation Salaff had with a working girl called Wai-gun (ibid., p. 449):

> (How was the decision reached for you to quit school?) My parents made the decision. I wasn't involved in the discussions. ... My brother, who is only a year younger, got to go to school longer because he is a boy. He has the responsibility in the future to rear a family, thus his further education will help him in getting a job; it's more important to him than to me. (But women work too.) I know that women do work now, but they didn't work so much then. Anyway, a woman's job is second to a man's. (How did you feel about the decision to end school?) Well, I am part of the family, too! I must share in its decisions, and take responsibility for running it!

This puzzle can be explained by vanity affiliation. In a society with a strong gender bias against women, the vanity in terms of social recognition that a man receives from high educational achievement is much greater than what a woman receives from the same achievement. In this case, the vanity a woman receives from her brother's success through vanity affiliation could be greater than what she would receive from her own success. I now further clarify this point using the following numerical example.

Suppose that in a society with a strong gender bias against women, a man who is accepted into a prestigious university receives a vanity score of 1000. Suppose that the man has a sister. Through vanity affiliation, the sister can obtain a vanity score of 200 from her brother's success. If the sister has the opportunity to obtain a good secondary-school education and studies hard to get into the same prestigious university, she would achieve a vanity score of 150. Note that this scenario is possible in a society that has a strong gender bias and heavily discounts women's success. In this case, the woman would rationally choose a strategy that led to her brother's academic achievement rather than a strategy that led to her own success. Of course, the woman may strongly desire the disappearance of such a gender bias. However, if she cannot change the bias through her own effort, she has no choice but to choose a strategy that effectively reinforces it.

I recall a remark that a colleague made several years ago. He said that he and many of his friends always bought the most fashionable mobile phones for their teenage children. However, the parents always used old-fashioned mobile phones. The logic of this situation is the same as that of the preceding one. Teenagers receive a large amount of positive or negative vanity from their peers when consuming luxurious items such as mobile phones. This also has a strong effect on their parents through vanity affiliation. In particular, many parents feel concerned that their children may be looked down upon by their classmates for having a lower-quality mobile phone. In contrast, my colleague and his friends are family-oriented men who have little incentive to impress their peers through fashion. They choose to buy the best mobile phones only for the sake of their children.

Moreover, to increase the vanity affiliation between the working girls and their siblings, their parents encouraged their involvement in the discipline and decisions made on their siblings' education. For example, Salaff (1976, p. 450) states:

> Girls who help pay for the schooling of younger children can also often select the school and figure in directing the careers of their siblings as well. The eldest daughter of a merchant who travelled frequently spoke of her influence in selecting the careers of her brothers ... Daughters may also discipline their younger brothers and sisters ... one eldest sister, a factory worker who was paying her brother's school bills, beat the child after he failed the school year. Similarly, Ci-li wished to enforce the younger children's responsibility to the family and chastised them when they did not study, whereas her mother was less strict.

While a sibling's education may be the most important reason for the willingness of working daughters to make economic sacrifices, they are also concerned about another aspect of vanity: their families' conspicuous consumption. With working daughters contributing their earnings to their parents, their families' purchasing power increased considerably. They could buy additional durable goods, such as televisions, refrigerators and washing machines. Possessing these durable goods not only significantly improved their standard of living but also their vanity, as the goods symbolized social status in Hong Kong during the 1970s. Moreover, and perhaps more importantly, the daughters' incomes enabled their parents to purchase 'decent' housing for their families (Salaff, 1976).

Furthermore, Chinese society is gregarious. In particular, in the city-state of Hong Kong, most families have a large number of relatives and friends. Thus their expenditures on social events, such as banquets in celebration of family members' birthdays, are often an important indicator of their social status. Working daughters' income contributions allowed Hong Kong families to give a greater number of more expensive banquets, which yielded more vanity for the families. Moreover, to enhance the vanity affiliation of the working daughters, they were often asked to play active roles in such events (Salaff, 1976).

In addition to sacrificing their earnings, many working daughters in Hong Kong also sacrificed by delaying their marriages. After getting married, a woman was constrained by her husband in submitting her earnings to her parents. Further, after having children, a woman's main vanity affiliate shifted from her siblings to her children, which induced her to withdraw or greatly reduced her economic contribution to her parents. Foreseeing this, Hong Kong parents often tried to persuade their daughters to delay marriage. Salaff (1976, pp. 452–3) offers the following observation:

> A member of A-li's family remarked, 'As we have so many children in our family, mother's really worried about how to support us all … she gets frightened when anyone mentions the word: "Marriage!"' Mae-fun's elder sister married at age 25, and Mae-fun as the second oldest child was expected to remain at home until at least that age. She said, 'Mother said I can marry whomever I wish, but even after I find someone, I must postpone the marriage for some years. With elder sister having married, we just can't afford to lose another in marriage now.' Such obligations to family are the major reason for the dramatic rise in marriage age in recent years.

# 15. Old-age support, family protection and population theory

## 15.1 VANITY AND FILIAL PIETY

Filial piety occupies the central core value in the cultures of many East Asian countries, such as South Korea, Japan, Taiwan and traditional China. It is a social norm promoted by Confucian philosophy, and it emphasizes that an individual should pay a great amount of respect to their parents. In particular, filial piety requires a person to be obedient to their parents and to provide financial support to them in their old age. Chapter 14 summarized Salaff's fairly detailed case study of filial piety in the behaviour of the working daughters of Hong Kong.

This chapter aims to examine filial piety more generally. It explores answers to the following two fundamental questions. First, what material basis is required for the norm of filial piety to emerge? Second, why are people willing to adhere to this social norm?

Economists tend to believe that there is an economic rationale for any social custom to exist in the first place, and filial piety is no exception. Economists' research indicates that, in ancient times, people's adherence to filial piety substantially improved almost everyone's welfare.

Today, most people work during their youth into middle age and then retire in old age, often between the ages of 60 and 65. Without a large amount of income transfers from the government, people's income drops considerably after retirement. However, people can save during their working years. Meanwhile, highly developed financial systems provide people with a variety of investment vehicles. At the very least, risk-averse individuals can choose a safe investment strategy of putting their money into a large bank in the form of time deposits. In most countries, a large bank is usually 'too big to fail'. Thus one's savings in a large bank are effectively insured by the government.

However, people in ancient times were not so fortunate. At the time, silver, gold and land had stable stores of value. However, the rule of law was usually not well established and private property rights were not well protected. Consequently, these items were vulnerable to theft and robbery. Other valuable items such as rice and livestock had clearly worse stores of value for long-term savings.[114] Thus, in such circumstances, old people would simply not be able to survive once they lost the capacity to work. In addition, well-organized nursing homes did not exist in ancient times, and old people had very miserable lives when their ability to take care of themselves deteriorated.

All these problems are resolved to a large extent when children are willing to take care of their parents. In circumstances where the return on savings is low and very uncertain, raising children who have filial piety obligations provides a potentially effective way of financing old-age consumption. In other words, filial piety in ancient times might have emerged as a response to underdeveloped financial and legal systems.

The next important question is: how can filial piety be enforced? Although parents and children are genetically related, the theory of evolution offers no help in answering this question. True, it is simply human nature for parents to raise their children. Indeed, all animals have a natural instinct to raise and protect their offspring, even if it puts their own lives at risk. All these facts can easily be justified from an evolutionary perspective. However, the same argument cannot be made to justify children taking care of their elderly parents. While parents pass their genes on to their children, the children do not pass their genes on to their parents. What arguments can then be made as to why children took on the responsibility of looking after their elderly parents in most ancient societies?

The answer can be derived from the analysis of the dynamic inter-actions between parents and children using the 'game theory' developed by John Nash. Ehrlich and Lui (1991) analyse a self-enforcing implicit contract in which parents invest in their children and in return obtain material support from their children in old age. In such intergenerational interactions, there are two potential 'beliefs'. The first is that the children take care of their elderly parents, and the other is that the children do not take on that responsibility when the time comes. Both beliefs can be self-fulfilling. Suppose that the current belief in the society is that children will take care of their elderly parents. Then, children will have the incentive to take on the responsibility when their parents are old. If they did not do so, the current 'belief' in the society would switch to a different belief that children do not take on the responsibility, which would lead to their own children (i.e. the grandchildren) not taking on the responsibility in turn. Thus, based on the concept of game theory, filial piety emerges as a 'social contract' that leads children to take care of their elderly parents.

However, life is full of uncertainty, and many unforeseeable special circumstances may lead children to deviate from being filial towards their elderly parents if the aforementioned social contract is the only constraint. Thus vanity may play an important role in ensuring that the 'belief' that benefits everyone during intergenerational interactions is sustained. Indeed, in the preceding analysis, the belief that children ignore their parents is also theoretically possible. In such cases of multiple equilibria, economists usually resort to 'culture and tradition' in determining the exact equilibrium.

Moreover, culture and tradition may not randomly select the equilibrium. In the preceding example, it is reasonable to argue that culture and tradition usually select the belief that children take care of their parents in old age, leading to the equilibrium that most society members prefer. In practice, the belief can be selected by educating society members about the value of filial piety. For example, in ancient China, filial piety was considered an important virtue. A member who had the reputation of not being filially pious to his parents was often ostracized by the society and could not be appointed as a government official. In other words, filial piety itself is a major source of vanity in some societies. As such, the consumption patterns of one's parents may become an important aspect of the child's conspicuous consumption. In fact, in extreme cases, the funeral of a parent in China today sometimes becomes an opportunity for demonstrating one's social and economic status. Some examples are provided as follows.

On 30 November 2010, a rich man in Chongqing set up an enormous banquet for his mother's funeral that consisted of more than 500 dinner tables and more than 5000 people.[115] In Veblen's terms, the funeral not only served as a ritual for mourning the mother, but was also used by the son for engaging in conspicuous consumption. Indeed, the report states: 'Hearing the news, people in the city of Chongqing could not help asking each other: "which rich man is now showing off his wealth?"'

There have been similar occurrences. On 17 November 2007, in Lufeng City of Guangdong province, about 3000 people participated in the funeral of the mother of a senior city government official.[116] In fact, such occurrences are quite common for senior government officials in small Chinese cities and counties. The officials often use these occasions to achieve multiple important purposes.

First, such a big funeral can demonstrate an official's strong filial piety, which is currently promoted by the Chinese central government. Second, it is an occasion to show off an official's power and status – his vanity. Of course, many junior officials do not want to miss the opportunity to flatter their superiors. In the case of the funeral of the senior official's mother, the public and media observed sarcastically that many participants (mainly junior government officials) cried and expressed a grief than was far deeper than that of the senior official himself.[117] (The public added that, if the senior official died, no one would attend his funeral in the first place.) Third, government officials can take advantage of such occasions to receive a large amount of money in the form of comforting 'gifts', usually given by businessmen who need his help, with much less concern for bribery charges.

## 15.2  RULE OF LAW AND FERTILITY

In association with economic development, most countries have experienced significant changes in their 'institutions'. In particular, the rule of law is much better established and property rights much better enforced in modern societies compared with ancient societies, in developed countries compared with developing countries and in more-developed urban areas compared with less-developed rural areas of the same country. These institutional changes may also significantly affect people's fertility choices and child gender preferences.

When a rule of law is lacking, a family has to depend mainly on its members to defend its properties, and more often than not on its honour or vanity. As a result, families may have an incentive to have more children. To better understand this argument, let us first examine the bargaining theory developed by John Nash. While the movie *A Beautiful Mind* shows that Nash developed non-cooperative game theory, which this book has utilized extensively, he also developed the bargaining theory, another important contribution that is explained as follows.

Nash considers a scenario in which a task must be performed by two persons, and asks the following question: 'How do the two persons who perform the task divide the value of the joint product?' A tempting answer may be that it depends on the relative contributions of the two persons. However, when the input of either of the two parties is necessary for the completion of the task, it is often difficult to assess the relative contribution. An illuminating example is that it takes a man and woman to 'produce' a child, and the woman usually endures much more time, effort and pain in the process. However, it is difficult for the woman to argue that she has more than a 50 per cent right to the child.

Based on some basic axioms, Nash (1950b) proves in a rigorous framework that a person's share of the joint product depends on their bargaining power. Where does one's bargaining power come from? Nash answers that a person's bargaining power depends on their 'outside option', which Nash defines as what the person would get by not joining the other person in the production. Consider a simple numerical illustration. Two persons, John and David, can make $1000 by working on a project together. Neither of them can work on the project alone. However, if they do not work on the project, they can both continue their regular jobs. John is regularly a software engineer, and he would otherwise earn $300. David is regularly a janitor, and he would otherwise earn $100. If they worked on the project, they would give up their regular jobs. In such a scenario, according to the Nash bargaining theory, John would receive a bigger share of the $1000 because his 'outside option' is greater than David's (i.e. $300 > $100).

Consider a scenario in which two village households, X and Y, compete for the right of a piece of land when neither of them can resort to the rule of law. In this example, the bargaining process between the two families over the piece of land is in the shadow of violent conflicts. Suppose that there are eight adult males in household X and four in household Y. Further, assume that every adult male has similar physical strength and fighting skills, and that there is no firearm. In this scenario, household X would have the advantage over household Y in a fight because household Y is outnumbered. Therefore, if a violent conflict were to break out, a member in household Y would be injured more seriously than a member in household X on average. In other words, the outside option is worse for household Y than for household X. This means that household X has more bargaining power than household Y in competing for the piece of land, which in turn implies that household X would receive a greater share of it. If we further assumed that the average injury to household X would be much smaller than the average injury to household Y in a violent fight, we could conclude that household X would get most of the piece of land. In the Nash bargaining framework, violence never really materializes. However, the ability to fight determines a person's bargaining power and hence their share of the payoff.[118]

Some observations and empirical studies support the preceding theoretical analysis. For example, Panayotou (1994, p. 151) observes that

> most contributions by children consist of capturing and appropriating open-access natural resources such as water, fodder, pastures, fish, fuel wood, and other forest products, and clearing open-access land for cultivation ... the number of children (is) the decisive instrument in the hands of the household: the household's share of open-access property depends on the number of hands it employs to convert open-access resources into private property.

In addition, by comparing the countries with low levels of economic freedom and rule of law and countries with high levels of those measures,

Norton (2002) shows that the fertility rates in the former are more than twice those in the latter. Further, he shows that this finding is robust after controlling for per capita income. Thus Norton (2002) concludes that an important determinant of fertility is the quality of the 'institutions', as measured by the protection of private property rights.

In some circumstances, the property right of land may be fairly well enforced. However, even if one discounts property disputes, there are often other disputes between neighbours. It is often hard for the government to settle such disputes, particularly in remote villages. For example, if a member of a family feels that they have been insulted by a member of the other family, whether they will obtain an apology depends on whether the other family fears revenge. If the size of the insulted member's family is small, making it unlikely that the family would win in a potential fight, then the other family may feel free to make insults and bully. In other words, the basic dignity of the family members in a remote village may depend on the size of the family. The single-child policy has been implemented in China since the early 1980s. While its implementation is fairly easy in urban China, it often meets major obstacles in rural areas, particularly in cases of families without sons. An important reason is that, in remote rural China, a family is often bullied by its neighbours if it does not have a son.

This logic provides another explanation for why the demand for children was high in ancient times and remains high in regions/countries where the rule of law is not well established. Indeed, history is full of examples of major figures achieving military success due to having large numbers of male children and close male relatives. One such example is Nurhachi, who built a kingdom in the vast territory in Manchu (modern-day Northeast China) by conquering and uniting various Jurchen tribes. Later on, his children conquered the entire country and built the Qing Dynasty. Nurhachi's rise to prominence was aided by his 16 sons, all of whom were brave and intelligent fighters and served as his generals. They partially accounted for the military efficiency of Manchus in the conquest of Northeast China and later on the entire country. Another notable example is Genghis Khan, the founder of the Mongol Empire. As noted in Chapter 11, Genghis Khan's numerous children and grandchildren built the largest contiguous empire in human history.

Moreover, the basic logic of this section provides another explanation for why people have an incentive to adhere to filial piety, in particular respecting their parents and grandparents. For example, in traditional China, the head of an extended family was its oldest male member, and the head had absolute authority over all other members. When the rule of law is not well established, a household must depend on its own members for its defence. However, an individual member usually has the incentive to 'shirk' in a fight to avoid injury. If every member of a family behaved likewise, the family would not comprise a strong unit in combat. To discipline its individual members into fighting bravely and making individual sacrifices, the family must have a strong authority that can credibly award or punish its members.[119] In traditional Chinese societies, such an authority is usually the most senior male of an extended family.

# 16. Gender bias, gender gaps and population theory

## 16.1 WHY IS THERE A GENDER BIAS AGAINST GIRLS?

In many societies, parents exhibit a strong bias in favour of boys. This bias is particularly pronounced in traditional societies. Meanwhile, parental gender bias has also been shown to exist even in very liberal societies of developed countries. For example, Dahl and Moretti (2008) demonstrate that many parents in the USA favour boys over girls and provide the following evidence. First, a woman is much less likely to get married if her first child is a girl. Second, among the women who take ultrasound tests during pregnancy, the mothers who have sons are more likely to be married before the delivery. Third, the couples whose first-born children are girls are much more likely to divorce later on.

How do we explain this observed parental gender bias? The analysis in Chapter 15 provides one answer to this question: boys are better able to help protect the property and honour of a family when the rule of law is not well established. For example, in rural China today, a significant proportion of households do not have sons due to the single-child policy. Members of such families are often bullied by neighbours, particularly when the fathers of the households become old.

Another explanation is related to the problem of domestic violence and wife beating. For example, Broude (1994, p. 312) states:

> Wife beating has a long history. In ancient Babylonia a husband could beat his wife … The woman cannot complain and cannot always prevent beatings by behaving well, as her spouse may also abuse her for no apparent reason. In Tanzania, Hadza wives are sufficiently nervous about beatings from their husbands that no woman will stay alone in camp with her spouse … In Oceania, a Manus husband will hit a wife who does not 'hear his talk,' that is, who fails to heed his commands … Chinese wives are required to show deference to their mothers-in-law, with whom they live, in all matters, and a wife who disobeys her husband's mother will be beaten by her spouse.

In fact, even in societies where the rule of law is well established, spousal abuse towards women is far from being eradicated. For example, Aizer and Dal Bó (2009, pp. 413–14) state:

> In 2001, women in the US reported 590 thousand incidents of rape, sexual and other assault at the hands of intimate partners and on average 4 women are killed each day by a partner. Though the number of reported assaults is high – it is likely an underestimate. Survey data suggest that only one half to one fifth of such assaults are reported to the police. Data gathered through personal surveys and medical professional assessments suggest that between 8 and 14% of women have been assaulted in the past year by an intimate, with lifetime prevalence estimated at 25–30% ... For women, intimate violence accounts for 33% of all homicides.

Although detailed stories of domestic violence are rarely heard because few women want to publicize their shame, such stories do surface occasionally. For example, in the September 2012 issue of *The New Yorker*, one article relates the experiences of J.K. Rowling, writer of the 'Harry Potter' fantasy series. It is stated in the article that Rowling was seriously abused by her former husband after about one year of marriage: 'He [Ms. Rowling's former husband] was once quoted in the *Daily Express* describing their last night; he said that he had dragged her out of their home at five in the morning and slapped her hard.'[120] For parents, the thought of this happening to their own daughter is hard to take.

Moreover, note that it was Rowling's former husband rather than she who told the story to the media. In other words, it was the perpetrator rather than the victim who publicized the pain and humiliation inflicted, meaning that Rowling was too ashamed about it to seek justice.

Due to these kinds of concern, people tend to prefer to have sons rather than daughters. If parents had only daughters, they would feel bad if the daughters were abused and bullied by their spouses. In other words, a woman who is abused by her spouse provides a source of negative vanity to her parents. Foreseeing this, parents prefer to have male children.[121] While there is not yet a direct empirical test of this theoretical implication, some indirect evidence does exist. For example, Washington (2008) demonstrates that, in the USA, if a congressperson has more daughters, they are more likely to vote liberally. Oswald and Powdthavee (2010) show that, in Britain, parents who have more daughters tend to be more left wing.

The potential problem of domestic violence also provides an explanation for the oft-observed fact that women are usually emotionally closer to their parents than men. One explanation is that, if a woman is beaten by her husband, she can obtain more help from her parents and brothers if she maintains a closer relationship with them. For example, Broude (1994, p. 313) offers the following observation:

> Among the Yanomamo, the brothers of a woman may intercede and arrange for the sister to become the wife of another man if her husband is judged to be too brutal in his treatment of his wife ... and a woman's female relatives may band together and beat the husband with their digging sticks if his abuse of his wife becomes too severe ... Public opinion can also serve to inhibit the level of violence that a husband is willing to visit upon his spouse ...

With a better establishment of the rule of law and a continuous increase in women's economic status, domestic violence towards women becomes increasingly less severe.[122] If the penalty against wife beating is sufficiently severe, few men will assault their wives physically. Moreover, when women's relative earnings increase, they are given more bargaining power over their husbands,[123] which reduces the likelihood that their husbands will bully them. For example, using US data taken from 1990 to 2003, Aizer (2010) shows that, when the wage gap between women and men became smaller, domestic violence against women indeed decreased significantly. Using Taiwanese data, Zhang and Chan (1999) find that a dowry improved the bride's welfare, as measured by the time taken to perform household chores. Moreover, there is ample evidence that husbands and wives do not pool all their income, and that a wife has more power in consumption decisions if she has a higher income.[124]

However, it may take some time for the gender bias to completely disappear, even in a society with a perfect rule of law and zero gender wage inequality. People may still prefer to have boys even when the material advantages of having boys over girls disappear. The culture dictates a higher social status to those who have sons, and assigns a vanity value to parents who have them. Thus the gender bias will not be eliminated overnight. The case of female virginity was discussed in Chapter 6, and the same logic applies to gender biases. Even if domestic violence disappeared, it would take time for a new culture to evolve to the point where a parental gender bias towards girls no longer existed.

## 16.2  NARROWING GENDER GAPS IN EARNINGS

The previous section observed that women have more bargaining power at home when the wage gap between women and men decreases. Moreover, as later chapters explain, gender inequality is crucial to understanding many aspects of family behaviour.

The good news is that a narrowing gender gap in wages has indeed been observed in many developed countries in the past few decades.[125] Moreover, the difference in educational attainment between women and men has continuously decreased. In fact, it now appears that a greater proportion of female students can be found at universities in most developed countries and even some developing countries.

Galor and Weil (1996) provide an economic theory for why this is the case. They conceive of two production factors, including brawn (physical labour) and brains (mental labour), to gauge relative productivity between women and men. By nature, a man tends to be endowed with more brawn than a woman. However, no evidence shows that a man's brainpower is greater than that of a woman on average. At the very least, the gender difference in brainpower is much smaller than that in physical strength. Assuming that capital is complementary to mental labour and substitutable with physical labour, Galor and Weil show that capital accumulation, which leads to economic growth, also reduces the gender gap in wages.

Based on the insights of Galor and Weil (1996), in Fan and Lui (2003) we extend their theory and put forward the following testable hypotheses. First, consider an economy in which there is a large number of occupations with various brawn and brains requirements. The gender gap is smaller in sectors and occupations in which physical labour is used less intensively. Second, brawn is a more important production factor in manufacturing industries than in service industries. Thus gender wage gaps should be smaller in the service sector than in the manufacturing sector. Third, most developed countries have experienced a structural change from a manufacturing-oriented economy to a service-oriented economy, which should reduce the gender wage gap. Fourth, *ceteris paribus*, men are more likely to choose to work in the manufacturing sector than women. Fifth, an individual with more education has more brainpower, and hence is more likely to choose to work in the service sector.

We test these hypotheses based on data taken from Hong Kong's 1981 and 1991 population censuses. The Hong Kong data are ideal for testing the theory for two reasons. First, between 1981 and 1991, Hong Kong experienced very dramatic structural changes that turned it from a manufacturing-oriented economy into a service-oriented economy.[126] The structural changes occurred due to the outsourcing of production from Hong Kong to Mainland China that mainly took place in the 1980s. Since China initiated the 'reform and open-door' policy in 1978, Hong Kong has been the dominant supplier of foreign direct investment in the country due to its geographical proximity and cultural ties with Southern China. For example, by 1990, 3–5 million workers in Mainland China were reportedly working directly or indirectly for Hong Kong, and the territory itself had a total workforce of about 3 million.[127]

Second, empirical researchers often face the difficulty of disentangling economic factors from social and political factors when explaining changes in gender inequality. Social and political developments often parallel economic development. For example, one may argue that a narrowing gender wage gap is mainly caused by the enactment and better implementation of laws that protect women's rights in the workplace. However, in Hong Kong, the laws and regulations on sex discrimination were not introduced until 1999. Thus Hong Kong provides a unique natural setting in which to test the theoretical argument of Fan and Lui (2003), as policy interventions were absent during the appropriate time.

Controlling for education and experience, we estimate that, in 1981, women earned 33 per cent less than men, an earnings disadvantage that decreased to 24 per cent by 1991. This means that, in Hong Kong, the gender gap narrowed by nine percentage points in a decade. We also examine the gender wage gaps across different production sectors, and find that the primary and manufacturing sectors recorded much higher income differentials than the service sector. Moreover, among the different service sector subsets, female workers in the financing, insurance, real-estate and business services, which demand the least amount of brawns, enjoyed the highest female–male earnings ratios.

One could argue that there is a wide variety of industries within the manufacturing sector (or any other sectors). While some manufacturing industries are labour intensive and therefore require more physical labour inputs, other industries are skewed towards mental labour inputs. In response to such a concern, we test our theory by analysing the gender gaps across occupations. We find that the female–male earnings ratios were highest for professionals and clerks. Women in these two occupations received an average income of more than 90 per cent of that of their male counterparts. This finding is consistent with the theory, as physical strength is immaterial for these occupations in determining labour productivity. However, female workers who engaged in elementary occupations such as plant and machine operation received less than 50 per cent of the income of male workers. This income differential was probably a result of the gender difference of brawns, which matters greatly in these occupations. In a more recent study, Pitt et al. (2012) yield a similar finding. Based on data collected from rural Bangladesh, they find that the economic returns to years of schooling and physical strength vary by occupation and that brawn-intensive occupations offer significantly fewer mental rewards.

Lui and I (in Fan and Liu, 2003) also show that the gender earnings gap for a certain occupation remained fairly stable between 1981 and 1991. We show that the observed narrowing aggregate gender gap resulted from the much greater proportion of female workers compared with male workers who moved from the manufacturing sector to the service sector during this period of structural change in the Hong Kong economy.

Moreover, we demonstrate that, for both men and women, the average number of schooling years for primary and manufacturing workers was much lower than that for workers in the mental-labour-intensive sectors. Further, comparing years of schooling by occupation, we find that, for both genders, the average educational attainment of professionals was much higher than that of physical-labour-intensive occupations. In sum, our empirical findings in Fan and Lui (2003) are strongly supportive of our five theoretical predictions.

Empirical studies in other countries also examine the causes of narrowing gender gaps. For example, using US data, Weinberg (2001) offers a somewhat similar story and focuses on a narrower angle in his examination of the role of increased computer use in the increase in demand for women workers since 1970. He shows that increases in computer use can account for over one half of the growth in demand for women workers. Thus his findings suggest that technological progress may be a reason for the increase in women's relative economic status. In short, Weinberg (2000) and Fan and Lui (2003) indicate that the narrowing gender gap is closely related to women's changing comparative advantage.

A greater equality in the earnings between male and female workers has important implications for family issues. According to the analysis in the previous section, we know that parental gender bias against girls will decrease. Indeed, in many developed countries today, couples mostly prefer to have a mix of both male and female children. For example, in advertisements featuring an 'ideal' family, a pair of good-looking parents is often portrayed as having a boy and girl (and a dog).

When the parental gender bias against girls is reduced, the fertility rate tends to decrease. To illustrate the logic of this argument, consider a scenario in which a family has a 'target' for a certain number of 'desirable' children, such as three. In the case of an extremely strong parental gender bias against girls, only male babies are considered desirable. Supposing that gender selection technology is unavailable and that the natural chance of giving birth to a boy is 50 per cent, then it is expected that a family will have about six children. On the other hand, suppose that the parental gender bias against girls completely disappears.

In this case, a family is expected to have precisely three children. Thus the reduction of a parental gender bias against girls might have considerably accelerated the observed demographic transition.

When fertility declines, the 'quality' of a child becomes the major source of vanity for its parents. Meanwhile, along with the substantial reduction of parental gender bias against girls, daughters may well act as the vanity affiliates for their parents. Not too long ago, girls received much less education than boys on average. For example, Fan and Lui (2003) report that in 1981 the average years of schooling for male and female workers in Hong Kong were 5.05 and 3.87, respectively. However, in most developed countries today, women have already completely closed this gap and often overtake men in educational attainment (e.g. Goldin et al., 2006).[128] Again, using Hong Kong as an example, Fan and Lui (2003) report that in 1991 the average years of schooling for male and female workers increased to 8.95 and 9.2, respectively. In just ten years, women slightly overtook men in the average number of years of schooling in Hong Kong. The structural changes in Hong Kong favoured women's comparative advantage, which sharpened the women's incentives to accumulate human capital. Moreover, because women are endowed with less brawn, they may have more of an incentive to increase their schooling to enhance their brainpower.

# 17. 'Conspicuous careers', overworked society, and family

## 17.1 THE 'SUPERSTAR' CONDITION AND 'CONSPICUOUS CAREERS'

When one refers to a 'superstar', familiar celebrities from television shows, movies, sports and music come to mind. Indeed, watching and reading about superstars are major leisure activities for many people, and the private lives of superstars often occupy newspaper headlines. The media creates the superstar condition to a large extent. While many celebrities often complain that the media overly interferes with their private lives, they also often use the media to increase their fame.

It is well known that the salaries of many superstars are astronomical. For example, in 1997 and 1998, Michael Jordan brought in salaries of US\$30 million and US\$33 million, respectively. There is an appropriate nickname for these superstars: the rich and famous.

Why do superstars make so much money? Rosen (1981) was the first to investigate this question. He begins his analysis with the observation that, as technology progresses, the best performers in a given field are able to serve every customer in a large market at a low cost. The best examples are the professional sports and music industries. In Shakespeare's time, an actor could perform for a few hundred audience members in a theatre at once, regardless of his acting skills. With the development of broadcasting technologies, billions of audience members can now enjoy an actor's performances conveniently through movies, television and DVDs at a low price. Continuous progress in electronics technology has allowed more people to enjoy professional sports and music performances via television and the Internet. Meanwhile, as television and Internet technology improves, the difference between watching live performances and enjoying them on television and the Internet is becoming smaller, and in many circumstances the views provided by the latter can be even better.

The expansion of commercial activities (programmes and advertisements) on television and the Internet to a wider audience has also allowed superstars to become richer. For example, an article in the *New York Times* compares football legend Pelé with more recent football sensation Portuguese forward Cristiano Ronaldo.[129] In 2010 dollars, Ronaldo's salary was US$17 million and Pelé's was only US$1.1 million. The article concludes that 'Pelé was not held back by the quality of his game, but by his relatively small revenue base.'

I mention the 'superstar' condition because it is finding its way into many occupations in modern societies. Although real superstars represent only a tiny fraction of the population, it is argued that the contemporary world has become a society in which winners take all (e.g. Frank and Cook, 1995). Indeed, careful observers may notice that many people now often demand the 'best' when it comes to making important decisions for themselves and their children. For example, in an important legal case, everyone wants the best lawyer. When people are seriously ill or require important surgery, they desire the best doctor. On an important date with an attractive woman, a man demands the best food and services from the best restaurant. During important social occasions, people want to impress others by wearing brand-name clothing. When children are born, their parents want to buy them the best milk powder and send them to the best schools. (In Chapter 5, it was suggested that many people remain unmarried because they demand the best-looking man/woman as a marital partner.)

Holding other things constant, everyone would clearly like to choose the best commodity. However, this desire can be greatly exacerbated by vanity, which induces people to choose the best commodity even if its price is substantially higher than that of the second-best commodity and even if the quality difference between the best and second-best commodities is very small. In China, a country fascinated by 'national glory' in the Olympic Games, there is an enormous difference between the gold and silver medals, although the difference between gold and silver medallists can comprise only a fraction of a second in a racing competition. In the NBA final, there is a great difference between a champion and the losing team. In most modern societies, such a mentality – vanity – pervades many aspects of people's lives.

Insistence on the 'best' is often a vain demand of consumers. As a result, the income inequality within a certain occupation and for people with similar education and talents has become greater (e.g. Frank and Cook, 1995). The notion that winners take all further enhances people's desire to succeed in their career development, as successful individuals command many more financial rewards and prestige. Consequently, in a modern economy, a new notion appears that successful individuals carry much more prestige, and therefore people are much more motivated to pursue career success. I now put forward a new concept, 'conspicuous career', which means that people achieve a high social status or vanity from a successful career. I use the term 'conspicuous career' as an analogue to Veblen's (1899) 'conspicuous consumption'. Many people gain vanity from both.

In fact, in some occupations, such as academia, a conspicuous career may confer only more honour and prestige rather than financial reward. Even in this case, a conspicuous career is many people's dream. A friend of mine obtained his PhD from the University of California in the early 1990s. Due to his outstanding academic performance, he immediately received job offers for assistant professorships from a number of US universities. While Harvard University was among them, it offered the lowest salary of all. He contacted the university and attempted to bargain for a higher salary. Harvard did not reply to him directly, but instead a Harvard professor called his dissertation adviser. The professor relayed the following message: 'Harvard does not bargain for salaries. Tell your student to accept the offer.' Of course, my friend then immediately did so. His decision was easy to understand: despite the lower salary, Harvard would provide him with the most conspicuous career.

## 17.2  'CONSPICUOUS CAREERS' AND THE LABOUR MARKET

Parallel to this increasing demand for the 'best' along with economic development, continuous technological progress and major structural changes have transformed most developed countries into economies that are dominated by service industries. Chapter 16 showed that this structural change favours women's comparative advantage and has led to a narrowing gender gap in earnings. Moreover, the relationship between technological progress and the demand for sophisticated mathematical/ technical skills appears to be an inverted U-curve (see Figure 17.1).

When the level of industrial technologies is low, people rely mainly on their physical strength for production. As technological progress increases, skilled technicians and engineers become critical to the success of many firms. However, with further technological progress, only a small fraction of occupations demand sophisticated mathematical/ technical skills.

The discipline of economics provides a useful illustration. It is a consensus that Adam Smith established modern economics with his two books *The Wealth of Nations* and *A Theory of Moral Sentiments*. While

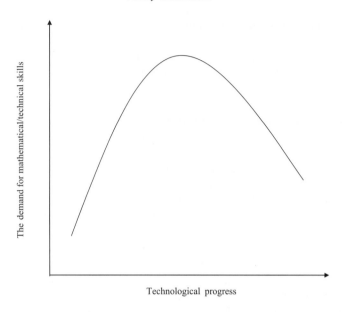

*Figure 17.1    The relationship between technological progress and demand*
*for mathematical/technical skills*

extremely insightful, neither of these two books consists of any mathematics. Indeed, classical economists such as Ricardo, Mills and Veblen
all made their pioneering contributions without any mathematical deriva-
tions. However, from the 1950s until the 1990s, the discipline of
economics became increasingly mathematical. A new theory must be
'formalized' with mathematical equations to be accepted as an economic
theory. Further, statistical methods are more often explored with increasing mathematical complexity to deal with complicated observations.
Before the 1980s, an economist had to be familiar with computer
programming to conduct data analyses, even in the most direct application of the standardized statistical tools. However, this trend has
reversed in recent years. Only a small fraction of new PhD students
currently work on pure economic theory and econometrics. Most new
economists focus on applied research that collects and analyses data.
Computer software such as Stata has become so powerful that an
economist does not require much knowledge of mathematics and statistics to complete the work.

  With such technological progress and structural changes, it appears
that work effort has become the single most important ingredient for
success. Indeed, as Winston Churchill once said, 'Continuous effort – not

strength or intelligence – is the key to unlocking our potential.' This implies that an increasing number of people have become serious contenders in this 'winners-take-all' environment. Not surprisingly, labour market competition has become increasingly severe in recent decades, at least in developed economies.

The superstar condition has profound effects on people's pursuit of vanity. In modern societies, people are not only concerned about whether they will find a good-looking spouse and whether their children will get into a good university, but are also trying hard to have successful or 'conspicuous' careers. A friend of mine comes from a middle-class family in Hong Kong. She has a younger brother, and her mother works as a housewife. While my friend has always been close to her mother, during her teenage years she was annoyed by one of her mother's habits. She and her brother were a constant topic when her mother chatted with others, particularly with close friends. My friend's parents are apparently very proud of their two children, who are both very good-looking and intelligent. One day, my friend complained to her mother that she felt uncomfortable to be the subject of so many conversations between her mother and others. Her mother replied, 'What do I have? I only have you and your brother!' My friend never complained again. Today, most women no longer work as housewives. While they are often overly busy, they enjoy having both a family and a career.

Maslow's theory interprets the pursuit of career development as the need for self-actualization, which is at the top of the hierarchy of needs. It should be noted that success is an important component in almost any kind of self-actualization. For example, if a woman's self-actualization involves becoming a fashion designer, she usually wants to be a *famous* fashion designer. If a man wants to be a professional basketball player, he usually wants to be a star in the NBA. Thus Maslow's theory and the theory of this book have the same implications for most of the issues discussed in this chapter, although they interpret them differently.

There is a much greater division of jobs in service industries, which not only allows individuals to make use of their idiosyncratic talents more efficiently but also caters to their pursuits of their spiritual dreams ('self-actualization' in Maslow's terms or 'vanity' according to this book's definition). This is in sharp contrast to a factory worker, who usually treats his occupation purely as a job. Indeed, we may say that, in modern times, many people want to have a 'career' rather than simply a 'job'. A career, particularly a conspicuous career, differs from a job in one crucial aspect: that of self-actualization or vanity.

## 17.3 OVERWORKED SOCIETY

In undergoing continuous technological progress and structural changes, most service-industry jobs require neither substantial physical strength nor complicated mathematical/technical skills, but do reward hard effort. Thus work effort becomes the most crucial ingredient for career success, which implies that an increasing number of people are becoming potential winners in a 'winners-take-all' society. The superstar condition, which is most pronounced in the sports and entertainment industries, is now prevalent in many occupations to varying degrees. The material reward and vanity that accompanies having a conspicuous career motivates many people to work hard.

In many prestigious occupations that lead to conspicuous careers, new employees face the rule of 'up or out'.[130] In an organization, an employee will, after a certain period of working, either be promoted upwards into a senior position or be fired. Therefore, those in such occupations have to work hard even to keep their current jobs.

In academia, the 'up or out' rule takes the form of the so-called 'tenure system'. While both teaching and research are considered important, most academicians can meet the teaching standard. As a result, more often than not, one's research output is the only determinant for whether one will obtain tenure, that is, a continuous contract at a university. This has spawned the 'publish or perish' cliché in academics. An assistant professor must meet a certain target in terms of both the number and quality of publications to secure a continuous contract at a university and usually at the same time to be promoted to be an associate professor. In other words, if an assistant professor can succeed in publications, they become a so-called 'superstar'. Otherwise, they will perish professionally.

Most developed countries have experienced a structural change from a manufacturing-oriented economy to a service-oriented economy. There is one essential difference in the means of production between the manufacturing and service industries. In a manufacturing industry factory, workers often operate in the same production line, which entails a similar effort from each worker. However, people work much more independently in white-collar jobs in service industries, and one can invest more effort at work independent of the work effort of others. There are usually many fewer workers in an office (service industry) than in a factory (manufacturing industry), and an individual who shares an office with co-workers can work harder than the others if they choose to do so.

In addition, the nature of 'work' has changed over time. For most of human history, the input of labour has indeed involved labouring and sweating. Peasants work in fields, hunters fight with animals and workers operate production lines. Because these jobs generally take a toll on the body, few people really enjoy working *per se*, particularly after doing so continuously for hours. In modern times, working in the services sector, which provides most of the employment, is often enjoyable. In fact, 'workaholism' is not an uncommon affliction. For example, Gary Cross (1993, p. viii) states in the preface to his lengthy book: 'Like most privileged academics, free time and money for me are not exclusively compensation for the pains and sacrifice of work. They are in some degree incidental to the pleasure of intellectual life.'

Moreover, working in some occupations is pleasant and carries comfort and prestige. While people working overly long hours in investment banking is often cited as an example, the people in this industry frequently travel on business. They take business- and first-class flights and stay in luxurious hotels. Indeed, this way of working provides a great sense of self-esteem, status and achievement, which this book calls vanity, and hence those in such occupations may simply enjoy working.

## 17.4   WORK AND FAMILY

What are the implications of overworking for marriage and family issues? As described earlier, the major functions of marriage and family are to pursue vanity and to banish boredom. In the contemporary world, at least in developed countries, these two functions can both be fulfilled by one's outstanding performance at work. Indeed, if some people are frustrated by humiliation and rejection in the dating world, they will naturally focus more on work. Even desirable men and women who are attractive to the opposite sex often find that maintaining a stable romantic relationship entails a great deal of energy and time. Consequently, they often prefer a casual sexual relationship rather than committing to a long-term relationship or marriage. This provides an additional explanation for the declining marriage rates in many developed countries today.

An immediate implication of overworking is that married couples must compromise to meet the demands of their most time-intensive activities: bearing and raising children. It is often observed that people delay the age at which they have children. Women are often advised that it would be better for them and their children if they gave birth before 30 years of age. However, many career-focused women choose to have children when they are nearly 40. At that age they often have difficulty getting pregnant, and, even if successful, may give birth to children who are prone to long-term health risks. A woman's ideal period for bearing and raising children often overlaps with her ideal period for career development.

Take the career path of a university professor as an example. A woman obtains her bachelor's degree at 22 years of age. After graduating from college, she works at a firm for two years. She then gets into a PhD programme, which usually takes five years to finish. If she is lucky, she will graduate in five years and land an academic job at a university. Her 'tenure clock' then starts to tick. If she is again lucky enough, she will publish enough material in six years and secure tenure at her university. By that time, the woman, who has experienced a smooth career development path, will already be 35 years old. If she meets some difficulties in the PhD programme and her publication endeavours, which most people experience, it will take more years for her to achieve tenure, even if she ultimately succeeds. This example illustrates why many career women delay childbearing and choose to have few children. This is often the cost of pursuing success in a conspicuous career.

# 18. The value of time in consumption and population theory

Chapter 17 introduced a new concept, the 'conspicuous career', which refers to the vanity many people obtain from their jobs. The nature of work has changed over time. Many now find their jobs pleasant and often spend long hours working. In this chapter, we discuss the value of time from another perspective: its role in consumption activities.

## 18.1 THE VALUE OF TIME IN CONSUMPTION

In modern societies, many people are both busy at work and hectic in life. While many are obsessed with material possessions, they also find time itself to be extremely valuable, not only for work and career pursuit but also for consumption. For example, if one wants to go to a theatre to see a play or to travel abroad, one requires both sufficient free time and enough money.

Time becomes increasingly valuable in consumption mainly due to the continuing expansion in the varieties of consumption goods. In particular, the development of the service industry is providing more ways for people to enjoy life. However, time input is almost always necessary for one to enjoy these services.

The following offers some examples. With the continuous development of air transportation, an increasing number of people can now afford to travel to different places for sightseeing. However, travelling requires both money and time. In the small Hong Kong district of Causeway Bay, thousands of restaurants provide enormous varieties of food that cater to all types of consumers. However, one requires a great amount of time to dine in even a small fraction of the restaurants in this tiny district alone. In many countries today, the rich often own vacation houses on mountains or beaches. However, such possessions are not enough to generate a great deal of happiness, and these individuals require holiday time to live in the houses and thereby appreciate the value of their possessions.

In his classic contribution, Veblen (1899) assigns 'conspicuous leisure', which means the visible leisure for the purpose of displaying one's high status in the society, a prominent role in the pursuit of social status or vanity. With this additional consideration, time becomes even more valuable for consumption in modern societies.

However, throughout most of human history, time has not been a very scarce consumptive resource for most people. For example, when an economy is underdeveloped, its entertainment industry may lack electricity and other crucial ingredients for its existence and development. Most people engage in agricultural production, and they all stop working after sunset.

In such scenarios, at least after dark, most people are usually fairly idle. One famous song from the 1980s about a young girl's treasured memory of her mother who knitted her a pair of gloves for the cold weather also describes idle life in rural China. The lyrics (translated into English) include the following lines: 'Time goes by so slowly in idleness. How wonderful would it have been if we could listen to the radio?' In such circumstances, people are constrained only by financial and material resources rather than by time.

Sketch comedy is popular in China. Almost all the country's comedians come from the Northeast, such as 'superstar' and household name Benshan Zhao, who appears regularly on the CCTV New Year's Gala. Most Chinese comedians are produced in the Northeast because the region endures a long and bitter winter during which peasants cannot work on their farms.[131] In such an environment, everyone belongs to the 'leisure class'. Without radios and televisions, a culture has emerged in which people create an enjoyable atmosphere at home and in the villages by singing and telling jokes. The harsh natural environment in Northeast China gave birth to a unique culture of Chinese sketch comedy that in turn has generated many good comedians.

## 18.2 MONEY AND TIME FOR THE 'QUANTITY' AND 'QUALITY' OF CONSUMPTION

In his seminal contribution 'A theory of the allocation of time', Becker (1965) introduces time into the consumption theory of economics. In a previous study (Fan, 1997b), I extend Becker's theory by looking into the 'quantity' and 'quality' of consumption separately. I make two key assumptions. First, the consumption of 'quantity' (or variety) is time-intensive. Second, the consumption of 'quality' is money-intensive. The intuition for these two assumptions is as follows.

First, time is a necessary input for consumption. The more quantity or variety a person wants to consume, the more time is required. Consider the examples of going to the theatre and travelling. Stories about busy and rich people who have never travelled abroad or even seen a movie for a long time, despite having the money to do so, are common. Another good example is the buffet lunch, which restaurant owners offer in the knowledge that it takes time for a customer to eat and that an ordinary customer can only eat so much food during lunchtime.

Second, the consumption of quality often entails spending a great deal of money but not much additional time. For example, if one wants to obtain more enjoyment from watching a live music performance, one can spend more money on a better seat, and no extra time investment is required.[132] In this case, the quality received increases based solely on the extra money spent. In China, there is an old saying about the price of quality: 'one penny, one quality'. Indeed, economic development has been associated mainly with continuous improvements in product quality rather than in quantity expansions.

Moreover, if we follow Becker (1991) in considering children as 'durable goods' for their parents according to their quantity and quality, then the two assumptions made in Fan (1997b) also apply to children. First, economists' substantial empirical research shows that, in a modern society, children are expensive for their parents mainly in terms of the value of time. According to some estimates, the cost of a mother's time often contributes about two-thirds of the cost of bearing and raising children.[133] For example, giving birth to a child entails a nine-month period of pregnancy on the part of the mother, regardless of the child's quality. One cannot reduce the length of the pregnancy period significantly, regardless of wealth or social status. In addition, a great deal of time and energy are required on the part of the parents to take care of an infant.[134]

Second, along with secular economic growth, expenditure on education per student has continuously increased in terms of both the absolute amount and proportion of average incomes. By increasing educational resources, children can obtain access to better educational materials and better-trained teachers, thereby enhancing their cognitive and emotional development.

## 18.3 MONEY, TIME AND DEMOGRAPHIC TRANSITION WITH ECONOMIC DEVELOPMENT

Based on the two assumptions made in the preceding section, I (Fan, 1997b) developed a theory that enriches the study of the interaction between the quantity and quality of children. The basic argument is as follows. When people are poor, they are 'time abundant' and constrained only by their financial resources. In fact, I show that time becomes a scarce resource for people only after their income reaches a certain level. In such an environment, children are not only a source of social status for parents but also an effective way to reduce boredom. Indeed, when people have too much time, raising and playing with children alleviates their idleness, making them happier. In such an environment, the fertility rate tends to increase as incomes rise. This argument helps explain why fertility rates and people's income were fairly strongly positively correlated throughout human history until the last 200 years.[135]

However, the situation is very different in modern societies with high levels of economic development. Time becomes more valuable with economic development. While secular technological progress and capital accumulation increase the incomes and wealth of most people, everyone is still endowed with a fixed supply of 24 hours in a day. Thus, when incomes increase, people become increasingly 'money abundant' and 'time scarce', for the time endowment is constant for every individual. As people become richer, they buy more things and thus spend more time consuming them.

Because the consumption of the quantities of material goods is time intensive, the increase in the quantities and varieties of people's consumption are limited by their constant time endowments. However, because a greater money input can always increase quality, an increase in incomes generally results in people increasing their expenditure on consumption quality. Such an increase in quality is sometimes seen mainly in terms of famous 'brands', such as Louis Vuitton handbags. Indeed, from the perspective of firms, increasing marketing expenditure is an important way to improve people's perception of product quality. A successful advertisement substantially increases the vanity obtained by possessing a certain product, which in turn significantly increases many people's willingness to pay for the product.

Moreover, by the same logic, an increase in income influences people to increase their expenditure on the quality of their children rather than have more children. With a continuous increase in consumption goods and services in terms of both variety and absolute amount, people find that time is becoming increasingly valuable in achieving enjoyment and happiness, as it allows them to consume greater varieties of goods and services. For example, the development of the entertainment industry, particularly in cities, enables people to enjoy the conspicuous leisure of a nightlife. Because having many children is a time-intensive activity, people find they are much happier having fewer children, as it gives them more time for material enjoyment and affords them the kind of happiness that accompanies a freer nightlife.

Theodore W. Schultz, a Nobel laureate in economics, offers the following insightful comments about time (1974, p. S4):

> Advances in useful knowledge, embodied in human and nonhuman capital, have gradually destroyed the assumption of the fixed supply of the 'original properties of the soil.' In the process, it is the scarcity of human time and its high value that dominate, and it is the 'fixed supply of human time' consisting of 24 hours per day and of a man's lifetime that becomes the critical factor in analysing the economic behavior of people, including their fertility.

This insightful statement becomes increasingly important with economic development. Nowadays, many people require time and concentration to pursue success in their conspicuous careers. They also require time to enjoy the ever-expanding variety of goods and services they can afford thanks to their increasing earnings. Moreover, they require time to enjoy conspicuous leisure, and thus often have to sacrifice the time required to bear and raise children. In big cities where many varieties of tempting goods and services and plenty of opportunities for conspicuous careers are on offer, many people choose not to have children at all. In Hong Kong, Macau and Singapore, the fertility rate is about 0.8–0.9. However, considering that a low-income family usually has more than one child, the fertility rate for university graduates would be less than 0.5; that is, two women with university education are expected to have fewer than one child between them. In fact, childlessness is a common condition in developed countries.[136]

# 19. A 'population problem': theory and policy

Death is life's biggest tragedy and an absolute certainty. The world population reached an estimated seven billion people in 2011. In 150 years all these people will be dead, yet seven billion or more will have taken their place. Some demographers predict that the world population will reach 10 billion by 2150.[137] These people will be completely new. In fact, those who will be born in the next 12 months cannot be predicted. About 300 million sperm are released in a man's ejaculate[138] to meet thousands of a woman's eggs. The probability that a certain sperm will match a certain egg, develop it into an embryo that will later result in a birth is much less than 1 in 1 billion, even when the man's and woman's identities are known ahead of time. This means that every person's birth is the result of an event with an extremely small probability of less than 1 billionth and possibly less than 1 trillionth. In this sense, every person should feel extremely lucky to be alive. In other words, every person is brought into being by God – the Goddess of Fortune.

Given these facts, examining 'population problems' to investigate optimal population levels and compositions seems impossible. From an ethics perspective, researchers on this topic are vulnerable to criticisms when they try to judge whether a certain fraction of the population or even a single individual should be born. However, as illustrated by the strict implementation of the one-child policy in China, population growth and economic development are closely related.[139] Thus the study of population problems cannot be ignored in economics.

## 19.1 DIFFERENTIAL FERTILITY AND THE 'POPULATION PROBLEM'

The research on social welfare in economics focuses mainly on a society's current members. Based on this approach, most of the economics literature finds it hard to argue that a population problem exists at all in the contemporary world. For example, in a model that has become a standard tool in population economics, Barro and Becker (1989) show that the dynastic model of an altruistically linked family generates a population growth rate that maximizes the utility of the 'representative individual'. Indeed, most of the literature on the 'optimal population' is based on the 'representative individual' framework, implying that it is hard to argue that the government can do anything to improve social welfare when the representative individual is rational.

The arguments beyond the 'representative individual' framework are usually debatable. Some argue that the birth rate in many European countries is too low, implying that the pay-as-you-go social security system will not be sustainable in the future.[140] However, the pay-as-you-go social security system may not offer a good policy in the first place. Further, a large percentage of the young people in European countries are unemployed. In Spain, for instance, the unemployment rate among those aged 16–24 was 53 per cent in the second quarter of 2012. From an economics perspective, this high youth unemployment rate makes it harder to argue that there are too few young people in European countries. On the other hand, some argue that the world is overpopulated, citing that natural resources such as energy and land are limited and cannot sustain such a large population.

These unsettled debates are beyond the scope of this book. In this chapter, I focus on a narrow angle – population composition – to tackle the population problem. In particular, this chapter, which is based on studies by de la Croix and Doepke (2003) and Fan and Stark (2008b), examines the expected average welfare of generations yet to be born.

De la Croix and Doepke (2003) emphasize the negative correlation between income and fertility, and argue that a rise in inequality increases it, lowers the average education level and depresses the growth rate. Moreover, they estimate that the fertility-differential effect accounts for most of the relationship between inequality and growth across countries.

In Fan and Stark (2008b) we base our framework on that of Rawls (1971), who develops the idea of the 'veil of ignorance' or the 'original position' as the starting point of a welfare analysis. According to Rawls (1971), the 'veil of ignorance' refers to the following: 'no one knows his place in society, his class position or social status; nor does he know his fortune in the distribution of natural assets and abilities, his intelligence and strength, and the like'. Rawls's idea is essentially best applied to the individuals yet to be born.

Based on Rawls's assumption, Fan and Stark (2008b) define social welfare as an index of expected happiness for a person yet to be born. Holding physical appearance and health constant, a better-educated individual is generally happier than a less-educated individual due to higher income level, among other factors. Thus the social welfare index will be higher if future generations have a greater chance of being better educated. If the difference in fertility rate between better-educated (and hence richer) people and less-educated (and hence poorer) people becomes smaller, then this goal will be achieved.

As analysed in previous chapters, better-educated parents are likely to have much lower fertility rates than less-educated parents. While vanity is a major concern for every member of a society, and children are a main source of vanity, the ways to pursue vanity differ significantly between better- and less-educated parents. Better-educated and richer parents find it advantageous to focus on the quality of their children rather than having more children. For example, better-educated individuals are much more likely to strive for conspicuous careers in their occupations. Further, they are likely to end up in occupations they truly enjoy, and hence are often likely to become workaholics. Moreover, richer people require more time for their consumption activities. Thus better-educated and richer parents have less time for family activities, and will thus reduce more the activities that are most time consuming – bearing and raising children.

Less-educated and poorer parents often obtain vanity from having children *per se*, partly because their children often have less of a chance at being 'successful' in the future. For example, a less-educated couple may feel proud to have three children, and feel superior to couples (with similar backgrounds) with two children or fewer[141] Alternatively, a less-educated couple may feel proud to have two sons and one daughter, and feel superior to couples (with similar backgrounds) who have only one son or none at all. As a result, vanity may lead less-educated couples to have many children to achieve a high social status among their peers. Thus the fertility rate of less-educated and poorer parents is much higher than that of better-educated and richer parents. Fan and Stark (2008b) note that this fertility differential is precisely an important source of a society's population problem as a whole.

Fan and Stark (2008b) show that, from the perspective of maximizing social welfare, richer and better-educated parents often have too few children and poorer and less-educated parents have too many children. The basic logic is that if better-educated parents have more children or less-educated parents have fewer children, the proportion of better-educated individuals in the next generation will be higher.

It should be noted that Stark and I focus only on the difference in education across individuals. Our work does not truly belong to 'eugenics', the aim of which is to improve human genetic traits in general (e.g. Currell and Cogdell, 2006). The difference is vividly illustrated by Paul Krugman's (1993, p. 25) self-reflection:

My formal charge in this essay is to talk about my 'life philosophy'. Let me make it clear at the outset that I have no intention of following instructions, since I don't know anything special about life in general. I believe it was Schumpeter who claimed to be not only the best economist, but also the best horseman and the best lover in his native Austria. I don't ride horses, and have few illusions on other scores. (I am, however, a pretty good cook.)

In fact, the population problem that Fan and Stark (2008b) analyse has long been recognized by the general public and policy-makers. For example, Singapore has devoted much attention to this issue. In an important speech at the National Day Rally on 14 August 1983, Lee Kuan Yew, then prime minister of Singapore, expressed such a concern: 'We must further amend our policies, and try to reshape our demographic configuration so that our better-educated women will have more children to be adequately represented in the next generation.'

## 19.2  HOW TO MITIGATE THE 'POPULATION PROBLEM'

How can the government mitigate or correct this population problem? There are no easy answers. A straightforward suggestion is to provide a pecuniary incentive to well-educated young couples to have more children. Fan and Stark (2008b) examine a scheme in which better-educated individuals would receive an income transfer from the government for each child they have. To be fair, the tax required for the income transfer would arrive from the group of better-educated individuals as a whole. However, this scheme does not often work well. As analysed in the previous chapters, many well-educated individuals choose to have few children or even none at all because they are busy with work and life. They are constrained by time in their career pursuits and their pursuit for pleasure in consumption. However, they often have more than enough money to spend. Consequently, an income transfer from the government rewarding them for having one more child, which is only a small fraction of their earnings, usually has little or no effect on their fertility decisions.

Fan and Stark (2008b) find a more effective scheme for mitigating the population problem through helping less-educated parents enhance their efficiency at educating their children through early childhood education programmes. This policy suggestion is inspired by the Head Start Program in the USA, which 'aims to improve the learning skills, social skills, and health status of poor children so that they can be in schooling on an equal footing with their more advantaged peers' (Currie and

Thomas, 1995, p. 341). Several empirical studies such as those by Currie and Thomas (1995), Currie (2001) and Garces et al. (2002) show that early childhood education programmes have significant positive effects on improving participants' learning efficiencies and hence increasing their educational attainments.

This is a somewhat surprising result, as the original aim of the 'Head Start Program' is not to address the population problem. However, this policy can be effective. As discussed previously, the main incentive to have children may be that parents aim to obtain vanity from their children's achievements. The children of parents with low educational backgrounds often have a very small chance of excelling in educational attainment. As a result, these parents often hope that their children have a 'natural' ability to become superstars in sports or music. Poor parents find having more children the only way to enhance their chances of having a gifted child. However, if the government could help poor parents sufficiently in giving their children a decent chance to succeed in the 'ordinary' way (through education), it is likely that these parents would have fewer children. In this case, less-educated parents would be motivated to spend more time educating their children, particularly on aspects for which there are no substitutes, such as good behaviour and character. In other words, when children from disadvantaged family backgrounds have a greater chance at being successful, their parents are likely to respond by spending more time and effort on their education and consequently reducing their fertility.

The rest of this chapter suggests three policy proposals that are not considered by Fan and Stark (2008b): (i) implementing a system of public education; (ii) imposing strict population control on the entire population; and (iii) implementing a 'work-sharing scheme' to limit the time spent working. The following three sections elaborate these policies, respectively.

## 19.3  PUBLIC EDUCATION

Richer and better-educated people tend to have fewer children. The different fertility choices between the rich and poor may be important for persistent income inequality across generations. Under the private educational system, a child from a poorer family obtains less educational resources because it has more siblings. This further hinders the perspective of intergenerational mobility for children with disadvantaged family backgrounds.[142]

With the consideration of differential fertility, income redistribution from the rich to the poor may be particularly important in equalizing educational resources, which may increase intergenerational mobility, efficiency and equity. An efficient and practical form of income redistribution that may largely reduce the inequality of educational resources is public education. Under complete public education, children from poor and rich families are taught by the same teachers and receive access to the same educational facilities. Of course, children with better-educated parents may continue to have some advantages. For example, as discussed in a later chapter, these children tend to exhibit more intelligence in their schoolwork on average. However, there would be more intergenerational mobility enabling the children from poor families to succeed. For example, if some children from poor families are very intelligent, they will not be handicapped by a lack of educational resources in achieving outstanding academic performances.

Moreover, under reasonable conditions, Fan and Zhang (2013) show that the fertility gap between the better- and less-educated parents would narrow under the system of public education, mitigating the population problem identified in this chapter.

## 19.4  SINGLE-CHILD POLICY

This policy proposal is analysed by Fan and Stark (2003), who show that the imposition of an upper limit on the fertility of each household can improve social welfare in the long term. It is empirically motivated by the single-child policy that China has implemented since 1980.

Since the advent of its economic reform in 1978, the Chinese government has recognized the close interaction between population and economic growth, and has been determined to curtail the growth rate of its population through its 'one couple, one child' policy.[143] While this policy of restricting fertility is subject to criticism on moral grounds, it has two positive consequences from an economics perspective.

First, through the familiar trade-off between the quantity and quality of children, a restriction leads parents to invest more in the quality of their children. Consequently, a substantial increase in human capital of the young generation has fuelled spectacular economic growth in China.[144]

Second, without the population policy, better-educated Chinese parents would choose to have far fewer children than less-educated parents, as they would in any other country. Therefore the single-child policy has been much more of a constraint to less-educated parents than to better-educated parents. As a result, a possibly unintended outcome of the single-child policy is that it considerably mitigates the population problem analysed by Fan and Stark (2008b).[145]

## 19.5   'WORK-SHARING' SCHEME

This policy proposal aims to address the population problem by modestly adjusting the time some busy people allocate to work, consumption and family. As analysed in Chapters 17 and 18, many people devote themselves to the constant pursuit of conspicuous careers. Meanwhile, they love to enjoy the ever-expanding variety of goods and services and may be tempted to demonstratrate conspicuous leisure. Therefore, they often have little time and energy for family life and raising children.

In *The Overworked American*, Juliet B. Schor (1991) shows a significant increase in the working hours for many Americans. In particular, her estimation indicates that, on average, the working hours of an American woman increased by 22 per cent from 1969 to 1987. Similar evidence can be readily found in other countries. For example, in September 2001, the Democratic Alliance for the Betterment of Hong Kong, a Hong Kong political party, conducted a survey on the working hours of 655 full-time employees. The following are some of the survey's questions and the corresponding results, which confirm Schor's argument on overworked societies.

Question 1: *How many days do you work overtime per week?*

Answers:

| Number of days | Percentage of respondents |
| --- | --- |
| 0 | 38.1 |
| 1 or 2 | 27.3 |
| 3 or 4 | 20.3 |
| 5 or more | 14.3 |

Question 2: *On average, how many hours of overtime do you work every day?*

Answers:

| Number of days | Percentage of respondents |
| --- | --- |
| Less than 1 | 23 |
| 1 to 2 | 51.3 |
| 3 to 4 | 19.6 |
| 5 or more | 6 |

Question 3: *Do you receive any extra pay for working overtime?*

Answers:

| Answers | Percentage of respondents |
| --- | --- |
| Yes | 21.9 |
| No | 78.1 |

While overworking is one problem of a society, unemployment is often another. Thus some policy-makers put forward a 'work-sharing' scheme. In many Western countries, work-sharing schemes have been proposed as a policy instrument to reduce unemployment. The basic logic of this policy proposal is that a reduction in hours per worker spreads the available work around and hence increases employment. For example, the following is from a recent newspaper article about this policy motion:[146]

> Britain is struggling to shrug off the credit crisis; overworked parents are stricken with guilt about barely seeing their offspring; carbon dioxide is belching into the atmosphere from our power-hungry offices and homes. In London on Wednesday, experts will gather to offer a novel solution to all of these problems at once: a shorter working week. A thinktank, the New Economics Foundation (NEF) … argues that if everyone worked fewer hours – say, 20 or so a week – there would be more jobs to go round, employees could spend more time with their families and energy-hungry excess consumption would be curbed.

The work-sharing scheme may present some implementation problems.[147] However, if the policy were well carried out, it would reduce the working time of some better-educated people, inducing them to have more time for family and possibly have more children. While the earnings of those people may be reduced, this does not present a problem. Their reduced earnings would also reduce their consumption activities, which also demand time. Therefore people would have even more time for family and hence be likely to have more children.

PART IV

Vanity, husband–wife relationships, and intergenerational relationships

# 20. Vanity and divorce

Divorce, the legal ending of a marriage, is a common occurrence. In the USA, the divorce rate rose steadily from 2.5 per 1000 people in 1966 to a peak of 5.3 in both 1979 and 1981 before dropping back to 3.4 in 2009.[148] Note that a large fraction of the population is unmarried (e.g. young children) and that old people usually do not divorce. Thus the refined divorce rate for young and middle-aged married couples, which is defined as the number of divorced couples over the total number of married couples for these age groups, should be much higher than the preceding numbers. Further, these figures indicate that a marriage is at risk of divorce for a given year only. Over many years, even a low annual divorce rate results in a large proportion of couples ending their marriages in divorce. For example, Lillard and Waite (1990) estimated that, if the divorce rates of the 1980s continued into the future, more than half of first marriages in the USA would end in divorce, and remarriage with new partners would be more prone to dissolution.

## 20.1 COSTS AND BENEFITS OF DIVORCE

Why do so many people choose to divorce? Divorce is a major decision for most people. Thus it is reasonable to assume that people are rational and forward looking in making the decision to divorce. Based on this assumption, an individual chooses divorce only if their utility (i.e. happiness index) from a current marriage is less than their expected utility of future alternatives such as remarriage. In other words, divorce occurs for a couple only if its benefit is greater than its cost for the husband, wife or both parties. I discuss the potential costs and benefits of divorce as follows.

In many societies, an individual achieves much higher social esteem if they have a spouse and children. Indeed, the feeling of possessing a spouse and children is usually one of the most crucial aspects of vanity. If a couple divorces, they lose the social status of possessing a spouse before remarriage occurs. Meanwhile, as the family is now broken, they receive much less social status from having children. That few men are enthusiastic about donating sperm illustrates the logic of this argument.

If people are greatly concerned about the survival of their genes, we would expect that most men would compete to donate sperm, and that many would in fact be willing to pay a large sum of money to the women who are willing to use their sperm. However, it is the men who are usually paid to donate their sperm,[149] and do so out of the urgent need for money or to help others. Only a very tiny proportion of men donate sperm for the happiness that accompanies having more offspring. One report notes the case of a serial sperm donor who fathered 14 children and revealed himself to be a virgin at the age of 36.[150] It is possible that this man used sperm donation as a substitute for getting married and having children.

Moreover, if a couple has children, divorce reduces their welfare in two important respects. First, empirical studies show that parental divorce significantly reduces the educational attainment and emotional development of children from previous marriages, regardless of whether the divorced parents remarry.[151] This finding is unsurprising. Like adults, children have self-esteem (or vanity). Much as parents obtain vanity from possessing children and a complete family, children obtain it from 'possessing' an unbroken family and both parents. After its parents divorce, a child is forced to live with only one parent. Consequently, in comparison with many of its classmates whose parents are not divorced, the child may feel inferior. In fact, in some Asian countries where the divorce rates are relatively low, children from single-parent families are often ridiculed by their peers. In addition, a divorce detracts from the time a father and mother devote to educating their children.[152]

Second, deciding which parent takes custody of the children after a divorce presents a problem. If one gives up custody, their social distance from the children becomes much larger, implying that the vanity one obtains from possessing the children becomes much weaker. In this case, a man's feelings towards his children from his previous marriage may be quite similar to his feelings for the children produced from his sperm donation, particularly if the divorce occurred when his children were little. However, the parent who takes custody of the children faces worse remarriage prospects. A prospective future marriage partner can consider the children from a former marriage as a financial burden and a potential source of dispute. More divorced couples compete for the custody of children in many Western countries compared with China, where many young couples fight in court to avoid custody.

Finally, there is often a huge reduction in financial resources when divorce occurs, particularly for women. For example, based on a national survey of 9055 people, Zagorsky (2005) finds that, in the USA, divorce reduced a person's wealth by about three-quarters on average compared with that of a single person. This huge financial loss may stem from a number of sources, such as the legal fee payments and emotional stress associated with divorce, which reduce one's productivity and earnings.

Given its high cost, why do many couples choose to divorce? It is because the benefits of divorce are sometimes significant for at least one of the parties. Consider the following hypothetical story. John and Stella married when John was 23 and Stella was 28. At the time of their wedding, John was good-looking and Stella was beautiful. Twenty years into their marriage, whereas John has developed a successful career, Stella has been worn down by the hard work of raising and teaching their children. At this stage in their lives, Stella is no longer attractive, and John is so charming that a large number of beautiful young women are available for his choosing. At a social gathering, many of John's friends brag to each other about the youth and beauty of their mistresses or new wives, making John feel inferior. Jennifer, a beautiful young woman in her early twenties, is madly in love with John. Although John feels indebted to Stella, he cannot withstand the temptation and begins a secret affair with Jennifer. As Stella knows John very well, she begins to notice something different about him, and soon discovers the affair. To divorce or not to divorce: that is the question. This story incidentally suggests that women should be cautious in deciding to marry younger men. Such marriages may be happy at the beginning, but after 20 years things may be very different.

Divorce sometimes occurs in situations where its cost is not very high. Consider another hypothetical story. Carole broke up with her long-time boyfriend at age 33. While it was heartbreaking, she finally got over it thanks to the valuable support from her family members and friends. Two years later, at age 35, she met another man named David. Although David was plain-looking, Carole was eager to have a child and thus accepted his marriage proposal. However, three months into the marriage, Carole meets Michael. Michael is tall, handsome and rich, and therefore fits Carole's ideal type. Although Michael knows Carole is no longer a virgin, he is attracted to her beauty. Carole divorces David quickly and marries Michael immediately.

This story illustrates the essential idea of the first economic theory of divorce developed by Becker et al. (1977), who argue that because the marriage market is not perfect, people must spend time and effort in searching for a marital partner. However, because no one can wait for the ideal person for ever, an individual may marry someone who is less desirable than themselves. Therefore a superior match who arrives in the future may upset a current marriage.

## 20.2 EXTRAMARITAL AFFAIRS AND DIVORCE

While the underlying reasons for divorce are often complicated, the substantial economics and sociology research arrives at a consensus: when divorce occurs, it is usually based on something unexpected. One main reason for divorce is extramarital affairs. Fan and Lui (2004) present an empirical study about the effect of extramarital affairs on divorce in Hong Kong. Since the opening up of China in 1978, the economies of Hong Kong and Mainland China have become increasingly integrated. For example, according to a Hong Kong government estimate, although Hong Kong's total population was only about 6.7 million in 1998, the amount of children born in China to Hong Kong parents numbered more than 1.6 million.[153]

Further, a sudden drastic degeneration of traditional morality occurred in China in the early 1990s. Because of the huge disparity in per capita income between the two regions, Hong Kong residents, even those from the low-income class, found it cheap and easy to engage in sexual affairs in Mainland China. Meanwhile, many Hong Kong men's participation in the marriage and sex markets in China resulted in a 'surplus' of women in the Hong Kong marriage market, further increasing the chance that extramarital affairs would take place. As a result, the divorce rate in Hong Kong increased drastically. For example, a 1998 survey indicates that about 60 per cent of the divorce cases in Hong Kong were related to extramarital affairs.[154]

These extramarital affairs introduced tremendous emotional stress and conflict.[155] In response to this increasingly serious social problem, Caritas Family Service in Hong Kong set up a 'Working Group on Extramarital Affairs' in December 1993 to provide counselling services to affected families. A by-product of this working group was a dataset on extramarital affairs and divorce in Hong Kong. The samples in this dataset were randomly chosen from those families that received counselling on extramarital issues at Caritas Family Service between 1 January 1994 and 1 April 1995, when the social problem of extramarital affairs seemed to be at its worst.

The dataset shows that 38 per cent of the affected couples divorced. Based on the dataset, in Fan and Lui (2004) we conduct a statistical analysis that yields several findings about the reasons for divorce. First, extramarital affairs result in a deterioration of marriage quality, which significantly increases the probability of divorce. Second, the presence of dependable children in a family lowers the probability of divorce. Moreover, the more children a couple have, the less likely divorce is to occur. Third, if a couple had a good relationship before the discovery of the extramarital affair, the parties are more likely to remain married in spite of it.

## 20.3 THE CUSTODY OF CHILDREN AFTER DIVORCE

The mother usually takes care of the children after a divorce. For example, in the USA, approximately 84 per cent of custodial parents are mothers and 16 per cent are fathers.[156] There are two main reasons for this arrangement. The first is based on the economics principle of comparative advantage, an idea that was first introduced by classical economist David Ricardo (1817). First used to explain international trade patterns, the principle of comparative advantage stipulates that, to achieve higher production efficiency, every country should specialize in the production and export of goods that give it comparative advantage.

Gary Becker later used this theory to explain the benefit of marriage. By a similar logic, he shows that the husband and wife of a household should spend more time and effort on the 'areas of production' in which each has comparative advantage. Whereas a husband is usually better at making money in the marketplace, a wife is usually better at taking care of children. Thus the theory of comparative advantage implies that each should spend more time and effort in these respective areas. This pattern of specialization refers to the usual 'sexual division of labour' within a marriage.

Even after a divorce, as long as a husband continues to give money to his former wife, this pattern of specialization remains efficient. He would do so for at least two reasons: (i) he is required by law to pay the alimony; and (ii) he is concerned about his children's welfare.[157] Because this pattern of arrangement entails that the wife spends more time with their children, she would naturally take custody in a divorce.

Second, remarriage prospects after divorce are usually much better for middle-aged men than for women. This stems mainly from the difference in beauty standards between men and women. As a woman grows older, wrinkles are more likely to appear on her face. If a woman has given birth or had an abortion, parts of her body such as her breasts may deviate significantly from many men's beauty standards.[158]

In contrast, age itself has much less of an effect on the deterioration of beauty for a man. While men also gain wrinkles as they get older, they have little effect on his beauty. In fact, a middle-aged man often has little disadvantage in terms of looks in comparison with a young man. Further, in many societies, the double standard of virginity continues to exist to varying degrees. In such societies, where many men are reluctant to marry women who have been married previously, no or little stigma exists for a divorced man.

Thus a woman is often willing to take custody of her children, as she considers it unlikely that she will find another husband who meets her standards. In contrast, a man may prefer not to take custody of his children, to improve his chances of marrying a 'higher-quality' woman.

# 21. Development and divorce

## 21.1 ECONOMIC DEVELOPMENT AND DIVORCE

An online search of 'the main causes of divorce' produces keyword results such as 'infidelity', 'physical abuse', 'emotional abuse' and 'incompatible personalities'. For example, an online search for 'valid reasons to divorce' reveals the following typical results:[159]

- Physical or Emotional Abuse: If they hit you once it will happen again. You should not stay in a marriage beyond that first punch, slap or shove. DO NOT make excuses for someone who hits you, DO NOT take the blame for someone hitting you. Violence is about a need to control and exert power over a spouse, it is not about loving a spouse. Domestic abuse comes in different forms. Your spouse may physically abuse you or emotionally abuse you. Yelling, screaming, name calling and put-downs are not acceptable forms of behavior. For your own safety and that of your children, you need to leave.
- Infidelity: Once a cheater, always a cheater. Infidelity is much like domestic abuse; it is a behavior that will repeat itself. A spouse will cheat for many reasons, what you, the victim of infidelity, need to understand is that there is never a good reason

Note that these 'valid reasons to divorce' have existed throughout human history. They have always been a part of husband–wife relationships. Thus the question is as follows: why is divorce only a condition of the past half-century?

In Fan (2001a), I provide an answer to this question, suggesting that divorce is a by-product of economic development. When an economy is underdeveloped and people's incomes are low, the cost of divorce prevents couples from divorcing irrespective of marriage quality. The intuition of this argument is straightforward: when people are poor, marriage quality is a luxury. Recall Malthus's population theory, which states that most households throughout human history have lived at or close to the subsistence level. In such cases, the considerable reduction of a household's total income from a divorce would result in some members of the household starving, implying that divorce is very unlikely to occur. Even when survival is not a serious concern, if a typical household's income is low, money that would otherwise be used for a divorce could be used to purchase crucial consumption items that substantially benefit the household's welfare. Thus a couple would choose not to divorce despite a bad marriage.

However, when an economy develops and people's incomes increase beyond a certain threshold level, couples will consider divorce if their marriage quality is bad. The logic is simple: relative to food consumption, the quality of a marriage is a luxury good. Much in the way poor people do not drive BMWs, people do not find it beneficial to divorce when the economy is underdeveloped, such as in ancient times. However, as the economy develops, some may find it appropriate to adopt the 'luxury' of divorce in the midst of a bad marriage. In an abstract sense, marriage quality is a luxury when incomes are low but a necessity when incomes are high. Just as people will purchase a mobile phone when their income reaches a certain level, they will consider paying the cost of divorce to end a bad marriage.[160] Thus divorce is a product of the contemporary world, and it is mainly determined by the economic fundamentals of a society.

## 21.2  SOCIAL DEVELOPMENT AND DIVORCE

Divorce can also be a product of social development. Once a social norm exists, it is hard for a single individual to break it. Divorces were a very rare occurrence 200 years ago. Even if a person was very wealthy and could easily afford the associated costs, divorces were very hard to conduct. If one chose to divorce, one would incur the cost of a major social stigma – negative vanity. Thus the first group of individuals who chose divorce made significant self-sacrifices. One such person was Caroline Norton, who 150 years ago had an important impact on the UK's Marriage and Divorce Act.[161]

The threshold income level of divorce may be much lower in developing countries compared with developed countries, perhaps due to the influence of the latter's cultural elements (e.g. Hollywood). Divorce in developed countries substantially reduces the stigma of divorce in developing countries, even when the divorce rates in developing countries are low. Therefore people in developing countries may begin to accept divorce as a social norm even when income levels are low. In fact, some people in developing countries worship the 'fashions' in rich countries, and may consider divorce such a fashion.

Moreover, a change in divorce laws has reduced the cost of divorce. It should be noted that the change in divorce laws might have been a response to increasing demand for divorce in unhappy marriages.[162] As described previously, this increasing demand is caused by significant social and economic development.

## 21.3  DIVORCE, FERTILITY AND WOMEN'S LABOUR MARKET PARTICIPATION

Divorce has a significant effect on other family issues such as fertility and women's labour market participation. In Fan (2001a), I present a theoretical analysis of the interactive effects of divorce and fertility. First, as discussed earlier, divorce is costly to a couple: it lowers a couple's expected future income. Divorce also breaks up a 'complete' family. Because people obtain much more vanity from having a 'complete' family, which may be the main reason inducing people to get married in the first place, a divorce substantially reduces the benefit of having children. Thus these considerations reduce fertility.

In turn, this decreased fertility also increases the probability of divorce, which further reduces fertility. Children are often the main concern when a conflicting couple decides whether to divorce. When a couple does not have children, a small conflict may result in a quick divorce. The presence of children may induce parents to behave well and respect their marital partners, leading to fewer marital conflicts. Without the concern for children, some couples may not care as much about the effect of their behaviour on their partners, leading to a greater likelihood of divorce.

A similar logic can help us understand the interactive effects of divorce and woman's labour market participation. Due to the commonality of divorce, many women feel that men are unreliable. Consequently, women seek more economic independence by working in the marketplace and trying to develop their own careers.[163] When women have their own careers, they become 'pickier' about their marriage quality, increasing the likelihood of divorce.

Woman's labour market participation also increases the incidence of extramarital affairs. In traditional societies, women work only at home, lessening the chance for married men and women to meet and interact extensively. However, when women work, men and women can easily become acquainted through close interactions in the workplace, increasing the chance that an extramarital affair will take place, particularly for the men and women who feel unsatisfied with their current marriages. Moreover, many women look up to the men with the most conspicuous careers at their workplaces, presenting another channel for woman's labour market participation to increase the probability of divorce.

Moreover, once many women are working, a woman may find it dangerous to be a housewife. If a woman becomes a full-time mother who takes care of her children at home, she usually dresses casually, as there is little point in appearing attractive to her children. In contrast, working women usually dress beautifully out of necessity, as many (male) customers prefer to interact with beautiful women. Indeed, companies often institute dress codes for their employees.

A husband whose wife works at home may notice the sharp contrast: whereas the ladies at his company are attractive, his wife has become unappealing to him. As a result, the husband may be tempted to pursue a woman at work. The title of the famous drama *Desperate Housewives* is apt.

In sum, divorce, fertility and women's work are closely interrelated. Indeed, it is observed that increases in divorce and women's labour market participation and decreases in fertility usually occur simultaneously in countries around the world.

# 22. Family background and children's education

Many of the previous chapters have highlighted that children are their parents' most important vanity affiliates. In other words, most parents strongly hope that their children will be successful, which would yield vanity for the parents and fulfil their own dreams. Indeed, an accomplished child often brings its parents much more vanity than a luxurious car.

However, the modern world is a highly competitive environment in which only a fraction of young people will achieve success. In 2011, Amy Chua, a professor at Yale Law School, published a book entitled *Battle Hymn of the Tiger Mother* in which she described strict parenting techniques that she believes were crucial to her daughters' high educational achievements. The global attention the book received due to its controversial elements illustrates people's paramount concern for their children's educational attainment and the fierce competition involved in ensuring they enter elite universities. This chapter describes how family background affects children's educational attainment and career success.

## 22.1 HISTORICAL VIEW

A positive correlation of social and economic status between parents and children has long been recognized. There is a large amount of empirical literature on intergenerational mobility that dates back to the classical writings of Galton (1869, 1889).[164] Galton first studied the correlation of height between parents and children. He made two findings. First, taller parents tend to have taller children. Second, the height advantage (or disadvantage) of a 'dynasty' relative to the height of the entire population of a society tends to decrease over time. The first finding can be arrived at from daily observation. However, Galton's second finding was (and perhaps continues to be) unknown to most people. He finds that such a height advantage (or disadvantage) of a dynasty decreases by one-third for each generation. For example, if the average height of a man's parents is six inches greater than the average height of their society, then he is likely to be four inches taller than the average male.

Galton launched a more ambitious project to study whether human ability is hereditary. To tackle the issue, he designed a clever experiment by counting the number of relatives of so-called 'eminent men' – famous people. He reasoned that, if human ability were hereditary, we would observe a greater proportion of eminent men among an eminent man's relatives than among the general population. In his project, Galton carefully analyses the obituaries of *The Times* newspaper, where he traces the lineage of many eminent men in Europe. He finds strong evidence that the number of eminent relatives drops from the first- to second-degree relatives, and again from the second- to third-degree relatives. This finding offers interesting evidence of the inheritance of abilities.

There is a simple empirical strategy for estimating intergenerational earnings mobility. In fact, there is little essential difference between the start-of-the-art methodology in modern economics and the methodology Galton used more than 100 years ago. However, economists can now access many more data and accurate earnings measures over long periods of time. The literature reports a positive correlation of earning ability between parents and children that differs across countries. Among developed countries, the correlation is high in the USA and relatively low in Northern Europe.

A more difficult question relates to why the earning abilities between parents and children are positively correlated. Galton's research provides a straightforward answer: as height matters to earnings, taller (and hence richer) parents tend to have taller (and hence richer) children. This is also clearly true for other aspects of physical attractiveness that are rewarded in the labour market.[165] In fact, the logic may apply to any other predetermined traits such as intelligence and personality, as long as a positive intergenerational correlation for these traits exists.

In recent decades, economists have developed a number of theories to look for more sophisticated answers to the preceding question. They focus on examining whether people make conscientious choices that result in persistent income inequality across generations. The following provides a summary of some of these theories.

## 22.2 PARENTAL INCOME AND CHILDREN'S EDUCATION

Becker and Tomes (1979, 1986) and Loury (1981) offer pioneering studies of intergenerational earnings mobility in the economics literature.

They assume that parents care about both their children's incomes and their own material consumption. In other words, they effectively make the same assumption as that emphasized in this book, although they do not state parents' vanity as a reason. They further show that richer parents spend more on their children's human capital investment, and consequently that the children tend to have higher earning abilities. To the extent that money matters for education outcomes, rich families have an advantage in investing in children's education.

Moreover, Galor and Zeira (1993) present a theoretical analysis showing that when credit markets are imperfect and expenditures on children's education are indivisible, only the children whose parental income is above a certain threshold level receive education. Because there is often a large earning gap between those who receive an education and those who do not, parental earnings may matter significantly to children's future earnings. From the perspective of occupational choice, Banerjee and Newman (1991) demonstrate that, in the countries with serious capital market imperfections, whereas wealthy people can become entrepreneurs, poor people have no other choice but to become workers. Thus the children of rich entrepreneurs become entrepreneurs and the children of poor workers become workers. Due to this barrier to becoming an entrepreneur, the income gap between entrepreneurs and workers may be very large. Therefore these two studies show that, when credit markets are imperfect, parental income is often an important determinant of whether one will be successful in pursuing a conspicuous career.

In developed countries, credit markets are well established and education is often provided by the government. As a result, parental income *per se* is less important. However, a family's background may still play an important role in determining one's education opportunities. For example, many elite universities in the USA overtly favour students with strong family backgrounds. The following recent report provides an illustration:[166]

> consider the case of China. There, legions of angry microbloggers endlessly denounce the official corruption and abuse which permeate so much of the economic system. But we almost never hear accusations of favoritism in university admissions, and this impression of strict meritocracy determined by the results of the national Gaokao college entrance examination has been confirmed to me by individuals familiar with that country. Since all the world's written exams may ultimately derive from China's old imperial examination system, which was kept remarkably clean for 1300 years, such practices are hardly surprising. Attending a prestigious college is regarded by ordinary Chinese as their children's greatest hope of rapid upward mobility

and is therefore often a focus of enormous family effort; China's ruling elites may rightly fear that a policy of admitting their own dim and lazy heirs to leading schools ahead of the higher-scoring children of the masses might ignite a widespread popular uprising. This perhaps explains why so many sons and daughters of top Chinese leaders attend college in the West: enrolling them at a third-rate Chinese university would be a tremendous humiliation, while our own corrupt admissions practices get them an easy spot at Harvard or Stanford, sitting side by side with the children of Bill Clinton, Al Gore, and George W. Bush.

## 22.3 PARENTAL INTELLIGENCE, PARENTAL EDUCATION AND CHILDREN'S EDUCATION OUTCOMES

In most developed countries, financial resources are hardly a main constraint on education.[167] In many Northern European countries, for example, education (including preschool education) is completely free, and students are even provided with a stipend to go to college. However, family background continues to matter to a child's education, as it determines the child's intelligence to a large extent.

Researchers as far back as Galton (1869) have observed a positive correlation of height between parents and children. It is plausible that such a strong positive correlation also exists in terms of intelligence. However, rigorous evidence to this effect is difficult to find for the simple reason that intelligence cannot be accurately measured. While IQ is a common measure of intelligence, one can attain a higher IQ score by studying harder or focusing on materials related to the IQ test.

Plenty of anecdotal evidence suggests that intelligence is genetically hereditary. The following story illustrates the argument that parental intelligence affects children's intelligence. In the 1980s, a small group of people in China who were not well educated became rich largely due to their exogenous geographical locations and certain special policies. In fact, some accrued wealth simply because they could not find jobs for a variety of reasons (e.g. criminal records) and were forced to start private businesses that became financially successful. They found beautiful wives and sent their children to special aristocratic schools. However, their children often performed badly academically.

After the lessons learned in the 1980s, the new rich changed their mate selection strategy in the 1990s. While beauty remains important, rich men, who have their choice of women, desire their wives to be intelligent and educated by prestigious universities. Indeed, an intelligent mother is likely to have an intelligent child for two main reasons. First, intelligence is most likely genetically hereditary. Second, a mother is often the most important teacher during her child's preschool education.

Whether education or intelligence is the more important parental trait contributing to a child's educational achievements is an important question. However, the economics and social science literature provides no definite answer, as one's intelligence cannot be well measured. It is most likely that both are important.[168] Moreover, if parental education is important in children's human capital formation, then there is a clear long-term benefit to receiving education. Even if education does not pay off during a special period such as one of economic transition, it may nevertheless make sense for a person to receive a good education for the benefit of her child's human capital accumulation.[169]

## 22.4  FAMILY BACKGROUND AND STUDY EFFORT

In addition to intelligence, study effort is an important determinant of educational attainment. For example, a 1986 article in the *New York Times* attributes the relative economic success of Asian Americans to their high study effort. In particular, it states: 'a recent survey of students in San Francisco... found male Asian-American students spent an average of 11.7 hours a week doing homework, compared with 8.0 hours for whites and 6.3 hours for blacks.'[170] More recently, based on the American Time Use Survey, which provides detailed data measuring the time use of thousands of individuals from 2003 to 2009, Ramey (2011) reports that the average hours per week spent by Asian, white, black and Hispanic high-school students are 13.0, 5.6, 3.4 and 4.6, respectively. In other words, Asian high-school students spend considerably more time studying than the students of other ethnic groups in the USA, which provides an important explanation for the substantially higher academic achievements of Asian Americans relative to the national average.

Why some students study significantly less hard than their classmates is an important question, and this section offers the following answers.[171] First, a greater study effort may result in a better grade, which may help one enter a good university and subsequently find a good job. However, many jobs do not depend on academic performance. Second, if a student is not good at studying, they may not like exerting the required effort. These two points are elaborated as follows.

First, while some jobs require a good education, a formal education is not always important. For example, a doctor's or professor's productivity is mainly determined by their educational attainment. However, many jobs (e.g. janitor, cab driver, cashier, bartender) do not require a high level of education. In particular, one can take an unskilled job and earn a living with one's physical endowments, even if one has few years of schooling. For example, a 1990 report by the National Centre on Education and the Economy points out that of the USA's 117 million jobs at the time, 40 million (34 per cent) did not require a high-school education (*The Economist*, 22 August 1992). Because the attendance levels in primary and secondary education are near 100 per cent in the USA, these 40 million jobs effectively did not require the workers to have any human capital beyond the 'basic' education that almost everyone had. While a college education is required for many other jobs (e.g. administrator, flight attendant, bank employee, social worker), these jobs usually do not depend on the workers' academic performances, and hence the applicants for those jobs are not asked about their grades or even about the reputations of their colleges. In fact, even if graduates from a more reputable college have a better chance of getting these jobs, their career perspective usually depends much more on other skills such as interpersonal skills than the grades they achieved at school or their cognitive skills in general.

Second, effort and intelligence are often positively correlated. If a student has a high level of intelligence, they will have a high willingness to exert effort in studying. Because an intelligent student is often praised by their teachers at school, they not only enjoy studying but also gain social esteem from their excellent academic performance.

However, if a student has a low level of intelligence, they will have a low willingness to exert effort in studying. As a result, they may choose to play sports, engage in more social activities and study less diligently. In the future, they will take a job that does not require a high knowledge of mathematics or other kind of formal education, or a job that does not require much formal education at all. Thus low intelligence may discourage an individual from accumulating human capital even if the education is completely free. In other words, low intelligence may induce a low study effort.

This reasoning implies that both intelligence and study effort may show strong positive correlations between parents and children, implying that income inequality will persist across generations. While one may argue that a child does not have such foresight, parents can foresee the future for their children. If they see that it will be hard for their children to proceed far with their schooling, they may not spend the effort required to discipline and guide their children to try hard at their academic performance. After all, education is not the only path to success, and children who exhibit poor school performance may develop an alternative perspective.

While this book emphasizes adult vanity, it should be noted that children have vanity too. If some children are slow to learn, they are likely to receive low grades for course work. The children may be criticized by teachers for poor performance or even ridiculed by class-mates. Consequently, they will probably hate studying and spend little effort on it. If they are athletic and good-looking, they will be much happier participating in sports activities and engaging in socializing. Thus intelligence and effort also interact positively through the vanity effect.

# 23. Parental behaviours and the quality of children

## 23.1 RELIGIOUS PARTICIPATION, SOCIAL CAPITAL AND CHILDREN'S EDUCATION

It is widely recognized that children's behaviour in general and their study efforts in particular matter greatly to their educational attainment. Chapter 22 showed that students' study effort may be closely related to their intelligence. However, it may not be the only determinant. In particular, children's good habits may also matter greatly to their future career success, and parents can often play an important role in guiding children to behave well and develop good habits.[172]

What can parents do to induce good behaviour and diligent study efforts from their children? In Fan (2008), I provide an answer to this question by suggesting that parental behaviour can affect children's 'social capital', which in turn influences their cognitive and non-cognitive development. While Fan (2008) focuses on parents' religious participation, the essential idea can be applied to their other social behaviours.

In a seminal contribution to sociology, Coleman (1988) emphasizes that social capital greatly affects an individual's human capital formation. Along this line of research, in Fan (2008) I analyse an important and largely ignored form of social capital in the creation of human capital: religion. I argue there that many people participate in religious activities not only due to their religious beliefs, but also because religion is conducive to their children's human capital formation.

A number of empirical studies show consistently that religion has a significant positive effect on children's educational attainment and future earnings.[173] Further, sociologists' extensive research indicates that youths raised in religious homes are less likely to engage in criminal activity, use drugs or alcohol and have premarital sex.[174] Indeed, many religions emphasize the virtues of hard work, honesty, seriousness and responsibility, all of which are conducive to children's acquisition of cognitive and non-cognitive skills.[175]

In response, parents' religious participation is often affected by the concern for their children's cognitive and moral development. For example, in his influential writing on the sociology of religion, Wilson (1978, pp. 262–3) notes:

> Religious training is something that all but two percent of American parents feel they should give their children ... [Parents] see [the church] as a place of character building for their children ... Children are frequently the most important consideration in choosing a particular church ... Couples with growing children have the highest rate of church attendance.

As shown by sociologists' and psychologists' research, parents' religious participation is essential for their children's religious training. For example, McCleary and Barro (2006, p. 152) note the following:

> the incentive to bring children to services tends to induce greater involvement of adults, who are likely to want to participate in the process of inculcating in their children and in ensuring that religious values and traditions are transmitted across generations.

Also, Nock (1992, p. 333) summarizes:

> American parents believe it important that their children receive moral and ethical guidelines from their church. This is why church attendance is highest among parents with young children ... children are much more responsive to the behavioral models than to instruction. They are much more likely to imitate what they see parents and others do than what they hear parents and others say ...

Based on these observations and arguments, I present an economic analysis in Fan (2008) in which people participate in a religion due to the concern for their children's human capital formation as well as their own religious beliefs. I assume that an individual's human capital is jointly determined by their family background and social capital. An individual's family background is represented by their parental human capital, and their social capital is measured by their 'religious capital', which is influenced by their frequency of religious participation.

In such a framework, if the parental human capital is too low, the children may not want to exert effort studying in any case. (This logic was explained in Chapter 22.) In response, the parents may attend few religious activities if their religious beliefs are weak. This result is consistent with a stylized fact about education and religion in the USA: education is the most statistically important factor explaining church attendance, and religious attendance rises sharply with education across individuals.[176]

However, Fan (2008) shows that, when parental human capital is above a certain threshold level, parents' religious participation is negatively correlated with their education level if the parental human capital and social capital are substitutes in their child's human capital formation. Together with the previous result, this result helps to explain an important stylized fact about education and religion revealed by Glaeser and Sacerdote (2008): in the USA, while religious attendance rises with education across individuals, it declines significantly with education across denominations.

In the literature, Weinberg (2001) analyses that parents use external incentives such as pecuniary rewards and/or corporal punishment to induce their children to exert efforts in study. In contrast, Fan (2008) suggests that religious education constitutes a kind of internal enforcement mechanism for children to learn to follow moral rules and exert effort in studying. In fact, as stressed by Smith (1776), one of the most economically significant functions of religious belief is to provide strong incentives for individuals to follow a moral code. Smith explains that religion effectively complements legal rules and other incentives that cause individuals to control their own behaviour.[177] Thus, in a sense, in Fan (2008) I extend Smith's observation from adults to children in noting that religion may help children exert more self-control and develop good habits, which may ultimately help them greatly in their education and career pursuits.

## 23.2  PARENTAL BEHAVIOUR AND THE 'MARRIAGE PREMIUM PUZZLE'

Parental behaviour may affect children in many ways, and religion is not the only way to influence children. In an article entitled 'Does Fatherhood Matter for Men?' Eggebeen and Knoester (2001) find substantial differences between fathers and non-fathers in many different types of behaviour, such as those relating to social connections and community group involvement. For example, whereas fathers are more likely to participate in service-type organizations, attend church and maintain intergenerational family ties, non-fathers are likely to go to bars or engage in other pleasure pursuits. The authors arrive at the following conclusion (p. 392): 'Fatherhood can profoundly shape the lives of men.' In an earlier chapter, I noted that some men may trade promiscuity for the right to possess a wife and children. The argument here essentially indicates that some men may be willing to trade promiscuity or a propensity for other bad habits for vanity, that is, the vanity of their children's high educational attainment.

Moreover, when a man adopts better habits, such as treating others politely and being responsible, his productivity at work increases. Thus this reasoning provides an explanation for why married men tend to earn more – the so-called 'male marriage premium puzzle'.

Empirical studies consistently document that a married man tends to earn significantly more money than a single man with the same qualifications (in terms of education, height, experience, race etc.), and the male marriage premium is estimated to range from 10 per cent to 35 per cent.[178] This presents a puzzle, as one might expect that not having the burden of a family would allow a single man to put much more time and effort into his work and career compared with a married man. However, the opposite is true.

There are two main explanations for the male marriage premium puzzle in the economics literature. First, it is argued that the men who earn more money are perhaps more likely to get married. But this argument does not explain the whole puzzle. For example, Ginther and Zavodny (2001) mitigate this problem of estimation by examining cases of shotgun weddings, and find that this argument explains 10 per cent of the male marriage premium at most.

The second argument is that there is often a sexual division of labour during a marriage in which women focus on the work at home, which allows men to focus their effort and attention on their professional work and hence to obtain higher earnings. However, most single men do not have children, meaning that work at home requires little of their time and effort. Even if a single man must occasionally perform household chores, he usually works much less than a married man at home. Indeed, a married man cannot entirely depend on his wife to take care of his children; further, he must devote time and attention to his wife. Thus this hypothesis cannot explain much of the male marriage premium puzzle.

This section provides a new explanation. As stated at the beginning of this section, married men with children need to be 'role models' to their children. Children often learn from the behaviour of their parents rather than their words. To behave well consistently, a man must develop good habits. In *The Seven Habits of Highly Effective People*, which business-school MBA students often use as a textbook, Covey (1989, p. 22) states:

> Habits are powerful factors in our lives. Because they are consistent, often unconscious patterns, they constantly, daily, express our character and produce our effectiveness or ineffectiveness. As Horace Mann, the great educator,

once said, 'Habits are like a cable. We weave a strand of it everyday and soon it cannot be broken.' I personally do not agree with the last part of his expression. I know they can be broken. Habits can be learned and unlearned. But I also know it isn't a quick fix. It involves a process and a tremendous commitment. Those of us who watched the lunar voyage of Apollo 11 were transfixed as we saw the first men walk on the moon and return to earth. Superlatives such as 'fantastic' and 'incredible' were inadequate to describe those eventful days. But to get there, those astronauts literally had to break out of the tremendous gravity pull of the earth. More energy was spent in the first few minutes of lift-off, in the first few miles of travel, than was used over the next several days to travel half a million miles. Habits, too, have tremendous gravity pull – more than most people realize or would admit. Breaking deeply imbedded habitual tendencies such as procrastination, impatience, criticalness, or selfishness that violate basic principles of human effectiveness involves more than a little willpower and a few minor changes in our lives. 'Lift-off' takes a tremendous effort, but once we break out of the gravity pull, our freedom takes on a whole new dimension.

Many men are willing to spend much effort on breaking their bad habits only after they have children. When they behave badly, such as by smoking or swearing, in front of their children, it will be very hard to teach their children not to do so. They can eliminate such behaviour in front of their children only if they develop good habits. This is why Eggebeen and Knoester (2001, p. 392) conclude that 'fatherhood can profoundly shape the lives of men'.

If a man develops good habits, he will carry them to the workplace. They will influence him to be more polite, responsible and sensitive to others' feelings, characteristics that will contribute to his productivity. Therefore good habits increase a man's workplace productivity and hence his earnings.

# 24. Intergenerational transfers of wealth

It is important to understand intergenerational transfers; they matter greatly to consumption and saving, which are crucial to economics. For example, aggregate consumption accounts for more than half of the gross domestic product (GDP) in almost every country in the world. Thus fluctuations in consumption are a major source of business cycles. Further, investment funds come from saving, which implies that saving is a main determinant of economic growth.

## 24.1 IMPORTANCE OF INTERGENERATIONAL TRANSFERS FOR SAVING

Most of us have enough experience and have made enough observations to know that consumption and saving decisions are often made by entire households rather than individuals. Children are particularly a factor in such decisions. The need to save may arise mostly from a concern for children and grandchildren. Some empirical studies show that intergenerational transfers account for 50–80 per cent of the capital accumulation in the USA.[179] In particular, a significant fraction of down-payments for first-time housing purchases in the USA are made by parents.[180] In Asian countries that have much higher saving rates, this should be more important.

The classical economist Alfred Marshall (1920, p. 228) made the well-known statement that in his time, 'men labour and save chiefly for the sake of the families and not for themselves ...'. This statement may suggest that saving may be more related to a concern for children at low economic development levels. As noted in Chapter 4, China's high saving rate is mainly a result of many parents wanting to help their children purchase expensive flats in Chinese cities.

One report made on 4 February 2012 in China vividly illustrates that people are willing to make tremendous sacrifices for their children and grandchildren. A man in his sixties became ill. He had been receiving medical treatment for three years, but his illness did not improve much. In the very early morning of 2 February 2012, his daughter-in-law was awoken by his painful groaning. The old man waved her close and tearfully told her the following before dying:

> My illness cannot be cured ... I have been a burden to you in recent years ... Now the children (his grandchildren) are still in school. Please do not spend money on me anymore, and save the money for my grandchildren's education. I hope they will be successful.

His daughter-in-law spotted a bottle of pesticide nearby. It was later confirmed that the old man had committed suicide by drinking it.[181]

## 24.2  ECONOMIC THEORY OF 'ALTRUISM' VERSUS EMPIRICS OF PRIMOGENITURE

The question becomes how to characterize the relationships between parents and children. In economics and other social sciences, there is a consensus that parents and children are linked by parental 'altruism' towards their children. However, in economics, it is commonly assumed that intergenerational altruism takes the specific form of parents caring about their children's happiness and giving money to their children to increase that happiness (e.g. Barro, 1974; Becker, 1974). This specific assumption has generated a great deal of controversy.

Children's happiness as a sole concern for parents may be a good ideology. Indeed, if children perceive such an attitude from their parents, a good relationship is usually maintained after the children grow up. However, the philosophical foundation for this intention of the parents is questionable. While it is true that the chance of a child's survival is sometimes related to its happiness, survival probability and happiness are often two totally different things.

In China, parents often state publicly that they only want their children to be happy, regardless of their education and career achievements, and that the children can do whatever they wish. However, it is also common knowledge that such statements are usually untrue.

Indeed, many empirical studies in economics rigorously test whether intergenerational transfers are intended to increase children's happiness, and these studies consistently reject this hypothesis.[182] Some economists argue that assuming utility/happiness dependence is problematic because it implies that there is no intergenerational conflict.[183] For example, the children of rich parents often wish their parents had given them more money when they were young so that they could have more fun. Parents usually give their children most of the money when the children are much older and have largely lost their interest in and ability to pursue pleasure. If a college student asks his parents for $10 000, the parents will usually ask him about the purpose. If the money is to be used for the student's educational expenditure, many parents will agree. However, if the money is to be used for pleasure pursuits such as travelling, few parents will agree.

For example, Pollak (1988, p. 241) argues:

Many parents spend substantial resources on their children's college educations. Suppose your college-age daughter announces that she would rather use the money for something else, for example, to contribute to Green Peace or to buy a Mercedes. As a parent I would find such an announcement distressing, and I suspect most parents would; my guess is that in most families the daughter would not get the money for Green Peace or for the Mercedes. Why? (ii) Anecdotal evidence suggests the importance of financial help from parents in providing down payments for home purchases; some confirmation – it has been suggested that 'data' is the plural of anecdote – is provided by statistics from the National Association of Realtors (1986, p. 25) showing that gifts are the source of 19 percent of the funds used for down payments on first houses. Suppose you were planning to give your son the money for the down payment on his first house, but that he would rather use the money for something else, for example, to contribute to Green Peace or to buy a Mercedes. I suspect that few of the parents who were willing to give their son the money for the down payment would give him the money for Green Peace or for the Mercedes. Why? (iii) Anecdotal evidence suggests that parents with substantial wealth are sometimes concerned that their children will misuse, squander, or waste resources that are transferred to them. To mitigate these concerns, parents sometimes establish trust funds that limit children's control over resources and thus their opportunities to misuse them. What lawyers call 'spendthrift trusts' are specifically designed to restrict children's control over resources, often well beyond the children's minorities and the parents' lifetimes. Why?

Of course, these examples do not mean the parents are wrong. They imply only that intergenerational altruism is different from the argument that parents give money to their children to increase the children's happiness.

Primogeniture may be the best illustration of the assumption that parents' concern for their children's happiness is not the main explanation for intergenerational transfers. Primogeniture is a system in which only one child, usually the eldest son, inherits his parents' wealth entirely while his siblings receive little or even nothing. This system, which has been implemented throughout human history, cannot be explained by the assumption that parents are concerned for their children's happiness. If parents cared about all of their children's happiness, why do they give their wealth to only one child?

Consider the following simple numerical example. A man has five sons. His wife is dead and he knows that he will soon die as well. He has $5 million to pass on to his children. The sons have very similar tastes and endowments, implying that they would experience similar levels of increased happiness upon receiving money from their father. These levels are specifically described in Table 24.1.

*Table 24.1  A numerical example*

| Money received from the father | $1 million | $2 million | $3 million | $4 million | $5 million |
|---|---|---|---|---|---|
| The amount of increased happiness | 10 | 18 | 24 | 28 | 30 |

Table 24.1 shows that the additional amounts of happiness the sons would gain from each additional $1 million are 10, 8, 6, 4 and 2, respectively. That the additional amount of happiness decreases as the money received increases reflects the law of diminishing marginal utility in economics, which was discussed in detail in Chapter 5. In this example, we can see that, if the father is truly concerned about the happiness of his children, he should give each son $1 million. In this case, the total amount of happiness his children attain from receiving the bequests is

$$5 \times 10 = 50$$

However, in the case of primogeniture, the total amount of happiness attained from receiving the bequests is

$$30 + 0 \times 4 = 30$$

In a more general framework, Chu (1991) demonstrates that primogeniture contradicts the theory that intergenerational transfers stem from parents' concern for their children's happiness *per se*. On the basis of anthropologists' extensive research, Chu proposes another explanation.

He argues that the altruism from parents to children arises from parents' concern for the survival of their genes. Based on this assumption, he explains that primogeniture emerged as family heads' optimal policy for minimizing the probability of their lineal extinction. Chu also demonstrates that this assumption provides a more satisfactory explanation for primogeniture than the common assumption that parents' utility depends on their children's utility.

## 24.3 'SURVIVAL OF THE GENE', VANITY AND BEQUESTS

Chu's (1991) essential idea is that the survival of the gene was the major motivation of bequests in ancient times.[184] In Fan (2005), I analyse this bequest motive by considering that parents and children are linked through their common desire to have grandchildren. Given that grandparents do not beget grandchildren directly, the concern for the survival of the gene induces grandparents to transfer some of their wealth to their children to aid them in bearing and raising grandchildren whom the grandparents care about. In ancient times, people's life expectancies were short, which meant that grandparents could not often raise their grandchildren directly. Thus bequests and expenditures on children's education provide a material basis for the survival of the gene.

Moreover, when survival is a major concern, a large proportion of bequests may result from people's precautionary motive. In low-income countries, people's income perspectives are usually very uncertain. For example, most of the populations in poor countries earn their livings from agriculture, and agricultural income is inherently volatile due to the large variability of weather, pests and natural disasters.[185] Thus, in the absence of substantial saving, the income of a household may often fall below the subsistence level. This may be an important reason why the infant mortality rates were high in ancient times. In response, some relatively rich households may have strong motivations to leave bequests to increase the chance of the survival of the gene. Bequests serve as a 'buffer stock' to help prevent the consumption of the members of a household from falling below the minimum survival level.[186]

However, one may argue that the concern for the survival of the gene belongs to the past. Most people today are not on the verge of survival, and often give substantial bequests to their children. They do so out of vanity. In this case, transfers from parents to children are made to improve certain characteristics of the grandchildren, thereby increasing the vanity of the grandparents.[187] For example, considering the high cost of elite education, rich people may want to leave large bequest amounts to ensure that their grandchildren and great-grandchildren are well educated. In developing countries, firm owners usually receive high incomes and enjoy a high social status. However, because the financial markets are not well developed, most people must depend on their own savings to start their businesses. In this case, intergenerational transfers from parents are pivotal, and may help children develop conspicuous careers. In response, parents may have an incentive to leave bequests because they obtain happiness (a vanity affiliation) from the conspicuous careers of their children, grandchildren and great-grandchildren.

In fact, this idea is closely related to that of Pollak (1988), who proposes a theory of 'paternalistic preferences' in explaining bequests. For example, he states (p. 242):

> parents might want their children to attend college or own a house because it gives the parents pleasure or satisfaction, independent of their children's preferences. This might reflect the parents' own values and aspirations, or their concern with status ('my daughter the doctor') ...

This chapter extends Pollak's (1988) study by analysing bequests in a general framework of vanity economics.

Analysing bequests from a vanity economics perspective helps to explain the observed empirical evidence in three respects. First, it emphasizes that parents do not care about their children's happiness *per se*. Instead, parents and children are linked through their common concern for educating grandchildren; transfers from parents to children are intended to induce the children to spend more on the grandchildren and thereby increase their quality. This implies that intergenerational conflicts and intergenerational commonality coexist. While a generation wants to make transfers (bequests) to the next generation, the two generations have different preferences in terms of what to do with the transfers. This implication explains the intergenerational conflicts described in the previous section, and why parents ultimately leave large bequests despite intergenerational conflicts.

Second, Auerbach et al. (1992) document a significant increase in the annuitization of the USA's elderly in the past few decades, which implies a declining bequest motive. In the USA and other developed countries, the financial markets have been well developed and the governments have offered considerable higher education subsidies. Consequently, bequests have become much less important in determining whether children are successful in their development of conspicuous careers. Therefore many people may have much less of an incentive to leave bequests than before, or compared with people in developing countries.[188] However, it should be made clear that this diminishing bequest motive does not mean that parents in the USA and other developed countries lack sufficient incentive to provide their children with good education or even help them to purchase a house, both of which matter greatly to children's social and economic status and hence their parents' vanity. For example, Cox and Stark (2005) show that many parents provide their children with housing down payments in order to encourage them to have grandchildren.

Third, this explains primogeniture. In fact, Adam Smith (1776) and some anthropologists point out that primogeniture is motivated by vanity. In explaining primogeniture in ancient Western Europe, Smith (1776) makes the following statement: 'when land was considered as the means, not of subsistence merely, but of power and protection, it was thought better that it should descend undivided to one … To divide it was to ruin it.' What Smith means by 'power and protection' is best explained by vanity or social status.

In many dynasties in ancient China, the government selected officials through public examination. Ho (1962) and Freedman (1966) show that, in ancient China, in response to this examination system, a household often concentrated its educational resources on its most talented child. Moreover, the authors show that a number of families or a whole clan sometimes pooled their money to fund the educational expenditure required for a single 'gifted' child. The hope of the clan was that this child would perform well in the exam and become a prestigious government official, which would in turn bring much honour (i.e. vanity) to the family and clan.

Nakane (1967) examines primogeniture in historic Japan and concludes (pp. 10–11): 'succession by primogeniture also tends to appear in the wealthy sector of the family. The degree of institutionalization of the household becomes greater, and the line of succession becomes more important …'. If survival were the major concern, we would expect primogeniture to be more important for poor families. Thus Nakane's (1967) finding that primogeniture was especially emphasized by rich families in ancient Japan clearly indicates that vanity was a major concern and much more important for the upper class.

The preceding description and analysis suggest that, at times when survival is not a major concern, it is more appropriate to interpret primogeniture as a way of extending the vanity of a family line rather than simply the biological survival of its offspring.[189]

## 24.4  'SURVIVAL OF THE GENE', VANITY AND POLYANDRY

There is another social custom that appears to be totally irrelevant to primogeniture but is logically very similar. It is polyandry, which refers to a woman having more than one husband (regardless of formal marriages). While this is a rare social custom for the world as a whole, it was common in Tibet and continues to exist there and in parts of India and Nepal. What is the economic basis for this custom?

Its rationale is surprisingly similar to that of the custom of primogeniture. First, when an economy is very poor (e.g. its land is largely infertile), a man with a wife may not be able to produce enough food to raise a child. In this case, two men may be induced to have a wife together to be able to raise one child. In this circumstance, sharing a wife substantially increases the chances of survival of the gene. When both men are concerned with the survival of their genes, they may choose polyandry. Thus, in ancient times, when the average income was below the subsistence level, polyandry sometimes occurred.

Economic development has meant that survival is no longer a major concern. The vanity of family wealth has become the major reason for the continuation of the polyandry tradition. Indeed, in most societies within the culture of polyandry, the husbands of a family are almost always brothers of the same family. For example, a man of a polyandrous community in Nepal explains the rationale of polyandry as follows: 'You can even be rich living with a shared wife. Property has to be divided if you live with a separate wife. This makes you poor and you can't have enough food to eat.'[190] Further, one article points out that polyandry and primogeniture share the same logic:[191]

> Polyandry evolved, like many other marriage systems, as a pragmatic way of property management and population control. Like many other pre-birth-control cultures, the people in the parts of India that climbed the Himalayan mountain range had a limited amount of farming land and a lot of sons. Those in medieval Europe dealt with the problem by dividing their properties or by giving the property only to the eldest son while the others went to the army or the church.

In earlier chapters I stressed that the possession of a wife provides a man with vanity. However, the possession of wealth does the same. Which kind of vanity is more important? What is the relative weight between these two kinds of vanity? The answer depends on people's beliefs in a Nash equilibrium framework. There are usually multiple Nash equilibria, which means that the relative weight may take many values. In some societies, the relative weight given to the possession of a wife is low while that given to the possession of wealth is high, providing the conditions for polyandry to rise.

# 25. Family, vanity and consumption puzzles

## 25.1 THE CONSUMPTION PUZZLE: DO THE RICH SAVE MORE?

Modern macroeconomic research on consumption/saving starts with Keynes's (1936) well-known consumption function. The first argument of the Keynesian consumption function is that income is the major determinant of consumption and saving. It was an important argument at the time of its establishment, as most economists before 1930 emphasized interest rates as the major determinants. They believed that a higher interest rate indicated higher savings (as the financial reward for saving is higher). Thus Keynes's conjecture was a big breakthrough that was confirmed later on by a great deal of empirical evidence. Income is the primary determinant of how people choose to consume, and the effects of interest rates on consumption are ambiguous.

The Keynesian consumption function has two components. The first is autonomous consumption, which is the amount consumed when current income is zero. Keynes presents a reasonable argument. While an individual may not have any income (e.g. a full-time student or temporarily unemployed worker), they may still like to consume at a certain level. The second component is consumption increasing with income. The amount of the consumption increase is only a fraction of the income increase, and Keynes calls this fraction the 'marginal propensity to consume'. In other words, the marginal propensity to consume is between zero and one.

An important implication of the Keynesian consumption function is that the saving rate, which is defined as the ratio between saving and income, increases with income. Consider this simple numerical illustration: suppose that the autonomous consumption is 10 and the marginal propensity to consume is 0.5. Table 25.1 shows an individual's saving rates when their income increases from 10 to 50.

*Table 25.1 A numerical illustration*

| Income | 10 | 20 | 30 | 40 | 50 |
|---|---|---|---|---|---|
| Consumption | $10 + 0.5 \times 10 = 15$ | $10 + 0.5 \times 20 = 20$ | $10 + 0.5 \times 30 = 25$ | $10 + 0.5 \times 40 = 30$ | $10 + 0.5 \times 50 = 35$ |
| Saving | $10 - 15 = -5$ | $20 - 20 = 0$ | $30 - 25 = 5$ | $40 - 30 = 10$ | $50 - 35 = 15$ |
| Saving rate | $-5/10 = -50\%$ | $20/20 = 0\%$ | $5/30 = 17\%$ | $10/40 = 25\%$ | $15/50 = 30\%$ |

Table 25.1 shows that when an individual's income increases from 10 to 50, his saving rate starts off negative, becomes zero, becomes positive and then continues to increase. Because Keynes interprets saving as a luxury, he expects that the rich save a higher proportion of their income than the poor. He considers this proposition to be a basic, consistent 'psychological' law.

This prediction is confirmed by a number of empirical studies with cross-sectional data. It is intuitive when we consider the saving rates of very rich people. For example, relative to his income, Warren Buffett's daily consumption is trivial, meaning that his saving rate is close to 100 per cent. Dynan et al. (2004) find a strong positive relationship between saving rates and lifetime income. This empirical finding means that saving rates increase not only with current income but also with lifetime income.

However, while this predication is consistent with the cross-sectional evidence, it is not consistent with the time-series evidence. For example, Kuznets (1946) discovers that although people's incomes increased significantly from 1869 to 1938, the saving rate in the USA remained remarkably stable during the period. Many later studies also confirm Kuznets's finding based on more recent and larger datasets.[192] This puzzle can be further illustrated by an international saving rate comparison. If richer people have higher saving rates, why hasn't the USA, the wealthiest nation in the world, had a higher saving rate than many much poorer countries such as China?

In sum, saving rates are roughly constant with economic development, which contradicts Keynes's theory. This important 'consumption puzzle' motivated the celebrated contributions of Modigliani and Brumberg's (1954) life-cycle hypothesis and Friedman's (1957) permanent-income hypothesis, both of which were awarded the Nobel Prize in Economics.[193] The analysis and explanations of this consumption puzzle remain fundamental issues in the teaching of modern macroeconomics.[194]

## 25.2 LIFE-CYCLE HYPOTHESIS, INTERGENERATIONAL TRANSFERS AND THE CONSUMPTION PUZZLE

In macroeconomics textbooks, the consumption puzzle described in the preceding section is usually explained by the application of the life-cycle hypothesis. This hypothesis is based on the idea of a consumption-smoothing motive, which indicates that people usually want to have a relatively stable pattern of consumption over time, rather than high consumption at some times and low consumption at others. The intuition behind this idea is that, in an abstract sense, we treat consumption as different goods at different times. The consumption-smoothing motive is then readily derived by applying the law of diminishing marginal utility to each good.

The life-cycle hypothesis emphasizes that income varies systematically over people's lives. It also assumes that a person's consumption is determined by their lifetime income rather than current income only, and suggests that people save when incomes are high and consume their savings when incomes are low. In particular, it emphasizes retirement as the reason for saving, after which incomes drop considerably. To maintain the same or a similar level of consumption after retirement, people must save during their working years.

In his influential macroeconomics textbook, Mankiw (2013) presents a concise explanation for the consumption puzzle based on the life-cycle hypothesis.[195] It assumes that a person's lifetime income comes from two sources: labour earnings and initial wealth. The person works first and then retires. Assuming that a person does not receive income in retirement, we know that they can save only during their working years. If the person's initial wealth is held constant, it is easy to verify that their saving rate increases as their labour earnings increase. This is explained as a short-run situation. However, in the long run, initial wealth increases in proportion to labour earnings. It is again easy to verify that, in this case, the person's saving rate is independent of their labour earnings.

However, certain questions remain. Where does the initial wealth come from? Why does initial wealth increase proportionally with income? In fact, an important contribution of the life-cycle hypothesis is that it explains retirement as the reason for saving. Modigliani emphasizes in a number of influential papers that people have little incentive to leave bequests to their children.[196] This clearly makes the remaining questions more puzzling.

In Fan (2006), I offered a new explanation for this consumption puzzle by explicitly considering bequests. The basic intuition is as follows.[197] People are more concerned about their offspring's future wealth when they expect that the child's future income will be relatively low. In other words, bequests from parents to their children decrease with the children's future mean income and increase with parental income. This presents the following implications.

First, at a given point in time, rich people have higher saving rates out of the concern that their children will receive comparatively lower incomes. In other words, a household with a higher lifetime income saves more to leave more bequests to its offspring, who are likely to be worse off. Indeed, Menchik and David (1983) show that the rich (those in the top quintile) leave many more bequests than others in terms not only of absolute amount, but also a proportion of their lifetime incomes. Why do parents care about their children's income? Yet again, vanity serves as an explanation. Rich people want to perpetuate their social status into the future.

Second, over time, when an economy experiences growth and a rise in mean income, individuals reduce their bequests because their offspring are expected to be equally well off. Consequently, saving rates can be approximately constant over time if the effects of the increases in an individual's lifetime income and their offspring's future mean income on the individual's consumption cancel each other out.

This reasoning from the perspective of intergenerational transfers thus helps explain the consumption puzzle and reconcile the short- and long-run consumption functions. In simpler terms, the consumption puzzle can be explained by considering the incentive of individuals to smooth consumption across generations of a dynasty.

## 25.3 THE 'RETIREMENT CONSUMPTION PUZZLE'

The 'retirement consumption puzzle' may also be closely related to vanity, albeit in a totally different way. This puzzle is derived from the life-cycle hypothesis described earlier in this chapter, which implies that consumption should be continuous or 'smooth' over different periods of time. However, it is often observed that people's spending drops considerably upon retirement.

The economics literature offers a number of explanations for this puzzle. The most straightforward explanation is that, on retiring, some people may find that they have accumulated less wealth than anticipated before retirement, and consequently reduce their consumption (e.g. Hurd and Rohwedder, 2006).

In analysing food consumption data from more than 550 households in the USA, Lundberg et al. (2003) find that married-couple households reduce their expenditures on food consumed both at home and otherwise by about 8 per cent following the retirement of the male head of household, and that single-parent households experience no decrease in consumption. From the perspective of marital bargaining, the authors posit that wives prefer to save more to support an expected longer retirement period in comparison with their husbands. The bargaining power is determined by the current relative income between a husband and wife. Thus, when a husband retires, his bargaining power decreases, which leads to a lower level of current consumption and hence a higher saving level.

This chapter offers a new explanation for the retirement consumption puzzle from a vanity economics perspective. Consumption is a manifestation of social status. Meanwhile, there is a complementarity effect between this consumption manifestation and one's occupational status. For example, if a man is a CEO of a famous company, he is supposed to wear expensive clothing and drive a luxurious car to work.

The salary and benefits package of the managing director of the International Monetary Fund (IMF) serves as a useful illustration. When Dominique Strauss-Kahn (DSK) was prosecuted for rape in 2011, the media revealed the extravagant details of this package. For example, a reports states:

> DSK, as he is widely known, earned a modest salary by international banker standards, but his job came with an ample expense account. He earns about $420,000 a year in salary, plus pension contributions and generous benefits. On top of that, he receives about $75,000 'to enable [him] to maintain, in the interests of the Fund, a scale of living appropriate to [his] position' – essentially, money for a Washington, D.C., home fancy enough to entertain foreign dignitaries and the world's economic leaders.[198]

## 25.4  INCOME GROWTH, VANITY AND CONSUMPTION GROWTH

As described in the first section of this chapter, the life-cycle hypothesis implies that people prefer 'smooth' patterns of consumption rather than consuming a great deal at one time and little at other times. While the implication is intuitive, several empirical observations are inconsistent with this theoretical prediction, such as the retirement consumption puzzle discussed in the preceding section. In general, several studies show that a person's consumption is often strongly determined by their current income rather than their lifetime income alone.

For example, Carroll and Summers (1991) show that, while the 'consumption-smoothing motive' exists, the smoothness of a person's consumption is usually observed over periods of several years, not several decades – the person's lifetime. From a vanity economics perspective, this finding is easily explained. The logic is essentially that which explains the retirement consumption puzzle. When an individual's income increases, their social status generally rises, and they must therefore consume more to reflect the higher social status. For example, if a person develops a very conspicuous career, people will expect them to lead a luxurious life. If that person instead has a lifestyle that is consistent with their social status (e.g. dressing in low-quality clothing and driving a low-quality car), their social image will probably be hurt. If social image matters to the person's career, then their conspicuous career may be damaged.

Carroll and Weil (1994) provide a more puzzling finding. They compare households with different expectations of future income growth. The life-cycle hypothesis predicts that households with predictably higher income growth should consume more and save less than households with predictably low income growth. However, Carroll and Weil arrive at the precise opposite finding: households with predictably higher income growth save more. Carroll and Weil (1994) and Overland et al. (2000) provide an explanation for this finding based on the argument that many people develop a habit of consumption and that this habit changes gradually.

Vanity economics can conveniently provide a complementary and alternative explanation for Carroll and Weil's (1994) finding. To enhance its social status, a household often wants to purchase a 'big item'. As discussed in Chapter 3, the 'four big items' in China before 1978 were sewing machines, watches, bicycles and radios. In the 1980s, the new 'six big items' were colour television sets, refrigerators, cameras, electric fans, washing machines and tape recorders. More recently, big items comprise cars and apartments. If a household expects high income growth in the near future, it may save more to purchase the next big item on its consumption ladder. On the contrary, a household that expects low income growth may not be able to afford another big consumption item in the next few years, even if it tries hard to save. Consequently, such a household may simply consume more now.

# PART V

# Vanity and inter-family relationships

# 26. Vanity and social interactions

## 26.1 VANITY WITHOUT SOCIAL COMPARISONS

As noted at the beginning of this book, the definition of 'vanity' here includes self-esteem, which implies that significant vanity may exist even in the absence of direct interpersonal comparisons. This chapter begins by further highlighting this point with a story about female virginity, which previous chapters also use as an example.

Cian-er, the heroine in a recent popular Chinese television drama series entitled *Migration to the Northeast of China*, had a sweetheart on the show named Chuanwen. The characters were eager to get married, and hence Chuanwen's mother made the marriage proposal to Cian-er's father. However, the proposal was rejected because Chuanwen's family was too poor to pay the 'bride price'. (Cian-er's father needed the money for the marriage expenditure of Cian-er's brother.)

The four-year absence of Chuanwen's father had contributed greatly to the family's poverty. One day shortly after the marriage proposal, Chuanwen's mother received a letter from her long-absent husband. To the thrill of the whole family, Chuanwen's father was revealed not only to be alive and healthy, but also to have made a small fortune in Northeast China. In the letter, Chuanwen's father asked Chuanwen's mother to send their three children to his new home in Northeast China as soon as possible.

Chuanwen went to say goodbye to Cian-er, whose father had locked her in her bedroom. Although Chuanwen could not get into the house, he managed to talk to Cian-er and told her the story of his father's letter. He told Cian-er that he would soon leave by boat, and departed sadly. Not long after Chuanwen left, Cian-er found a clever way to escape from the locked room and ran to the port.

When Cian-er arrived at the port, the boat had just left. Seeing her on the shore, Chuanwen immediately jumped off the boat and swam. Although they were penniless, Chuanwen and Cian-er decided to make the migration on foot. They lived in Shandong Province, and Northeast China was a year's journey away. Making extremely tortuous journeys, the two obtained food for survival mainly through begging. Chuanwen became seriously ill, and Cian-er overcame a great deal of difficulty in saving his life. Although they were separated by an incident in the middle of the journey, both fortunately managed to arrive at their final destination.

However, a tragic event befell Cian-er after she separated from Chuanwen: an evil man took her virginity through coercion. Although she knew where her fiancé's family lived, the incident made Cian-er decide not to look for him. She later bumped into Chuanwen and his family in dramatic fashion, but marriage was not considered. Chuanwen's parents considered it an impossibility simply because Cian-er was no longer a virgin.

This story illustrates that the virginity of a bride is of great concern to a man and his family, even in cases where no one close to the family has any information about it. Vanity is, first and foremost, a form of self-esteem.[199] In a cultural environment where a wife's virginity is considered basic to her husband's dignity, Chuanwen and his parents would have experienced a loss of self-esteem and felt inferior to others if he had married a non-virgin.

It may be pointed out that this is only a fictional plot. However, such a story makes sense to Chinese viewers and hence must reflect reality. Chapter 6 presents a number of real stories about the importance of female virginity and supports the argument that a wife's virginity is important to a man's pride, even if no one else knows about it. The main difference between Chuanwen and Cian-er's story and other stories is that all the members of Chuanwen's family, including Chuanwen, his parents and brothers, are portrayed as 'perfect' characters with integrity.

## 26.2 VANITY WITH SOCIAL COMPARISONS

It must be emphasized that interpersonal comparisons substantially amplify vanity.[200] For example, as described in Chapter 9, many women in Asian countries tolerate their husbands' extramarital affairs as long as they know nothing about them. The deeper implication of this bottom line is that no one in the wife's social circle knows about her husband's affair. If none of her friends knows about the affair, the loss of vanity the woman experiences is relatively small. However, in cases where a woman's friends inform her about such an affair, most of the people in her social circle typically know about it or soon will, and the woman suffers a public humiliation. This enormously increases the negative vanity she experiences. In such a case, the woman will not tolerate her husband's extramarital affair. This example illustrates that social comparisons are often closely related to vanity.

In a similar vein, if an individual receives an honour, they prefer to reveal the information to as many people as possible. While receiving an honour in private is good for one's self-esteem, sharing the news with others greatly enhances the associated vanity. Indeed, this argument is the essence of Veblen's theory of conspicuous consumption. Moreover, in this sense, the study of vanity is closely related to the large amount of economics and social science literature on envy.

However, when the detail of interpersonal comparisons is considered, we may be dealing with a very complicated philosophical issue. For example, as noted in Chapter 19, even Paul Krugman, a Nobel laureate in economics, admits that Joseph Schumpeter may be the only great economist who was simultaneously the best lover and best horseman in his native Austria. Schumpeter was not the richest man in Austria, and, even if he were, there was no guarantee that his children and grandchildren would be of the best 'quality'. Indeed, certain people will always make us feel inferior in some ways.

Fortunately, interpersonal comparisons appear to be related only to certain 'reference groups'. For example, Frank (1985, p. 8) states:

> Negative feelings are much more evoked by adverse comparisons with our immediate associates than by those with people who are distant in place or time. We are little troubled when we hear that one of the Rockefellers, somewhere, has acquired a stately mansion. But we often become agitated indeed when we learn that one of our co-workers got a slightly higher pay raise than we did.

## 26.3 VANITY AND THE CHOICE OF SOCIAL INTERACTIONS

In terms of social distance theory, one's reference group in interpersonal comparisons usually consists of those with whom one often interacts, such as close neighbours and co-workers. The literature on interpersonal comparisons usually takes one's reference group as given. Fan and Stark (2007a) extend the literature by arguing that one's reference group depends to some extent on one's choices. For example, if John is particularly jealous of David, he can choose to avoid or reduce his social interactions with him. Consequently, a greater social distance is built between them over time, and hence David becomes an unimportant person in John's social comparison reference group. Therefore, after a time John will feel a little jealous towards David.

In Fan and Stark (2007a), we apply the theory to explain the puzzle that many migrants spend little effort assimilating into the mainstream culture of the host country despite the high economic return of assimilation and the low cost.[201] Our explanation is that many migrants are much poorer than natives. More assimilation results in a shorter social distance between migrants and natives, and thus leads the migrants to feel more jealousy towards the natives. In response, some migrants choose to assimilate less to reduce such jealousy. In other words, Fan and Stark (2007a) show that vanity may to some extent depend on people's social interaction choices, and that people may sacrifice pecuniary benefits for vanity.

The essential idea in Fan and Stark (2007a) can be applied to many other settings. For example, young people tend to hang out with friends (of the same sex) who more or less share a similar physical attractiveness. When they discuss their dating experiences, those who are less 'desirable' inevitably feel jealous towards those who are better-looking. This can become much worse if they participate in social activities in which the less 'desirable' person may witness their 'dream lover' totally ignoring them and flirting with their better-looking friends instead.

Another example is a bride's choice of bridesmaids. Because a wedding is an extremely important occasion for a bride, she often wants to choose pretty girls as her bridesmaids to enhance the glamour and happiness of the celebration. However, a bride also often wants to be 'the most beautiful girl in the world' at the wedding ceremony. Thus she is often reluctant to select more attractive girls as bridesmaids, particularly her maid of honour. Of course, an unexpected guest at the wedding may be stunningly beautiful and overwhelm the bride. However, if the bride barely knows the guest, the social distance between them is relatively great. Such a guest is unlikely to take centre stage at the wedding. Consequently, the bride will experience little negative effect on her vanity.

# 27. Vanity, family and migration

## 27.1 OCCUPATIONAL STIGMA, FAMILY AND MIGRATION

When I was a college student, I read the following article entitled 'The Double Life of Alfred Bloggs' from an English textbook, which motivates this section.[202]

> These days, people who do manual work often receive far more money than clerks who work in offices. People who work in offices are frequently referred to as 'white collar workers' for the simple reason that they usually wear a collar and tie to go to work. Such is human nature, that a great many people are often willing to sacrifice higher pay for the privilege of becoming white collar workers. This can give rise to curious situations, as it did in the case of Alfred Bloggs who worked as a dustman for the Ellesmere Corporation. When he got married, Alf was too embarrassed to say anything to his wife about his job. He simply told her that he worked for the Corporation. Every morning, he left home dressed in fine black suit. He then changed into overalls and spent the next eight hours as a dustman. Before returning home at night, he took a shower and changed back into his suit. Alf did this for over two years and his fellow dustmen kept his secret. Alf's wife has never discovered that she married a dustman and she never will, for Alf has just found another job. He will soon be working in an office as a junior clerk. He will be earning only half as much as he used to, but he feels that his rise in status is well worth the loss of money. From now on, he will wear a suit all day and others will call him 'Mr Bloggs', not Alf.

A man's vanity consists of dignity and self-esteem, which are often particularly important in front of those he cares about most, such as his wife or girlfriend. That is why Alfred Bloggs kept the secret of his low-status job from his wife. While he was successful, others may not be so lucky. Many people like to gossip, and it is difficult to keep rumours from spreading. For example, it is likely that one of Bloggs's colleagues knew one of his neighbours well. In such a situation, many people find a solution that often substantially mitigates this problem: migration.

For example, in the early 1980s, some senior Chinese professors had the opportunity to visit some universities in the USA. They were usually either sent by the Chinese government or supported financially by charitable foundations such as the Ford Foundation. They were given enough money to cover their daily expenses. However, many of them made use of opportunities to earn extra money to purchase the 'six big items' discussed in Chapter 3, such as televisions and refrigerators. On their meagre salaries in China, it would have taken them about 20 years to purchase these six items, even after saving 50 per cent of their salaries every month.

As it was illegal for a visiting scholar from China to work in the USA, most of the professors worked illegally in Chinatown restaurants, washing dishes and cleaning toilets. Although some of these people were world-class scholars in mathematics, physics and chemistry and were highly respected in China and by their peers at US universities, they willingly performed degrading work for the extra money.

There are numerous similar instances. For example, in a popular novel, John Irving (2005) vividly relates that if a woman from Amsterdam wanted to be a prostitute, she would go to The Hague, and women from The Hague would then come to Amsterdam.[203]

In Fan and Stark (2011), Stark and I develop a theory of migration as a response to occupational stigma. Our basic argument is that a person's negative vanity (or 'social humiliation') associated with performing a degrading job is greater when the information is revealed to those whose opinions they value. While it is impossible to avoid exposure completely when performing a degrading job, one wishes to minimize the chances of being seen by friends, family or acquaintances. Migration to a strange environment is often a strategy that provides such a disguise.

Performance of a degrading job in an individual's home town is likely to become known to one's friends and neighbours and cause them to experience a great deal of negative vanity. However, in a foreign country, performance of a degrading job is usually seen only by foreigners (usually with large social distances), implying a low amount of negative vanity from the occupational stigma. Thus our theory explains why migrants are often observed to take degrading jobs that natives usually do not want.

## 27.2  CONSPICUOUS CAREERS AND RETURN MIGRATION

Depending on whether an individual is successful in their career, they may choose to be close to the social circles that include their family and old friends or strangers (Fan and Stark, 2011). For example, in a number of developing countries such as India and China in the 1990s and Israel, Japan and Korea in the 1960s and 1970s, many nationals who obtained their PhDs in the USA returned home. Although those people could have earned much higher salaries in the USA and other Western countries, they nonetheless went back to receive considerably lower salaries in their home countries.[204] In the economics literature, this is referred to as 'return migration', and it is usually explained that the lower price levels in poorer countries may compensate for the reduction in earnings.[205]

Fan and Stark (2011) provide a new explanation from a vanity economics perspective. Suppose that a man has a conspicuous career – he gains a PhD from a prestigious US university and becomes a university professor. A conspicuous career provides a person not only with good earnings but also with honour or prestige (or vanity), which is often most important. While those with a conspicuous career is usually respected everywhere, they enjoy the prestige (or vanity) much more in their home town compared with a foreign country.

The less the social distance between a person and the people in their social circles, the more happiness they can obtain from a conspicuous career. For example, consider a Korean national who has a successful career in the USA and becomes a famous scholar. Looking around, he finds himself distanced psychologically from the people he meets every day. His colleagues and neighbours are friendly to him, and his academic contributions are well recognized by his university. However, he rarely thinks about them in his 'fantasy world' in general and his interpersonal comparisons in particular. He speaks Korean with his wife and children at home. One day, he is invited to be a keynote speaker at a conference in Seoul. He is well respected by the conference organizer. Before the conference, a minister of the Korean government invites him for dinner to honour his academic status. After the conference, he immediately returns home to see his parents and former classmates. His parents and close relatives are very proud of him, and his former classmates envy him. In particular, he feels a great sense of achievement when he meets an old classmate who bullied him in middle school. This former classmate is now a factory worker, and they belong to different social classes.

During the conference, he is offered a professorship at Korean University. The salary offered is much higher than those of his would-be colleagues at Korean University, but is only half his current salary. After considering the offer for two months, he decides to accept it. While he knows he would be respected more in Korea if he continued to hold his job in the USA, the amount of time he could stay in Korea every year would be too short. He ultimately decides that he is much happier being a professor in Korea. While this story is hypothetical, it illustrates the main incentives of the nationals of a poor country to return home despite having jobs that pay much higher salaries in the USA.[206]

## 27.3  'SEASONAL MIGRATION', FAMILY AND CONSPICUOUS CONSUMPTION

A similar logic applies to 'seasonal migration'. For example, many Polish people work in Germany, and most engage in short-term work that usually lasts no longer than three months a year. Okólski (2001, pp. 105, 109) observes that 'migrants increasingly... focus on one particular aim: namely earning money in the host country and spending it in the home country,' and characterizes 'mobility of this kind [as] a split living set-up, with economic activity pursued largely in the host country and family life taking place predominantly in the home country.'

Stark and Fan (2007a) analyse seasonal migration by considering wage rates and the costs of living in home and foreign countries in addition to the cost of separation. From a social distance perspective, this chapter adds an explanation to seasonal migration. When a man makes some money, he desires a good life with his family in his home country. The vanity associated with living a comfortable life is more pronounced in a home country than in a foreign country. In other words, the vanity a man derives from conspicuous consumption also depends on his social distance from his neighbours.

Also, if the man works in an occupation with a low social status, then the argument based on the theory of vanity economics is reinforced: working abroad substantially reduces the negative vanity (or humiliation) of taking such a low-status job. It is much harder for the people in the man's home town to observe his working activities abroad. In particular, it is much easier for the man to keep such secrets from his spouse, children and other loved ones. In contrast, the hard cash he brings back home from abroad is directly reflected in his purchasing power.

# 28. Epilogue

Gary Becker is often rated as the most prominent economist to expand the scope of economics. Indeed, he is the most important contributor to the fields of family and labour economics, which have become the core of modern economic research.[207] In his Nobel Prize speech, Becker summarized his approach as follows: '[it] assumes that individuals maximize welfare *as they conceive it*, whether they be selfish, altruistic, loyal, spiteful, or masochistic'. In particular, a cornerstone assumption he made in the study of fertility is that children are considered durable goods from their parents' perspective. As such, parents are naturally concerned about the quality of their children in the same way as they care about the quality of a television or other common durable goods.

Becker's path-breaking contributions stem not only from his intelligence and vision but also from his courage to challenge widely accepted and politically correct social norms or 'morality'. For example, again in his Nobel Prize speech, Becker offers the following recollection:

> Human capital is so uncontroversial nowadays that it may be difficult to appreciate the hostility in the 1950s and 1960s toward the approach that went with the term. The very concept of human capital was alleged to be demeaning because it treated people as machines. To approach schooling as an investment rather than a cultural experience was considered unfeeling and extremely narrow. As a result, I hesitated a long time before deciding to call my book *Human Capital*, and hedged the risk by using a long subtitle. Only gradually did economists, let alone others, accept the concept of human capital as a valuable tool in the analysis of various economic and social issues.[208]

It is easy to imagine the animosity Becker experienced in making some of his other arguments. For instance, he posits that people differ in their qualities from the perspectives of their parents or potential marital partners. This is in sharp contrast with the political ideology that 'all men are created equal'.

This book follows Becker's tradition and footsteps, and tries to analyse male–female relationships and parent–child relationships more deeply, broadly and concretely. For example, as it is assumed that parents conceive their children as durable goods, a similar logic leads me to argue that men and women are conceived as durable goods by their spouses. In his theory of conspicuous consumption, Veblen argues that durable goods often carry vanity for those who possess them. A natural extension is that people also obtain vanity from their spouses and children, including both the possessions themselves and their qualities.

## 28.1  *LADY CHATTERLEY'S LOVER, FREAKONOMICS* AND *VANITY ECONOMICS*

This book presents a systematic theory of the vanity economics of marriage, sex and family from numerous angles. In particular, it portrays the frequent close interactions and trade-offs between vanity and sex. In this epilogue, as a vivid illustration of the wide application of this theory, I would like to apply it to some major themes of D.H. Lawrence's classic novel, *Lady Chatterley's Lover*.

First published in 1928, the novel tells the life story of a young married woman named Constance (Connie). Connie's husband is Clifford Chatterley, a British aristocrat. Shortly after their wedding, Clifford becomes permanently paralysed below the waist due to a war injury, and loses his sexual functions. The couple grow bored with their sexless lives. Clifford talks to Constance about his fantasy of having a child running around their huge house. Due in part to this subtle encouragement, Connie has an affair with estate gamekeeper Oliver Mellors and becomes pregnant. To keep it secret, Connie takes a holiday in Venice, where she gives birth to the child. She returns home to find Oliver gone. Later on they meet in London, and Connie decides to have a new life with Oliver and never return to Clifford.

In light of the theory of this book, I would like to pose and then answer the following questions. First, why did Connie not divorce Clifford on discovering the loss of his sexual functions? Second, why did Clifford hint at Connie that he wanted her to have a child for the Chatterley family (albeit with another man)? Third, why did Connie ultimately decide to leave Clifford?

Vanity economics provides the following answers. First, Connie does not divorce Clifford at the beginning because she is concerned that their divorce would carry a stigma that would prevent her from remarrying into an upper-class family. In other words, her concern for the vanity she obtains from being upper class keeps her married to Clifford despite their sexless lives.

Second, Clifford obtains vanity from possessing a child. Of course, he would be much happier if he could father the child biologically. Due to this impossibility, his 'second-best' solution is to ask Connie to have a secret affair with another man so that she can give birth to a child. Although the child and Clifford are not genetically related, Clifford is happy to have a child who bears the family name. Moreover, if they could manage to keep things confidential, those in their social circle would never know or at least would be uncertain that Clifford was not the child's biological father. This would further enhance Clifford's social standing and the vanity and happiness he obtains from possessing a child and hence a more complete family.

Third, that Connie ultimately leaves Clifford stems from factors other than vanity. While vanity is often people's major concern, it is not the only source of happiness or unhappiness. In particular, sexual desire is another important aspect of human need. If Connie chose to live with Oliver, a man from the working class, she would have to forsake the vanity she obtains from being upper class. However, there are other sufficient reasons for her to be with Oliver. First, she would have an enjoyable sex life. (In fact, the descriptions of the sexual activities between Connie and Oliver were a major selling point of the novel.) She would also have a more 'complete' family in the sense that her child would be able to live with both biological parents. A man may naturally devote more attention and provide more protection to his biological child than to a non-biological child,[209] which would induce the child's mother to remain with the biological father. Indeed, it may be Lawrence's exact intention to show that more primitive human nature ultimately prevails despite our obsessions with vanity.

This book's main contribution is its extension of the analyses of vanity economics from the consumption of durable goods to the study of sex, marriage and family issues. However, the application of vanity economics can go beyond these issues. For example, the concern for vanity may be a reason why some people join criminal organizations. Levitt and Venkatesh (2000) miraculously obtained a detailed dataset describing the financial activities of a drug-selling street gang in Chicago. They find that most 'foot soldiers' in drug gangs receive a very low income that is only slightly above the legal minimum wage. This low wage obviously cannot justify the high risks associated with selling drugs. For example, a drug dealer can be robbed, seriously injured or even killed by other gang members. They may also be sent to prison for many years.

Levitt and Venkatesh (2000) argue that these drug dealers most probably expect 'promotion' within a gang, which would enhance their income significantly. However, this argument does not seem to be sufficient to explain the motivations of all drug dealers. For example, many drug dealers may not be very forward-looking, given that their futures are often highly uncertain.

The application of vanity economics offers an alternative and complementary explanation. First, a teenage boy is often bullied, particularly in bad neighbourhoods in the USA. (In fact, bullying is not rare even in 'good' US neighbourhoods.) Once a boy enters a criminal organization, he gains access to guns and armed gang members, and most of his classmates and acquaintances in the streets hesitate to bully him again. Thus the boy's vanity may increase substantially after joining a street gang. By extension, others will not dare to bully his family members, further increasing his vanity and happiness. Moreover, his enhanced social status may help him 'get the girls'.

Going back to the explanation offered by Levitt and Venkatesh (2000), the benefit of promotion for a drug dealer may not be solely pecuniary. A man may enjoy the prestige of being a gang leader, as it is often accompanied by respect from other gang members, neighbours and perhaps former classmates who used to bully him.

## 28.2  VANITY IS ANOTHER 'INVISIBLE HAND'

In *The Wealth of Nations*, Smith (1776) advances the well-known idea of the 'invisible hand'. In particular, he states, in relation to an ordinary person:

> By preferring the support of domestic to that of foreign industry, he intends only his own security; and by directing that industry in such a manner as its produce may be of the greatest value, he intends only his own gain, and he is in this, as in many other cases, led by an invisible hand to promote an end which was no part of his intention. Nor is it always the worse for the society that it was not part of it. By pursuing his own interest he frequently promotes that of the society more effectually than when he really intends to promote it.

A similar 'invisible hand' exists for the survival of animals and even plants. While many animals do not think about having offspring *per se*, their sexual desires naturally lead them to give birth to offspring and continue the survival of their species after their death. Consider the strategy of an apple tree to produce apples. When a monkey eats an apple, it often swallows the seeds. Thus, when the animal defecates in a different location, the indigestible apple seeds take root in that location and grow into another apple tree. In this case, it is the self-interest of the monkey rather than its benevolent intention that facilitates the multiplication of the apple tree.

The focus of this book is vanity, which is unique to human society. Vanity induces people willingly and often happily to make tremendous sacrifices, working like slaves to bear, raise and educate children and to earn more money, thereby ensuring the continuous development of human society. In fact, such an invisible hand is also noted by Adam Smith (1759), who makes the following statement:

> He is enchanted with the distant idea of this felicity. It appears in his fancy like the life of some superior rank of beings, and, in order to arrive at it, he devotes himself for ever to the pursuit of wealth and greatness. To obtain the conveniences which these afford, he submits in the first year, nay in the first month of his application, to more fatigue of body and more uneasiness of mind than he could have suffered through the whole of his life from the want of them ... Through the whole of his life he pursues the idea of a certain artificial and elegant repose which he may never arrive at, for which he sacrifices a real tranquillity that is at all times in his power, and which, if in the extremity of old age he should at last attain to it, he will find to be in no respect preferable to that humble security and contentment which he had abandoned for it ...

Chapter 2 quoted Esther Duflo as saying 'People here are obsessed with doing everything perfectly. If you raise a child, it must be a perfect child. They must go to the perfect college and be the best at their job.' Obviously, it is impossible that every child will turn out to be the best among its peers. But vanity does induce most parents to do their best in raising and educating their children.

In Chapter 10, from an evolutionary perspective, I characterize a 'principal–agent relationship' between a human being and their genes. When our major concern is survival, the desires most essential to the survival of the gene are related to food and sex, which motivate humans to live on and reproduce. However, humans have dominated the world for several thousand years. We could easily kill all the lions and tigers on earth. What is the point of further evolution? What is the further motivation of the development of humans and their civilizations? The answer provided by this book, together with the works of Adam Smith (1759, 1776), John Rae (1834) and Thorstein Veblen (1899), is vanity. In a sense, vanity is like an invisible hand that leads humans to pursue goals endlessly. In other words, self-esteem and 'the mere desire of superiority over others by whatever criteria' motivate humans to create many wonders of human civilization. In her influential book on nationalism, Greenfeld (1992, pp. 487–8) offers the following:

> National identity is fundamentally, a matter of dignity. It gives people reasons to be proud ... It would be a strong statement, but no overstatement, to say

that the world in which we live was brought into being by vanity. The role of vanity – or desire for status – in social transformation has been largely underestimated ...

Dawkins (2006) argues that humans are machines created by their genes, precisely like all animals. This book argues that humans differ from animals in an important respect: humans crave vanity, while animals do not do so at all. In other words, humans are both vanity machines and gene machines. As analysed in this book, the exact forms and magnitudes of vanity depend on the detailed functioning of a society. Thus humans are machines created not only by their genes but also by the society in which they live. While genes lead people to pursue hedonistic pleasures and to be concerned about the survival of their future generations, vanity is another important driver that explains both individual behaviour and social and economic progress.

Popular culture offers a famous example of a 'vanitas', which is a type of picture that can present two totally different images. At first sight, one may see a beautiful woman looking at her reflection in a mirror. However, from a different angle, the picture shows the image of a skull. This device is a classic indication that vanity is of little 'real' value. Most people care very much about vanity and, as the picture exemplifies, women's beauty in particular. The picture illustrates that, when one's dream is ultimately fulfilled, one may realize that the dream is nothing but vanity. However, the pursuit of this dream, which often entails much time and effort, may lead the individual to make important contributions to human society.

## 28.3   VANITY AND BEYOND

There often appears to be a close link between the distribution of vanity and the sense of inequality and social justice. Karl Marx's important writings, *The Communist Manifesto* and *Capital*, have been extremely influential around the world because they highlight the income inequality between the rich (capitalists) and the poor (workers). Indeed, people often have a strong aversion to being poor, which yields negative vanity in their social comparisons. For example, between 1949 and 1952, when the People's Republic of China was established, about one million 'landlords' were executed because they owned more land than others and were hence richer.[210]

Prominent philosopher John Rawls is another similar example. Wikipedia's entry on Rawls runs as follows:

*His magnum opus,* A Theory of Justice (1971), was hailed at the time of its publication as 'the most important work in moral philosophy since the end of World War II,' … His work in political philosophy, dubbed Rawlsianism, takes as its starting point the argument that 'most reasonable principles of justice are those everyone would accept and agree to from a fair position.' Rawls employs a number of thought experiments – including the famous veil of ignorance – to determine what constitutes a fair agreement in which 'everyone is impartially situated as equals,' in order to determine principles of social justice … English philosopher Jonathan Wolff argues that 'while there might be a dispute about the second most important political philosopher of the 20th century, there could be no dispute about the most important: John Rawls.'

Moreover, the well-known conclusion of the so-called 'Rawlsian social welfare criterion' is that social welfare corresponds with the welfare of the worst-off individual in society.[211]

An important appeal of the theories of Marx and Rawls is their emphasis on strict income equality. However, income is not the only source of welfare; nor is it the only source of vanity. In romance and marriage, physical appearance often matters much more than income. For example, the stigma associated with 'the short, the fat and the ugly' is often much greater than the stigma of being poor, at least in developed countries. What are the implications of the Rawlsian social welfare criterion when people differ substantially in physical appearance? The answers to this question are beyond the scope of this book, but offer an interesting avenue for future research.

Moreover, many people feel very miserable when they cannot achieve their vanity-related goals. In future research, it would be interesting to consider whether people care too much about their social status. For example, a serious religious belief and even persistent meditations may substantially moderate people's desires in their everlasting pursuit of vanity.

I would like to end this book by quoting the first paragraph of *Lady Chatterley's Lover*:

> Ours is essentially a tragic age, so we refuse to take it tragically. The cataclysm has happened, we are among the ruins, we start to build up new little habitats, to have new little hopes. It is rather hard work: there is now no smooth road into the future: but we go round, or scramble over the obstacles. We've got to live, no matter how many skies have fallen.

People's major concern in ancient times was survival, when it was feared that a fallen sky would end many lives. In modern times, people's major concern is vanity. As such, people with strong souls will be able to stand up again and again, no matter how many skies have fallen and knocked them down.

# Notes

1. For example, see Becker (1991), Stark (1995), Becker and Murphy (2000), Lazear (2000), Cameron (2003, 2009), Ermisch (2003), Bowles et al. (2005), Bowmaker (2005), Cigno and Rosati (2005), Levitt and Dubner (2005, 2009), Ariely (2008, 2010), and Gintis (2009).
2. http://en.wikipedia.org/wiki/King_Zhou_of_Shang.
3. Michael et al. (1994).
4. http://www.bbc.co.uk/news/world-12160538.
5. For example, see Freud (2000).
6. West et al. (1999) and Keightley and Eyre-Walker (2000).
7. I thank Yifan Zhang for suggesting this example.
8. http://www.ft.com/intl/cms/s/2/81804a1a-6d08-11e1-ab1a-00144feab49a.html.
9. 'Social distance' is a concept widely used in sociology and psychology (e.g. Karakayali, 2009; Matthews and Matlock, 2011), and was introduced into economics by Akerlof (1997).
10. http://dimemag.com/2011/07/the-evolutionary-yao-ming-effect/.
11. http://espn.go.com/new-york/nba/story/_/id/7608874/david-stern-says-never-seen-anything-jeremy-lin-frenzy.
12. http://en.wikipedia.org/wiki/Jeremy_Lin#Public_image.
13. http://www.guardian.co.uk/technology/2011/oct/06/steve-jobs-pancreas-cancer.
14. For example, see http://historum.com/speculative-history/31959-xu-fu-japan.html. While it is a speculation that Xu Fu was the first emperor of Japan, this story does reveal the magnificent size and equipment of Xu Fu's fleet.
15. Bagwell and Bernheim (1996) examine the conditions under which 'Veblen effects' arise in a game-theoretical framework.
16. 'The Luxury-Goods Trade', *The Economist*, 8 January 1993, pp. 95–8.
17. For example, see a recent media coverage on this issue: http://www.ibtimes.com/articles/267181/20111214/india-40-million-missing-girls-problem-gendercide.htm?page=all.
18. This example and its analysis are essentially similar to Cigno (1991).
19. Zhang (1994) shows that assortative mating also applies to the expected bequests from parents. Using a dataset of eighteenth-century Quebec, Hamilton and Siow (2007) show that social status was an important determinant of marriage matches.
20. This argument is made in Becker (1991) and Cigno (1991).
21. http://www.dailymail.co.uk/news/article-2257209/Wealthy-Indian-Datta-Phuge-spends-14-000-shirt-GOLD-impress-ladies.html?ito=feeds-newsxml#.
22. http://en.wikipedia.org/wiki/Duel.
23. http://en.wikipedia.org/wiki/Go_Hyun-jung.
24. http://tw.nextmedia.com/applenews/article/art_id/33928741/IssueID/20120101.
25. http://www.hudong.com/wiki/%E4%BB%98%E6%88%90%E5%8A%B1.
26. http://news.bbc.co.uk/2/hi/8147563.stm.
27. http://www.thesun.co.uk/sol/homepage/news/1249208/Hubby-divorces-non-virgin-bride.html.
28. http://zh.wikipedia.org/wiki/%E6%B6%82%E4%B8%96%E5%8F%8B.

29. http://www.theregister.co.uk/2012/02/17/chinese_virgin_website/.

30. http://en.wikipedia.org/wiki/Qin_Shihuang.

31. http://en.wikipedia.org/wiki/Tulip_mania.

32. http://en.wikipedia.org/wiki/Droit_du_seigneur.

33. '13-Year-old Virgin for Sale in India' (15 April 2008), http://www.medindia.net/news/indiaspecial/13-Year-old-Virgin-for-Sale-in-India-35445-1.htm.

34. 'Virginity For Sale: Utah Mom Pleads Guilty To Offering 13-Year-Old Daughter To Man', http://www.huffingtonpost.com/2011/10/25/virginity-for-sale-utah-m_n_1029054.html.

35. http://finance.stockstar.com/SS2012052800002917.shtml.

36. http://www.bgr.com/2011/06/28/teenage-girl-in-china-offers-to-sell-virginity-for-iphone-4/.

37. http://news.cnet.com/8301-17852_3-10246204-71.html#ixzz1me9yrs6L.

38. http://www.torontosun.com/2012/10/25/brazilian-girl-sells-virginity-for-780000.

39. http://www.washingtonpost.com/world/africa/morocco-outraged-over-suicide-of-rape-victim-forced-to-marry-rapist/2012/03/14/gIQAxBQzBS_story.html.

40. http://www.wisemuslimwomen.org/currentissues/stigmitizationofrape/.

41. http://en.wikipedia.org/wiki/Rape_trauma_syndrome.

42. http://countrystudies.us/india/84.htm.

43. For example, see Li et al. (2010).

44. http://news.ifeng.com/history/zhiqing/ziliao/detail_2013_07/10/27348913_0.shtml.

45. http://www.straight-talk.net/abortion/consequences.shtml.

46. http://en.wikipedia.org/wiki/Sexual_revolution_in_1960s_America.

47. http://collegiateway.org/colleges/ingram-1999/.

48. http://www.infoplease.com/ipa/A0005061.html.

49. http://en.wikipedia.org/wiki/Age_at_first_marriage.

50. http://www.cbsnews.com/2100-500368_162-1464262.html.

51. http://www.metrolyrics.com/i-just-had-sex-lyrics-the-lonely-island.html.

52. For example, Akerlof (1980) argues that the stigma of deviating from a social norm will decrease as more people do not adhere to the norm.

53. http://en.wikipedia.org/wiki/Edison_Chen_photo_scandal.

54. http://en.wikipedia.org/wiki/Personal_life_of_Wilt_Chamberlain.

55. For an article on men pursuing the quantity of sexual partners, see http://phtv.ifeng.com/program/kjwx/detail_2012_02/14/12498519_0.shtml.

56. When vanity is considered less, some men may choose to be sexually promiscuous, to remain single, and possibly to father many children (e.g. Willis, 1999, 2000).

57. Weiss (1997) provides an excellent survey of this literature.

58. http://v.ifeng.com/news/society/201103/ab40139a-1365-4f4b-b9b5-0d8081f80da9.shtml.

59. The following are two videos showing that singles felt awkward in Beijing and Taipei, respectively, during the period of Chinese New Year: http://news.sohu.com/20120123/n332900609.shtml and http://video.chinatimes.com/video-cate-cnt.aspx?cid=6&nid=72145.

60. http://finance.sina.com.cn/money/lcfa/20120104/102611122700.shtml.

61. 'China's "leftover women", unmarried at 27', 21 February 2013, http://www.bbc.co.uk/news/magazine-21320560.

62. http://en.wikipedia.org/wiki/History_of_human_sexuality.

63. Edlund and Korn (2002) develop an economic theory of prostitution, in which a key assumption is that a typical man's happiness increases with the number of his sexual partners.

64. For example, in 1994, per capita GDP was about US$400 in China, and about US$21509 in Hong Kong.

65. For example, Fan and Wei (2006) show that the degree of marketization in China is highly comparable to that in developed countries based on the analyses of price data. Also, Fan and Grossman (2001) and Coase and Wang (2012) analyse the evolution of the political institutions that led China to become a market economy.

66. For some studies on the integration of the economies between Hong Kong and Mainland China, see Tsang and Cheng (1997), Fan (1998), Fan and Cheung (2004), Cheung and Fan (2006), and Fan et al. (2006).

67. Source: *Ming Pao* (a Hong Kong newspaper, in Chinese), 12 September 1997, p. 1.

68. For example 'It's Doubtful China Meant One Country, Two Sets of Families – A Mainland Village Prospers As Hong Kong Men Keep House With No. 2 Wife', *Wall Street Journal*, 21 June 1999.

69. The phenomenon of *de facto* polygyny is also observed in other poor countries. For example, Gould et al. (2012) report that, in Côte d'Ivoire, about 46 per cent of married women between 18 and 40 were in a *de facto* polygynous marriage in 1986.

70. http://www.nytimes.com/2011/08/10/world/asia/10mistress.html?_r=2&pagewanted=all.

71. http://entertainments.dwnews.com/news/2012-05-07/58727228.html.

72. http://ck101.com/forum.php?mod=viewthread&action=printable&tid=2233993.

73. http://jezebel.com/5634082/the-bollywood-actress-as-prostitute.

74. http://www.tressugar.com/Myth-Bollywood-Actress-Turned-Prostitute-10883738.

75. http://www.jpmei.com/social_focus/1768.html.

76. See http://uk.news.yahoo.com/chinese-teenager-sells-kidney-iphone-212819458.html. Moreover, there is another similar story told in China. A young man sold his kidney, and he said that the first thing he did after the transaction was to buy a mobile phone for his girlfriend (http://news.ifeng.com/Mainland/detail_2012_05/29/14891213_0.shtml).

77. For example, a woman from a poor country can get much higher earnings by working as a prostitute in a rich country than taking an ordinary job in her home country. Also, Edlund et al. (2009) show that, even within a country, many prostitutes can have very high earnings relative to most other occupations.

78. http://edition.cnn.com/2009/WORLD/asiapcf/09/24/hongkong.teenage.prostitution/.

79. http://en.wikipedia.org/wiki/Coincidence_of_wants.

80. http://en.wikipedia.org/wiki/Enjo_k%C5%8Dsai

81. http://en.wikipedia.org/wiki/Enjo_k%C5%8Dsai.

82. http://en.wikipedia.org/wiki/Enjo_k%C5%8Dsai

83. For example, see the detailed descriptions in Polachek and Siebert (1993) and Ehrenberg and Smith (2009).

84. http://en.wikipedia.org/wiki/Indecent_Proposal.

85. http://en.wikipedia.org/wiki/Tiger_Woods#Car_accident_and_alleged_affairs.

86. http://www.nytimes.com/2012/12/02/opinion/sunday/new-love-a-short-shelf-life.html?pagewanted=2&_r=2&pagewanted=all&amp&.

87. For an early study of extramarital affairs in economics literature, see Fair (1978).

88. However, it is only for the convenience of exposition. The theory developed also applies to the opposite case in which wives participate in extramarital activities while husbands try to prevent them from happening.

89. Moreover, once the decision to divorce is made, it is often irreversible, at least to a large extent. In this case, there is an 'option' value for a woman to wait and see whether her relationship can improve. (Dixit (1989) presents an analysis of the 'option' value of an irreversible investment project.)

90. http://1000thingsaboutjapan.blogspot.hk/.

91. http://jiangfengjp.blog.ifeng.com/article/16511258.html.

92. For example, see Lundberg and Pollak (1993).

93. For example, see Rasmusen (1989).

94. For example, see Billy et al. (1993) and Binson et al. (1995).
95. For example, see Galor and Weil (1999).
96. http://findarticles.com/p/articles/mi_m1200/is_6_163/ai_97997816/.
97. http://en.wikipedia.org/wiki/Matrilineality.
98. For some empirical studies on the interaction between the quantity and quality of children, see Rosenzweig and Wolpin (1980), Behrman et al. (1989), Hanushek (1992), Angrist et al. (2005), Black et al. (2005a), Fernandez and Fogli (2009), and Qian (2009).
99. For example, see van der Eyken (1977) and Sahota (1978).
100. For example, see Bloom (1981).
101. For example, see Osberg (1984), Heckman (2006), and Almond and Currie (2011).
102. Fan et al. (2013) conduct an analysis on the interactions between parental and kindergarten inputs in preschool education.
103. Heckman (2006, 2011), Cunha and Heckman (2007, 2009), Cunha et al. (2010).
104. For example, see Hanushek et al. (2003), Zimmerman (2003), Angrist and Lang (2004), Whitemore (2005), Nechyba (2006), Ding and Lehrer (2007), Ammermueller and Pischke (2009), Duflo et al. (2011), and Lavy et al. (2012).
105. For example, see Evans et al. (1992), Gaviria and Raphael (2001), and Segal (2008).
106. For example, see Harley (1986) and the survey in Fan (1997a).
107. http://edition.cnn.com/2012/12/02/world/asia/hong-kong-ivy-league-admission/index.html?hpt=hp_c2.
108. See Ricardo (1817). However, in modern times, when the externality effect of human capital is important, Fan and Stark (2008a) show that, in developing countries, unrestricted rural-to-urban migration often reduces the average income of both rural and urban dwellers in equilibrium. They reach a different conclusion from David Ricardo because they emphasize the externality effect of average human capital in the modern knowledge-based economy, which might not have existed in Ricardo's time.
109. This theoretical prediction is empirically supported by Yi and Zhang (2010) based on the data of Hong Kong.
110. Grootaert and Kanbur (1995, p. 195) first note that 'Examples are… the employment of children to weave carpets because they have more nimble fingers and can tie smaller knots than can adults.'
111. In fact, health continues to be an important determinant of economic development even in the contemporary world (e.g. Strauss and Thomas, 1998; Weil, 2007).
112. However, an implicit assumption here is that the parents do not use the increased income from child labour in the competition of showing off their wealth by engaging in conspicuous consumption of luxurious goods, which may happen as an equilibrium outcome under some circumstances (e.g. see Moav and Neeman, 2012 for an analysis.). Indeed, in some poor countries, a household often spent a considerable amount on 'conspicuous consumption'. For example, Banerjee and Duflo (2007) report that a household's median spending on festivals in some regions of India was about 10 per cent of its annual income. In this case, children's labour market participation may not have positive impacts on children's human capital formation. Thus the positive impact of child labour on children's education is more likely to be observed in the cultures that emphasize education, such as some East Asian countries.
113. The information in this paragraph is based on Salaff (1976).
114. For example, see Nugent (1985).
115. http://unn.people.com.cn/GB/14804/13361756.html.
116. http://news.renminbao.com/100/4959.htm.
117. http://focus.cnhubei.com/original/200905/t683309.shtml.

118. See Anbarci et al. (2002) for a rigorous analysis of bargaining in the shadow of conflicts.
119. In other words, such an authority reduces the 'transaction cost' of the collaborations among household members in fighting a common enemy. (See Pollak, 1985 for a survey of the transaction cost approach to the study of families.)
120. http://www.newyorker.com/reporting/2012/10/01/121001fa_fact_parker?currentPage =all.
121. Of course, the gender bias against girls does not imply that no family will choose to have girls, even if the technology of gender selection is perfect. For example, Edlund (1999) argues that if parents hope that their children will be able to get married, then the gender bias will result in low-status families choosing to have daughters and high-status families choosing to have sons.
122. For example, see Stevenson and Wolfers (2006) and Doepke et al. (2012).
123. For example, see Manser and Brown (1980), McElroy and Horney (1981), McElroy (1990), Thomas (1990), and Browning et al. (1994).
124. For example, see Behrman (1997), Lundberg et al. (1997), Browning and Chiappori (1998), Duflo (2003), and Behrman and Rosenzweig (2006).
125. For example, see Goldin (1990), Blau and Khan (1992) and Wellington (1993).
126. Suen (1995).
127. Tsang and Cheng (1997).
128. Goldin and Katz (2002) argue that the power of modern contraceptive methods to a large extent explains the narrowing gender gap in education and earnings. Peters and Siow (2002) analyse how the perspective of competition in the marriage market induces parents to invest in children's human capital. Chiappori et al. (2009) posit that, when the market return to schooling increases, women will work less at home, which may induce more women to receive high education than men in some circumstances. Iyigun and Walsh (2007) show that empowering women through institutional reforms will result in lower fertility and women's higher earnings.
129. http://www.nytimes.com/2010/12/26/business/26excerpt.html?pagewanted=all.
130. For example, see O'Flaherty and Siow (1995).
131. http://www.chinaculture.org/gb/cn_zgwh/2005-07/13/content_70584_2.htm.
132. I thank Robert Pollak for suggesting this example.
133. For example, see Espenshade (1977).
134. Willis (1973) and Pollak and Wachter (1975) extend Becker (1965) in analysing fertility based on the theory of the allocation of time.
135. Becker (1991), Boyer (1989), and Wrigley and Schofield (1981).
136. For example, see the survey by Hotz et al. (1993). Choo and Siow (2006) show that the legalization of abortion reduced the economic gains to marriage, which may provide another explanation for the phenomenon of childlessness.
137. See http://en.wikipedia.org/wiki/World_population.
138. http://wiki.answers.com/Q/How_many_sperm_are_in_one_ejaculation.
139. For example, see Dasgupta (1995), Ehrlich and Lui (1997), and Becker et al. (1999).
140. For example, see van-Groezen et al. (2003) and Cremer et al. (2006).
141. For example, Manski and Mayshar (2003) and Li and Zhang (2009) find strong evidence that households compare with each other in making choices of fertility in Israel and China, respectively.
142. For example, see de la Croix and Doepke (2004), Cremer et al. (2011), and Fan and Zhang (2013).
143. For example, see Bianco and Hua (1988).
144. For example, see Heckman (2005) and Heckman and Yi (2012).

145. This reasoning may share an essential logic with Donohue and Levitt (2001), who show that the legalization of abortion reduced some unwanted births and hence considerably reduced crimes in the USA.
146. http://www.guardian.co.uk/society/2012/jan/08/cut-working-week-urges-thinktank? INTCMP=SRCH.
147. For example, see Fan (2007) and the literature reviewed therein.
148. http://en.wikipedia.org/wiki/Divorce_demography.
149. For example, in Spain in 2012, a woman receives €3000 for denoting eggs and a man receives €50 for denoting sperm each time (http://edition.cnn.com/video/ ?hpt=hp_bn6#/video/business/2012/07/31/soares-spain-sperm-eggs-for-sale.cnn).
150. http://usnews.nbcnews.com/_news/2012/01/18/10182852-serial-sperm-donor-reveals-hes-a-virgin?lite.
151. For example, see McLanahan and Bumpass (1988) and Hetherington et al. (1998).
152. Zhang et al. (2013) show that parental absence due to migration has adverse effects on the cognitive achievement of the children left behind. Also, a recent report in China states that many parents choose to divorce after their children finish the College Entrance Examination. This examination determines whether a high-school graduate can get into a university and what kind of university they can get into (http://edu.sina.com.cn/gaokao/2012-08-23/0911353020.shtml).
153. 'Business stance may backfire', *Asian Business*, Hong Kong, June 1999, p. 6.
154. Source: 'Divorce rate increased by four times within 16 years', *Oriental Daily*, 21 August 1998, p. A.16.
155. In fact, extramarital affairs not only increase marital instability; they even significantly increase the suicide rate of members of affected families. (Source: 'House-wife suicides increase tenfold', *South China Morning Post*, 28 August 1997, p. 1.)
156. http://singleparents.about.com/od/legalissues/p/portrait.htm.
157. Weiss and Willis (1993) show that a husband often does not give sufficient financial support to his former wife and his children after divorce. Thus such a division of labour is less efficient after divorce.
158. Moreover, a woman's perspective of remarriage can be further worsened because she often loses her fecundity after the age of 37 or so (e.g. Siow, 1998).
159. http://divorcesupport.about.com/od/isdivorcethesolution/a/Four-Valid-Reasons-To-Divorce.htm.
160. The quality of a marriage is often largely unknown beforehand, and is revealed only some time after marriage (e.g. Weiss and Willis, 1985, 1997).
161. http://www.dailymail.co.uk/femail/article-508936/The-wife-changed-history--asking-divorce.html.
162. For example, see Allen (1998).
163. Fernandez and Wong (2013) provide a quantitative assessment of the impact of divorce on women's labour market participation.
164. For example, see the surveys by Grawe and Mulligan (2002) and Lefgren et al. (2012).
165. For example, see Hamermesh and Biddle (1994), Averett and Korenman (1996), Biddle and Hamermesh (1998), and Hamermesh et al. (2002).
166. http://www.theamericanconservative.com/articles/the-myth-of-american-meritocracy/.
167. For example, see Hanushek (1996, 2010) and van der Klaauw (2008).
168. For example, see Lam and Schoeni (1993), Galor and Tsiddon (1997), Hassler and Mora (2000), Sacerdote (2002), Plug and Vijverberg (2003) and Black et al. (2005b).
169. For example, see Fan et al. (1999) and Behrman et al. (1999).
170. Source: 'Why Asians Are Going to the Head of the Class?', *New York Times* (3 August 1986): EDUC 18–23.

171. This analysis is based on Fan (2003).
172. For example, see Heckman (2006, 2011) and Heckman and Kautz (2012).
173. For example, see Evans and Schwab (1995), Neal (1997), Vella (1999) and Ewing (2000).
174. See, for example, the survey by Iannaccone (1998).
175. For example, see the review of Landes (2000) on the virtues of some religions and traditions.
176. For example, see Iannaccone (1998) and Glaeser and Sacerdote (2008).
177. See Anderson (1988) for a survey of Smith's writings on religion.
178. For example, see Korenman and Neumark (1991), Daniel, K. (1995), and Ginther and Zavodny (2001).
179. See, for example, Kotlikoff and Summers (1981), Kotlikoff (1988), and Gale and Scholz (1994).
180. See, for example, Pollak (1988) and Cox and Stark (2005).
181. http://www.chinanews.com/sh/2012/02-04/3644973.shtml.
182. For example, see Cox (1987), Altonji et al. (1992, 1997), Cox and Rank (1992), Hayashi (1995) and Wilhelm (1996).
183. In fact, Bernheim and Bagwell (1988) show that the assumption that parents' utility/happiness depends on their children's utility/happiness has the counterfactual implication that all the members of a society belong to a 'large happy family', which implies the irrelevance of all distributional policies and defies the existence of market economies.
184. The survival of offspring may also be a concern in developing countries of the contemporary world (Gersovitz, 1988). Becker (1976) and Bergstrom (1995, 1996) investigate wealth transfers among siblings due to their genetic relationship.
185. For example, see Deaton (1989).
186. For example, Deaton (1992) and Carroll (1997) are important studies of 'buffer-stock saving'. But they do not consider the subsistence constraint. The role of 'buffer stock' is probably more important when survival is a major concern.
187. A rigorous analysis is conducted in Fan (2001b). The bequest motive here is somewhat related to the argument of strategic bequest motive of Bernheim et al. (1985). But what these authors emphasize is that parents use bequests to induce children to do something to please the parents, such as making frequent phone calls to them. It is also related to Cole et al. (1992), which argues that the desire to enhance children's social status in the marriage market may induce parents to make a bequest.
188. Also, Weil (1994) shows that the children who expect bequests often increase consumption and reduce their own saving (long before receiving the bequests). This, in turn, may reduce parents' incentives to leave bequests. In fact, Menchik (1980) and Behrman and Rosenzweig (2004) show that the allocation of bequests among siblings often takes the form of equal divisions in the USA, which suggests that the bequests may be largely accidental from the perspective of the parents.
189. In fact, all the above quotations appear in Chu (1991), but Chu's main intention was to use them to argue against the theory that intergenerational transfers stem from parents caring about children's happiness *per se*. Chu's discussion relates little to the theory of vanity.
190. http://io9.com/5925324/polyandry-or-the-practice-of-taking-multiple-husbands.
191. Ibid.
192. See the survey by Modigliani (1986).
193. Milton Friedman was awarded the Nobel Memorial Prize in Economics in 1976 for the permanent-income hypothesis; Franco Modigliani was awarded the Nobel Memorial Prize in Economics in 1985 for the life-cycle hypothesis.

194. It is illustrated in several influential textbooks, such as Dornbusch and Fischer (1994), Gordon (2003) and Mankiw (2013).

195. Mankiw's presentation is a simplified version of Modigliani's Nobel Prize speech (Modigliani, 1986).

196. For example, see Modigliani (1986, 1988).

197. For a rigorous analysis, see Fan (2006, 2012).

198. http://www.slate.com/articles/business/moneybox/2011/05/dominique_strausskahns_lavish_life.html.

199. This argument may be related to the idea of 'identity' in Akerlof and Kranton (2000).

200. Becker (1974) argues that, in general, social interactions intensify emotions.

201. For example, Lazear (1999, p. S96) states: 'Multiculturalism ... seems to be on the rise in the United States ... In 1900, 85 percent of immigrants were fluent in English. Surprisingly, in 1990 the fluency rate among immigrants was only 68 percent, despite dramatic improvements in communication during the century.'

202. Alexander (1967, p. 18).

203. This example is taken from a working-paper version of Fan and Stark (2011).

204. See, for example, Zweig et al. (2008) and Dustmann et al. (2011).

205. For example, see Stark et al. (1997), Dustmann and Kirchkamp (2002), and Stark and Fan (2007a).

206. Fan and Stark (2007b, 2007c) and Stark and Fan (2007b, 2011b) study that many university graduates in developing countries often endure significant hardships, such as unemployment and underemployment, for better opportunities of studying in developed countries and then working in rich countries for much higher wages. The honour and prestige associated with the possible return migration would provide them with even greater incentives.

207. For example, see Pollak (2003).

208. See Becker (1993, p. 392).

209. For example, see Anderson et al. (1999) and Case et al. (2000).

210. http://www.historylearningsite.co.uk/china_1949_to_1953.htm.

211. Stark et al. (2012) show that the maximin criterion of Rawls (1971) can be obtained from the assumption of the veil of ignorance if and only if interpersonal comparisons are considered and people are strongly averse to income inequality.

# References

Aizer, Anna (2010), 'The gender wage gap and domestic violence', *American Economic Review*, **100** (4): 1847–59.

Aizer, Anna and Dal Bó, Pedro (2009), 'Love, hate and murder: commitment devices in violent relationships', *Journal of Public Economics*, **93** (3–4): 412–28.

Akerlof, George A. (1980), 'A theory of social custom, of which unemployment may be one consequence', *Quarterly Journal of Economics*, **94** (4): 749–75.

Akerlof, George A. (1997), 'Social distance and social decisions', *Econometrica*, **65** (5): 1005–27.

Akerlof, George A. and Rachel E. Kranton (2000), 'Economics and identity', *Quarterly Journal of Economics*, **115** (3): 715–53.

Alcott, Blake (2004), 'John Rae and Thorstein Veblen', *Journal of Economic Issues*, **38** (3): 765–86.

Alexander, Louis G. (1967), *New Concept English*, London: Longman.

Allen, Douglas W. (1998), 'No-fault divorce in Canada: its cause and effect', *Journal of Economic Behavior & Organization*, **37** (2): 129–49.

Almond, Douglas and Janet Currie (2011), 'Human capital development before age five', in Orley Ashenfelter and David Card (eds), *Handbook of Labor Economics, vol. 4b*, Amsterdam: Elsevier Science, pp. 1315–486.

Altonji, Joseph G., Fumio Hayashi and Laurence J. Kotlikoff (1992), 'Is the extended family altruistically linked? Direct tests using micro data', *American Economic Review*, **82** (5): 1177–98.

Altonji, Joseph G., Fumio Hayashi and Laurence J. Kotlikoff (1997), 'Parental altruism and inter vivos transfer: theory and evidence', *Journal of Political Economy*, **105** (6): 1121–66.

Ammermueller, Andreas and Jorn-Steffen Pischke (2009), 'Peer effects in European primary schools: evidence from the progress in international reading literacy study', *Journal of Labor Economics*, **27** (3): 315–48.

Anbarci, Nejat, Stergios Skaperdas and Constantinos Syropoulos (2002), 'Comparing bargaining solutions in the shadow of conflict: how norms against threats can have real effects', *Journal of Economic Theory*, **106** (1): 1–16.

Anderson, Gary M. (1988), 'Mr. Smith and the preachers: the economics of religion in the wealth of nations', *Journal of Political Economy*, **96** (5): 1066–88.

Anderson, Kermyt G., Hillard Kaplan, David Lam and Jane B. Lancaster (1999), 'Paternal care by genetic fathers and stepfathers II: reports by Xhosa high school students', *Evolution and Human Behavior*, **20** (6): 433–51.

Angrist, Josh D. and Kevin Lang (2004), 'Does school integration generate peer effects? Evidence from Boston's Metco program', *American Economic Review*, **94** (5): 1613–34.

Angrist, Joshua D., Victor Lavy and Analia Schlosser (2005), 'New evidence on the causal link between the quantity and quality of children', NBER Working Paper 11835, New York: National Bureau of Economic Research.

Ariely, Dan (2008), *Predictably Irrational: The Hidden Forces That Shape Our Decisions*, New York: HarperCollins.

Ariely, Dan (2010), *The Upside of Irrationality*, New York: Harper-Collins.

Arthur, W. Brian (1982), 'Book reviews', *Population and Development Review*, **8** (2): 393–7.

Ashraf, Quamrul and Oded Galor (2011), 'Dynamics and stagnation in the Malthusian epoch', *American Economic Review*, **101** (5): 2003–41.

Auerbach, J. Alan, Laurence J. Kotlikoff and David N. Weil (1992), 'The increasing annuitization of the elderly – estimates and implications for intergenerational transfers, inequality and national saving', NBER Working Paper 4182, New York: National Bureau of Economic Research.

Averett, Susan and Sanders Korenman (1996), 'The economic reality of the beauty myth', *Journal of Human Resources*, **31** (2): 304–30.

Bagwell, Laurie Simon and B. Douglas Bernheim (1996), 'Veblen effects in a theory of conspicuous consumption', *American Economic Review*, **86** (3): 349–73.

Baland, Jean Marie and James A. Robinson (2000), 'Is child labor inefficient?', *Journal of Political Economy*, **108** (4): 663–79.

Banerjee, Abhijit V. and Esther Duflo (2007), 'The economic lives of the poor', *Journal of Economic Perspectives*, **21** (1): 141–67.

Banerjee, Abhijit V. and Andrew F. Newman (1991), 'Risk-bearing and the theory of income distribution', *Review of Economic Studies*, **58** (2): 211–35.

Barro, Robert J. (1974), 'Are government bonds net wealth?', *Journal of Political Economy*, **48** (6): 1095–118.

Barro, Robert and Gary Becker (1989), 'Fertility choice in a model of economic growth', *Econometrica*, **57**: 481–502.

Basu, Kaushik (1999), 'Child labor: cause, consequence and cure, with remarks on international labor standards', *Journal of Economic Literature*, **37** (3): 1083–119.

Basu, Kaushik and Pham Hoang Van (1998), 'The economics of child labor', *American Economic Review*, **88** (3): 412–27.

Becker, Gary S. (1960), 'An economic analysis of fertility', in Universities-National Bureau (ed.), *Demographic and Economic Change in Developed Countries* (NBER Conference Series Vol. 11), Princeton, NJ: Princeton University Press, pp. 209–31.

Becker, Gary S. (1965), 'A theory of the allocation of time', *Economic Journal*, **75** (299): 493–517.

Becker, Gary S. (1974), 'A theory of social interactions', *Journal of Political Economy*, **82** (6): 1063–94.

Becker, Gary S. (1976), 'Altruism, egoism and genetic fitness: economics and sociobiology', *Journal of Economic Literature*, **14** (3): 817–26.

Becker, Gary S. (1991), *A Treatise on the Family*, Cambridge, MA: Harvard University Press.

Becker, Gary S. (1993), 'Nobel lecture: the economic way of looking at behavior', *Journal of Political Economy*, **101** (3): 385–409.

Becker, Gary S. and H. Gregg Lewis (1973), 'On the interaction between the quantity and quality of children', *Journal of Political Economy*, **81** (2): S279–S288.

Becker, Gary S. and Kevin M. Murphy (2000), *Social Economics: Market Behavior in a Social Environment*, Cambridge, MA: Harvard University Press.

Becker, Gary S. and Nigel Tomes (1979), 'An equilibrium theory of the distribution of income and intergenerational mobility', *Journal of Political Economy*, **87** (6): 1153–89.

Becker, Gary S. and Nigel Tomes (1986), 'Human capital and the rise and fall of families', *Journal of Labor Economics*, **4** (3): S1–S39.

Becker, Gary S., Edward L. Glaeser and Kevin M. Murphy (1999), 'Population and economic growth', *American Economic Review*, **89** (2): 145–9.

Becker, Gary S., Elisabeth Landes and Robert Michael (1977), 'An economic analysis of marital instability', *Journal of Political Economy*, **85** (6): 1141–87.

Behrman, Jere R. (1997), 'Intrahousehold distribution and the family', in Mark R. Rosenzweig and Oded Stark (eds), *Handbook of Population and Family Economics: vol. 1*, Amsterdam: Elsevier Science, pp. 125–87.

Behrman, Jere R. and Mark R. Rosenzweig (2004), 'Parental allocations to children: new evidence on bequest differences among siblings', *Review of Economics and Statistics*, **86** (2): 637–40.

Behrman, Jere R. and Mark R. Rosenzweig (2006), 'Parental wealth and adult children's welfare in marriage', *Review of Economics and Statistics*, **88** (3): 496–509.

Behrman, Jere R., Robert A. Pollak and Paul Taubman (1989), 'Family resources, family size and access to financing for college education', *Journal of Political Economy*, **97** (2): 398–419.

Behrman, Jere R., Andrew D. Foster, Mark R. Rosenzweig and Prem Vashishtha (1999), 'Women's schooling, home teaching and economic growth', *Journal of Political Economy*, **107** (4): 682–714.

Bergstrom, Theodore C. (1995), 'On the evolution of altruistic ethical rules for siblings', *American Economic Review*, **85** (1): 58–81.

Bergstrom, Theodore C. (1996), 'Economics in a family way', *Journal of Economic Literature*, **34** (4): 1903–34.

Bernheim, B. Douglas and Kyle Bagwell (1988), 'Is everything neutral?', *Journal of Political Economy*, **96** (2): 308–38.

Bernheim, B. Douglas, Andrei Shleifer and Lawrence H. Summers (1985), 'The strategic bequest motive', *Journal of Political Economy*, **93** (6): 1045–76.

Bhalotra, Sonia and Christopher Heady (2003), 'Child farm labor: the wealth paradox', *World Bank Economic Review*, **17** (2): 197–227.

Bianco, Lucien and Chang-ming Hua (1988), 'Implementation and resistance: the single-child family policy', in Stephen Feuchtwang, Athar Hussain and Thierry Pairault (eds), *Transforming China's Economy in the Eighties: vol. 1, The Rural Sector, Welfare and Employment*, London: Zed Books, pp. 147–68.

Biddle, Jeff E. and Daniel S. Hamermesh (1998), 'Beauty, productivity and discrimination: lawyers' looks and lucre', *Journal of Labor Economics*, **16** (1): 172–201.

Billy, John O.G., Koray Tanfer, William R. Grady and Daniel H. Klepinger (1993), 'The sexual behavior of men in the United States', *Family Planning Perspectives*, **25** (2): 52–60.

Binson, Diane, Stuart Michaels, Ron Stall, Thomas J. Coates, John H. Gagnon and Joseph A. Catania (1995), 'Prevalence and social distribution of men who have sex with men: United States and its urban centers', *Journal of Sex Research*, **32** (3): 245–54.

Black, Sandra E., Paul J. Devereux and Kjell G. Salvanes (2005a), 'The more the merrier? The effect of family size and birth order on children's education', *Quarterly Journal of Economics*, **120** (2): 669–700.

Black, Sandra E., Paul J. Devereux and Kjell G. Salvanes (2005b), 'Why the apple doesn't fall far: understanding intergenerational transmission of human capital', *American Economic Review*, **95** (1): 437–49.

Blau, Francine D. and Lawrence M. Khan (1992), 'The gender earnings gap: learning from international comparisons', *American Economic Review*, **82** (2): 533–38.

Bloom, Benjamin (1981), *All Our Children Learning*, New York: McGraw-Hill.

Bonnet, Michel (1993), 'Child labour in Africa', *International Labour Review*, **132** (3): 371–89.

Bowles, Samuel, Herbert Gintis and Melissa Osborne Groves (2005), *Unequal Chances: Family Background and Economic Success*, Princeton, NJ: Princeton University Press.

Bowmaker, Simon W. (2005), *Economics Uncut: a Complete Guide to Life, Death and Misadventure*, Cheltenham, UK and Northampton, MA, USA: Edward Elgar.

Boyer, George R. (1989), 'Malthus was right after all: poor relief and birth rates in Southeastern England', *Journal of Political Economy*, **97** (1): 93–114.

Broude, Gwen J. (1994), *Marriage, Family and Relationships: A Cross-cultural Encyclopedia*, Santa Barbara, CA: ABC-CLIO.

Browning, Martin and Pierre-André Chiappori (1998), 'Efficient intra-household allocations: a general characterization and empirical tests', *Econometrica*, **66** (6): 1241–78.

Browning, Martin, François Bourguignon, Pierre-André Chiappori and Valerie Lechène (1994), 'Income and outcomes: a structural model of intrahousehold allocation', *Journal of Political Science*, **102** (6): 1067–96.

Burbank, Jane and Frederick Cooper (2010), *Empires in World History: Power and the Politics of Difference*, Princeton, NJ: Princeton University Press.

Buss, David M. and Todd K. Shackelford (1997), 'Susceptibility to infidelity in the first year of marriage', *Journal of Research in Personality*, **31** (2), 193–221.

Cameron, Samuel (2003), *The Economics of Sin: Rational Choice or No Choice at All?*, Cheltenham, UK and Northampton, MA, USA: Edward Elgar.

Cameron, Samuel (2009), *The Economics of Hate*, Cheltenham, UK and Northampton, MA, USA: Edward Elgar.

Carnegie, Dale (1984), *How to Stop Worrying and Start Living*, New York: Pocket Books.

Carroll, Christopher D. (1997), 'Buffer-stock saving and the life cycle/permanent income hypothesis', *Quarterly Journal of Economics*, **112** (1): 1–55.

Carroll, Christopher D. and Lawrence H. Summers (1991), 'Consumption growth parallels income growth: some new evidence', in B. Douglas

Bernheim and John B. Shoven (eds), *National Saving and Economic Performance*, Chicago, IL: University of Chicago Press, pp. 305–48.

Carroll, Christopher D. and David N. Weil (1994), 'Saving and growth: a reinterpretation', *Carnegie-Rochester Conference Series on Public Policy*, **40** (1): 133–92.

Case, Anne, I-Fen Lin and Sara McLanahan (2000), 'How hungry is the selfish gene?', *Economic Journal*, **110** (466): 781–804.

Cheung, Kui-yin and C. Simon Fan (2006), 'Economic integration between Hong Kong and Mainland China: did trade hurt Hong Kong's unskilled workers?', in Robert Ash and Lok-sang Ho (eds), *China, Hong Kong and the World Economy: A Study of Globalization*, Basingstoke: Palgrave, pp. 186–99.

Cheung, Steven N.S. (1972), 'The enforcement of property rights in children and the marriage contract', *Economic Journal*, **82** (326): 641–57.

Chiappori, Pierre-André, Murat Iyigun and Yoram Weiss (2009), 'Investment in schooling and the marriage market', *American Economic Review*, **99** (5): 1689–713.

Chiappori, Pierre-André, Sonia Oreffice and Climent Quintana-Domeque (2012), 'Fatter attraction: anthropometric and socioeconomic matching on the marriage market', *Journal of Political Economy*, **120** (4): 659–95.

Choo, Eugene and Aloysius Siow (2006), 'Who marries whom and why', *Journal of Political Economy*, **114** (1): 175–201.

Chu, C.Y. Cyrus (1991), 'Primogeniture', *Journal of Political Economy*, **99** (1): 78–99.

Chua, Amy (2011), *Battle Hymn of the Tiger Mother*, New York: Penguin Press.

Chua, Beng Huat (2000), *Consumption in Asia: Lifestyles and Identities*, New York: Routledge.

Cigno, Alessandro (1991), *Economics of the Family*, Oxford: Clarendon Press.

Cigno, Alessandro and Furio Camillo Rosati (2005), *The Economics of Child Labour*, Oxford: Oxford University Press.

Coase, Ronald and Ning Wang (2012), *How China Became Capitalist*, New York: Palgrave Macmillan.

Cole, Harold L., George J. Mailath and Andrew Postlewaite (1992), 'Social norms, savings behavior and growth', *Journal of Political Economy*, **100** (6): 1092–125.

Coleman, James S. (1988), 'Social capital in the creation of human capital', *American Journal of Sociology*, **94**: S95–S120.

Covey, Stephen R. (1989), *The Seven Habits of Highly Effective People: Restoring the Character Ethic*, New York: Simon and Schuster.

Cox, Donald (1987), 'Motives for private income transfers', *Journal of Political Economy*, **95** (3): 508–46.

Cox, Donald and Mark R. Rank (1992), 'Inter-vivos transfers and intergenerational exchange', *Journal of Economics and Statistics*, **74** (2): 305–14.

Cox, Donald and Oded Stark (2005), 'On the demand for grandchildren: tied transfers and the demonstration effect', *Journal of Public Economics*, **89** (9–10): 1665–97.

Cremer, Helmuth, Firouz Gahvari and Pierre Pestieau (2006), 'Pensions with endogenous and stochastic fertility', *Journal of Public Economics*, **90** (12): 2303–21.

Cremer, Helmuth, Firouz Gahvari and Pierre Pestieau (2011), 'Fertility, human capital accumulation and the pension system', *Journal of Public Economics*, **95** (11–12): 1272–9.

Cross, Gary S. (1993), *Time and Money: the Making of Consumer Culture*, London: Routledge.

Cunha, Flavio and James Heckman (2007), 'The technology of skill formation', *American Economic Review*, **97** (2): 31–47.

Cunha, Flavio and James Heckman (2009), 'The economics and psychology of inequality and human development', *Journal of the European Economic Association*, **7** (2–3): 320–64.

Cunha, Flavio, James Heckman and Susanne M. Schennach (2010), 'Estimating the technology of cognitive and noncognitive skill formation', *Econometrica*, **78** (3): 883–931.

Currell, Susan and Christina Cogdell (2006), *Popular Eugenics: National Efficiency and American Mass Culture in the 1930s*, Athens, OH: Ohio University Press.

Currie, Janet (2001), 'Early childhood education programs', *Journal of Economic Perspectives*, **15** (2): 213–38.

Currie, Janet and Duncan Thomas (1995), 'Does head start make a difference?' *American Economic Review*, **85** (3): 341–64.

Dahl, Gordon B. and Enrico Moretti (2008), 'The demand for sons', *Review of Economic Studies*, **75** (4): 1085–120.

Daniel, Kermit (1995), 'The marriage premium', in Mariano Tommasi and Kathryn Ierulli (eds), *The New Economics of Human Behavior*, Cambridge: Cambridge University Press, pp. 113–25.

Darwin, Charles (1859), *The Origin of Species*, London: Murray.

Dasgupta, Partha (1995), 'The population problem: theory and evidence', *Journal of Economic Literature*, **33** (4): 1879–902.

Dawkins, Richard (2006), *The Selfish Gene*, Oxford: Oxford University Press.

Deane, Phyllis and W.A. Cole (1967), *British Economic Growth, 1688–1959: Trends and Structure*, London: Cambridge University Press.

Deaton, Augus (1989), 'Saving in developing countries: theory and review', in *Proceedings of the World Bank Annual Conference on Development Economics: vol. 1*, Washington, DC: International Bank for Reconstruction and Development/World Bank, pp. 61–96.

Deaton, Augus (1992), *Understanding Consumption*, New York: Oxford University Press.

de la Croix, David and Matthias Doepke (2003), 'Inequality and growth: why differential fertility matters', *American Economic Review*, **93** (4): 1091–113.

de la Croix, David and Matthias Doepke (2004), 'Public versus private education when differential fertility matters', *Journal of Development Economics*, **73** (2): 607–29.

DeLong, Brad (2005), *Macroeconomics*, New York: McGraw-Hill.

Ding, Weili and Steven F. Lehrer (2007), 'Do peers affect student achievement in China's secondary schools?', *Review of Economics and Statistics*, **89** (2): 300–312.

Dixit, Avinash K. (1989), 'Entry and exit decisions under uncertainty', *Journal of Political Economy*, **97** (3): 620–38.

Doepke, Matthias, Michèle Tertilt and Alessandra Voena (2012), 'The economics and politics of women's rights', *Annual Review of Economics*, **4** (1): 339–72.

Donohue, John J. III and Steven D. Levitt (2001), 'The impact of legalized abortion on crime', *Quarterly Journal of Economics*, **116** (2): 379–420.

Dornbusch, Rudiger and Stanley Fischer (1994), *Macroeconomics*, New York: McGraw-Hill.

Duflo, Esther (2003), 'Grandmothers and granddaughters: old-age pensions and intrahousehold allocation in South Africa', *World Bank Economic Review*, **17** (1): 1–25.

Duflo, Esther, Pascaline Dupas and Michael Kremer (2011), 'Peer effects and the impact of tracking: evidence from a randomized evaluation in Kenya', *American Economic Review*, **101** (5): 1739–74.

Dustmann, Christian and Oliver Kirchkamp (2002), 'The optimal migration duration and activity choice after re-migration', *Journal of Development Economics*, **67** (2): 351–72.

Dustmann, Christian, Itzhak Fadlon and Yoram Weiss (2011), 'Return migration, human capital accumulation and the brain drain', *Journal of Development Economics*, **95** (1): 58–67.

Dynan, Karen E., Jonathan Skinner and Stephen P. Zeldes (2004), 'Do the rich save more?', *Journal of Political Economy*, **112** (2): 397–444.

Easterlin, Richard A. (1974), 'Does economic growth improve the human lot? Some empirical evidence', in Paul A. David and Melvin W. Reder (eds), *Nations and Households in Economic Growth: Essays in Honor of Moses Abramovitz*, New York: Academic Press, pp. 89–125.

*The Economist* (1993), 'The luxury-goods trade', 8 January, pp. 95–8.

Edlund, Lena (1999), 'Son preference, sex ratios and marriage patterns', *Journal of Political Economy*, **107** (6): 1275–304.

Edlund, Lena, Joseph Engelberg and Christopher A. Parsons (2009), 'The wages of sin', Columbia University Economics Discussion Paper 0809-16, June.

Edlund, Lena and Evelyn Korn (2002), 'A theory of prostitution', *Journal of Political Economy*, **110** (1): 181–214.

Eggebeen, David J. and Chris Knoester (2001), 'Does fatherhood matter for men?', *Journal of Marriage and Family*, **63** (2): 381–93.

Ehrenberg, Ronald G. and Robert S. Smith (2009), *Modern Labor Economics: Theory and Public Policy*, Boston, MA: Pearson/Addison Wesley.

Ehrlich, Isaac and Francis T. Lui (1991), 'Intergenerational trade, longevity and economic growth', *Journal of Political Economy*, **99** (5): 1029–59.

Ehrlich, Isaac and Francis Lui (1997), 'The problem of population and growth: a review of the literature from Malthus to contemporary models of endogenous population and endogenous growth', *Journal of Economic Dynamics and Control*, **21** (1): 205–42.

Ermisch, John (2003), *An Economic Analysis of the Family*, Oxford: Princeton University Press.

Eskapa, Shirley (1984), *Woman Versus Woman*, New York: F. Watts.

Espenshade, Thomas J. (1977), 'The value and cost of children', *Population Bulletin*, **32** (1), 1–48.

Evans, William N. and Robert M. Schwab (1995), 'Finishing high school and starting college: do Catholic schools make a difference?', *Quarterly Journal of Economics*, **110** (4): 941–74.

Evans, William N., Wallace E. Oates and Robert M. Schwab (1992), 'Measuring peer group effects: a study of teenage behavior', *Journal of Political Economy*, **100** (5): 966–91.

Ewing, Bradley T. (2000), 'The wage effects of being raised in the Catholic religion: does religion matter?', *American Journal of Economics and Sociology*, **59** (3): 419–32.

Fair, Ray C. (1978), 'A theory of extramarital affairs', *Journal of Political Economy*, **86** (1): 45–61.

Fan, C. Simon (1997a), 'The economic value of language skills: with special application in Hong Kong', *Hong Kong Linguist*, **17**: 29–34.

Fan, C. Simon (1997b), 'The value of time and the interaction of the quantity and quality of children', *Seoul Journal of Economics*, **10** (2): 1–24.

Fan, C. Simon (1998), 'Why has China been successful in attracting foreign investment: a transaction cost approach', *Journal of Contemporary China*, **7** (17): 21–32.

Fan, C. Simon (2000), 'Economic development and the changing patterns of consumption in urban China', in Beng-Huat Chua (ed.), *Consumption in Asia: Lifestyles and Identities*, London: Routledge, pp. 82–97.

Fan, C. Simon (2001a), 'A model of endogenous divorce and endogenous fertility', *Journal of Population Economics*, **14** (1): 101–17.

Fan, C. Simon (2001b), 'A model of intergenerational transfers', *Economic Theory*, **17** (2): 399–418.

Fan, C. Simon (2003), 'Human capital, study effort and persistent income inequality', *Review of Development Economics*, **7** (2): 311–26.

Fan, C. Simon (2004a), 'Child labor and the interaction between the quantity and quality of children', *Southern Economic Journal*, **71** (1): 21–35.

Fan, C. Simon (2004b), 'Relative wage, child labor and human capital', *Oxford Economic Papers*, **56** (4): 687–700.

Fan, C. Simon (2005), 'Survival of the gene, intergenerational transfers and precautionary saving', *Journal of Development Economics*, **76** (2): 451–79.

Fan, C. Simon (2006), 'Do the rich save more? A new view based on intergenerational transfers', *Southern Economic Journal*, **73** (2): 362–73.

Fan, C. Simon (2007), 'Sticky wage, efficiency wage and Keynesian unemployment', *Pacific Economic Review*, **12** (2): 213–24.

Fan, C. Simon (2008), 'Religious participation and children's education: a social capital approach', *Journal of Economic Behavior and Organization*, **65** (2): 303–17.

Fan, C. Simon (2011), 'The luxury axiom, the wealth paradox and child labor', *Journal of Economic Development*, **36** (3): 25–45.

Fan, C. Simon (2012), 'Do the rich save more? A revisit to the theories of the consumption function', mimeo, Department of Economics, Lingnan University, Hong Kong.

Fan, C. Simon and Kui-yin Cheung (2004), 'Trade and wage inequality: the Hong Kong case', *Pacific Economic Review*, **9** (2): 131–42.

Fan, C. Simon and Herschel I. Grossman (2001), 'Incentive and "corruption" in Chinese economic reform', *Journal of Policy Reform*, **4** (3): 195–206.

Fan, C. Simon and Hon-Kwong Lui (2003), 'Structural change and the narrowing gender gap in wages: theory and evidence from Hong Kong', *Labour Economics*, **10** (5): 609–26.

Fan, C. Simon and Hon-Kwong Lui (2004), 'Extramarital affairs, marital satisfaction and divorce: evidence from Hong Kong', *Contemporary Economic Policy*, **22** (4): 442–52.

Fan, C. Simon and Oded Stark (2003), 'Heterogeneity and the population problem', mimeo, University of Bonn.

Fan, C. Simon and Oded Stark (2007a), 'A social proximity explanation of the reluctance to assimilate', *Kyklos (International Review for Social Sciences)*, **60** (1): 55–63.

Fan, C. Simon and Oded Stark (2007b), 'International migration and "educated unemployment"', *Journal of Development Economics*, **83** (1): 76–87.

Fan, C. Simon and Oded Stark (2007c), 'The brain drain, "educated unemployment", human capital formation and economic betterment', *Economics of Transition*, **15** (4): 629–60.

Fan, C. Simon and Oded Stark (2008a), 'Rural-to-urban migration, human capital and agglomeration', *Journal of Economic Behavior and Organization*, **68** (1): 234–47.

Fan, C. Simon and Oded Stark (2008b), 'Looking at the "population problem" through the prism of heterogeneity: welfare and policy analyses', *International Economic Review*, **49** (3): 799–835.

Fan, C. Simon and Oded Stark (2011), 'A theory of migration as a response to occupational stigma', *International Economic Review*, **52** (2): 549–71.

Fan, C. Simon and Xiangdong Wei (2006), 'The law of one price: evidence from the transitional economy of China', *Review of Economics and Statistics*, **88** (4): 682–97.

Fan, C. Simon and Jie Zhang (2013), 'Differential fertility, inequality and intergenerational mobility under private versus public education', *Journal of Population Economics*, **26** (3): 907–41.

Fan, C. Simon, Na Li and Xiangdong Wei (2006), 'Market integration between Hong Kong and Chinese mainland', in Robert Ash and Lok-sang Ho (eds), *China, Hong Kong and the World Economy: A Study of Globalization*, Basingstoke: Palgrave, pp. 170–85.

Fan, C. Simon, Jody Overland and Michael Spagat (1999), 'Human capital, growth and inequality in Russia', *Journal of Comparative Economics*, **27** (4): 618–43.

Fan, C. Simon, James Heckman, Xiangdong Wei and Junsen Zhang (2013), 'Parental inputs and kindergarten care in pre-school education', mimeo, University of Chicago.

Fernandez, Raquel and Alessandra Fogli (2009), 'Culture: an empirical investigation of beliefs, work and fertility', *American Economic Journal: Macroeconomics*, **1** (1): 146–77.

Fernandez, Raquel and Joyce Cheng Wong (2013), 'Divorce risk, wages and working wives: a quantitative life-cycle analysis of female labor force participation', mimeo (February), New York University.

Frank, Robert H. (1985), *Choosing the Right Pond: Human Behavior and the Quest for Status*, New York: Oxford University Press.

Frank, Robert H. (2011), *The Darwin Economy: Liberty, Competition and the Common Good*, Princeton, NJ: Princeton University Press.

Frank, Robert H. and Philip J. Cook (1995), *The Winner-Take-All Society: How More and More Americans Compete for Ever Fewer and Bigger Prizes, Encouraging Economic Waste, Income Inequality and an Impoverished Cultural Life*, New York: Free Press.

Freedman, Maurice (1966), *Chinese Lineage and Society: Fukien and Kwangtung*, London: Athlone.

Freud, Sigmund (2000), *Three Essays on the Theory of Sexuality*, in James Strachey (ed. and trans.), New York: Basic Books.

Friedman, Milton (1957), *A Theory of the Consumption Function*, Princeton, NJ: Princeton University Press.

Fyfe, Alec (1989), *Child Labour*, Cambridge: Polity Press.

Galbi, Douglas A. (1994), 'Child labour and the division of labour in the early English cotton mills', mimeo (June), Centre for History and Economics, King's College, Cambridge.

Gale, William G. and John Karl Scholz (1994), 'Intergenerational transfers and the accumulation of wealth', *Journal of Economic Perspectives*, **8** (4): 145–60.

Galor, Oded and Daniel Tsiddon (1997), 'Technological progress, mobility and economic growth', *American Economic Review*, **87** (3): 363–82.

Galor, Oded and David N. Weil (1996), 'The gender gap, fertility and growth', *American Economic Review*, **86** (3): 374–87.

Galor, Oded and David N. Weil (1999), 'From Malthusian stagnation to modern growth', *American Economic Review*, **89** (2): 150–54.

Galor, Oded and Joseph Zeira (1993), 'Income distribution and macroeconomics', *Review of Economic Studies*, **60** (1): 35–52.

Galton, Francis (1869), *Hereditary Genius: An Inquiry into Its Laws and Consequences*, London: Macmillan.

Galton, Francis (1889), *Natural Inheritance*, London: Macmillan.

Garces, Eliana, Duncan Thomas and Janet Currie (2002), 'Longer term effects of Head Start', *American Economic Review*, **92** (4): 999–1012.

Gaviria, Alejandro and Steven Raphael (2001), 'School-based peer effects and juvenile behavior', *Review of Economics and Statistics*, **83** (2): 257–68.

Gerke, Solvay (2000), 'Global lifestyles under local conditions: the new Indonesian middle class', in Beng-Huat Chua (ed.), *Consumption in Asia: Lifestyles and Identities*, London: Routledge, pp. 82–97.

Gerrig, Richard J. and Philip G. Zimbardo (2010), *Psychology and Life*, Boston, MA: Pearson/Allyn and Bacon.

Gersovitz, Mark (1988), 'Saving and development', in Hollis Chenery and T.N. Srinivasan (eds), *Handbook of Development Economics, vol. 1*, Amsterdam: North-Holland, pp. 381–424.

Gillis, Malcolm, Dwight H. Perkins, Michael Roemer and Donald R. Snodgrass (1996), *Economics of Development*, New York: W.W. Norton.

Ginther, Donna K. and Madeline Zavodny (2001), 'Is the male marriage premium due to selection? The effect of shotgun weddings on the return to marriage', *Journal of Population Economics*, **14** (2), 313–28.

Gintis, Herbert (2009), *The Bounds of Reason: Game Theory and the Unification of the Behavioral Sciences*, Princeton, NJ: Princeton University Press.

Glaeser, Edward L. and Bruce I. Sacerdote (2008), 'Education and religion', *Journal of Human Capital*, **2** (2): 188–215.

Glewwe, Paul, Hanan G. Jacoby and Elizabeth M. King (2001), 'Early childhood nutrition and academic achievement: a longitudinal analysis', *Journal of Public Economics*, **81** (3): 345–68.

Glewwe, Paul, Michael Kremer and Sylvie Moulin (2009), 'Many children left behind? Textbooks and test scores in Kenya', *American Economic Journal: Applied Economics*, **1** (1): 112–35.

Goldin, Claudia (1990), *Understanding the Gender Gap: An Economic History of American Women*, New York: Oxford University Press.

Goldin, Claudia and Lawrence F. Katz (2002), 'The power of the pill: oral contraceptives and women's career and marriage decisions', *Journal of Political Economy*, **110** (4): 730–70.

Goldin, Claudia, Lawrence F. Katz and Ilyana Kuziemko (2006), 'The homecoming of American college women: the reversal of the college gender gap', *Journal of Economic Perspectives*, **20** (4): 133–56.

Gordon, Robert J. (2003), *Macroeconomics*, Boston, MA: Addison-Wesley.

Gould, Eric D., Omer Moav and Avi Simhon (2012), 'Lifestyles of the rich and polygynous in Côte d'Ivoire', *Economics Letters*, **115** (3): 404–7.

Grawe, Nathan D. and Casey B. Mulligan (2002), 'Economic interpretations of intergenerational correlations', *Journal of Economic Perspectives*, **16** (3): 45–58.

Greenfeld, Liah (1992), *Nationalism: Five Roads to Modernity*, Cambridge, MA: Harvard University Press.

Grootaert, Christiaan and Ravi Kanbur (1995), 'Child labour: an economic perspective', *International Labour Review*, **134** (2): 187–201.

Hamermesh, Daniel S. and Jeff E. Biddle (1994), 'Beauty and the labor market', *American Economic Review*, **84** (5): 1174–94.

Hamermesh, Daniel S., Xin Meng and Junsen Zhang (2002), 'Dress for success – does primping pay?', *Labour Economics*, **9** (3): 361–73.

Hamilton, Gillian and Aloysius Siow (2007), 'Class, gender and marriage', *Review of Economic Dynamics*, **10** (4): 549–75.

Hanushek, Eric A. (1992), 'The trade-off between child quantity and quality', *Journal of Political Economy*, **100** (1): 84–117.

Hanushek, Eric A. (1996), 'Measuring investment in education', *Journal of Economic Perspectives*, **10** (4): 9–30.

Hanushek, Eric (2010), 'Education production functions: evidence from developed countries', in Dominic J. Brewer and Patrick J. McEwan (eds), *Economics of Education*, Amsterdam: Elsevier, pp. 132–6.

Hanushek, Eric A., John F. Kain, Jacob M. Markman and Steven G. Rivkin (2003), 'Does peer ability affect student achievement?', *Journal of Applied Econometrics*, **18** (5): 527–44.

Harley, Birgit (1986), *Age in Second Language Acquisition*, Clevedon, UK: Multilingual Matters.

Hassler, John and José V. Rodríguez Mora (2000), 'Intelligence, social mobility and growth', *American Economic Review*, **90** (4): 888–908.

Hatfield, Elaine and Susan Sprecher (1986), *Mirror, Mirror: the Importance of Looks in Everyday Life*, Albany, NY: State University of New York Press.

Hayashi, Fumio (1995), 'Is the Japanese extended family altruistically linked? A test based on engle curves', *Journal of Political Economy*, **103** (3): 661–74.

Hazan, Moshe and Binyamin Berdugo (2002), 'Child labor, fertility and economic growth', *Economic Journal*, **112** (482): 810–28.

Heckman, James J. (2005), 'China's human capital investment', *China Economic Review*, **16** (1): 50–70.

Heckman, James J. (2006), 'Skill formation and the economics of investing in disadvantaged children', *Science*, **312** (5782): 1900–902.

Heckman, James J. (2011), 'Integrating personality psychology into economics', NBER Working Paper 17378, New York: National Bureau of Economic Research.

Heckman, James J. and Tim Kautz (2012), 'Hard evidence on soft skills', *Labour Economics*, **19** (4): 451–64.

Heckman, James J. and Junjian Yi (2012), 'Human capital, economic growth and inequality in China', mimeo, University of Chicago.

Heckman, James J., Rodrigo Pinto and Peter Savelyev (2013), 'Understanding the mechanisms through which an influential early childhood program boosted adult outcomes', *American Economic Review*, **103** (6): 2052–86.

Hetherington, E. Mavis, Margaret Bridges and Glendessa M. Insabella (1998), 'What matters? What does not? Five perspectives on the association between marital transitions and children's adjustment', *American Psychologist*, **53** (2): 167–84.

Ho, Ping-ti (1962), *The Ladder of Success in Imperial China: Aspects of Social Mobility, 1368–1911*, New York: Columbia University Press.

Horrell, Sara, Jane Humphries and Hans-Joachim Voth (2001), 'Destined for deprivation: human capital formation and intergenerational poverty in nineteenth-century England', *Explorations in Economic History*, **38** (3): 339–65.

Hotz, V. Joseph, Jacob Alex Klerman and Robert J. Willis (1993), 'The economics of fertility in developed countries', in Mark R. Rosenzweig and Oded Stark (eds), *Handbook of Population and Family Economics*, Amsterdam: Elsevier Science, pp. 275–347.

Hunt, Edward H. (1973), *Regional Wage Variations in Britain 1850–1914*, Oxford: Clarendon Press.

Hunt, Edward H. (1986), 'Industrialization and regional inequality: wages in Britain, 1760–1914', *Journal of Economic History*, **46** (4): 935–66.

Hurd, Michael D. and Susann Rohwedder (2006), 'Some answers to the retirement-consumption puzzle', NBER Working Paper 12057, New York: National Bureau of Economic Research.

Iannaccone, Laurence R. (1998), 'Introduction to the economics of religion', *Journal of Economic Literature*, **36** (3): 1465–95.

ILO (1996), *Child Labor: Targeting the Intolerable*, Geneva: ILO.

Irving, John (2005), *Until I Find You*, New York: Random House.

Itzkoff, Seymour W. (1983), *The Form of Man: The Evolutionary Origins of Human Intelligence*, Ashfield, MA: Paideia Publishers.

Iyigun, Murat and Randall P. Walsh (2007), 'Endogenous gender power, household labor supply and demographic transition', *Journal of Development Economics*, **82** (1): 138–55.

Karakayali, Nedim (2009), 'Social distance and affective orientations', *Sociological Forum*, **23** (3): 538–62.

Keightley, Peter D. and Adam Eyre-Walker (2000), 'Deleterious mutations and the evolution of sex', *Science*, **290** (5490): 331–3.

Keynes, John Maynard (1930), 'Economic possibilities for our grandchildren', in *Collected Writings, vol. ix, Essays in Persuasion*, London: St Martin's Press.

Keynes, John Maynard (1936), *General Theory of Employment, Interest and Money*, London: Macmillan.

Korenman, Sanders and David Neumark (1991), 'Does marriage really make men more productive?', *Journal of Human Resources*, **26** (2): 282–307.

Kotlikoff, Laurence J. (1988), 'Intergenerational transfers and saving', *Journal of Economic Perspectives*, **2** (2): 41–58.

Kotlikoff, Laurence J. and Lawrence H. Summers (1981), 'The role of intergenerational transfers in aggregate capital accumulation', *Journal of Political Economy*, **89** (4): 706–32.

Krugman, Paul (1993), 'How I work', *The American Economist*, **37** (2): 25–31.

Kuznets, Simon (1946), *National Income: A Summary of Findings*, NBER, New York: Arno Press.

Lam, David and Robert F. Schoeni (1993), 'Effects of family background on earnings and returns to schooling: evidence from Brazil', *Journal of Political Economy*, **101** (4): 710–40.

Lamson, H.D. (1930), 'The standard of living of factory worker', *Chinese Economic Journal*, **7** (5): 1240–56.

Landes, David (2000), 'Culture makes almost all the difference', in Samuel P. Huntington and Lawrence E. Harrison (eds), *Culture Matters: How Values Shape Human Progress*, New York: Basic Books, pp. 2–13.

Lavalette, Michael (1998), 'Child labour: historical, legislative and policy context', in Bridget Pettitt (ed.), *Children and Work in the UK: Reassessing the Issues*, London: Child Poverty Action Group, pp. 22–40.

Lavy, Victor, M. Daniele Paserman and Analia Schlosser (2012), 'Inside the black of box of ability peer effects: evidence from variation in the proportion of low achievers in the classroom', *Economic Journal*, **122** (559): 208–37.

Lawrence, D.H. (1960), *Lady Chatterley's Lover*, Harmondsworth, UK: Penguin Books.

Lazear, Edward P. (1999), 'Culture and language', *Journal of Political Economy*, **107** (6): S95–126.

Lazear, Edward P. (2000), 'Economic imperialism', *Quarterly Journal of Economics*, **115** (1): 99–146.

Lefgren, Lars, Matthew J. Lindquist and David Sims (2012), 'Rich Dad, smart Dad: decomposing the intergenerational transmission of income', *Journal of Political Economy*, **120** (2): 268–303.

Levitt, Steven D. and Stephen J. Dubner (2005), *Freakonomics: A Rogue Economist Explores the Hidden Side of Everything*, New York: William Morrow.

Levitt, Steven D. and Stephen J. Dubner (2009), *Superfreakonomics: Global Cooling, Patriotic Prostitutes and Why Suicide Bombers Should Buy Life Insurance*, New York: William Morrow.

Levitt, Steven and Sudhir A. Venkatesh (2000), 'An economic analysis of a drug-selling gang's finances', *Quarterly Journal of Economics*, **115** (3): 755–89.

Levy, Victor (1985), 'Cropping pattern, mechanization, child labor and fertility behavior in a farming economy: rural Egypt', *Economic Development and Cultural Change*, **33** (4): 777–91.

Li, Hongbin and Junsen Zhang (2009), 'Testing the external effect of household behavior: the case of the demand for children', *Journal of Human Resources*, **44** (4): 890–915.

Li, Hongbin, Mark R. Rosenzweig and Junsen Zhang (2010), 'Altruism, favoritism and guilt in the allocation of family resources: Sophie's choice in Mao's mass send-down movement', *Journal of Political Economy*, **118** (1): 1–38.

Lillard, Lee A. and Linda J. Waite (1990), 'Determinants of divorce', *Social Security Bulletin*, **53** (2): 29–31.

Loury, Glenn C. (1981), 'Intergenerational transfers and the distribution of earnings', *Econometrica*, **49** (4): 843–67.

Lundberg, Shelly and Robert A. Pollak (1993), 'Separate spheres bargaining and the marriage market', *Journal of Political Economy*, **101** (6): 988–1010.

Lundberg, Shelly J., Robert A. Pollak and Terence J. Wales (1997), 'Do husbands and wives pool their resources? Evidence from the United Kingdom child benefit', *Journal of Human Resources*, **32** (3): 463–80.

Lundberg, Shelly, Richard Startza and Steven Stillman (2003), 'The retirement-consumption puzzle: a marital bargaining approach', *Journal of Public Economics*, **87** (5–6): 1199–218.

Lynch, Gary and Richard Granger (2008), *Big Brain: The Origins and Future of Human Intelligence*, New York: Palgrave Macmillan.

Malthus, Thomas Robert (1798), *An Essay on the Principle of Population*, London: J. Johnson.

Mankiw, N. Gregory (2013), *Macroeconomics*, New York: Worth Publishers.

Manser, Marilyn and Murray Brown (1980), 'Marriage and household decision-making: a bargaining analysis', *International Economic Review*, **21** (1): 31–44.

Manski, Charles F. and Joram Mayshar (2003), 'Private incentives and social interactions: fertility puzzles in Israel', *Journal of the European Economic Association*, **1** (1): 181–211.

Mantoux, Paul (1983), *The Industrial Revolution in the Eighteenth Century*, Chicago, IL: University of Chicago Press.

Marshall, Alfred (1920), *Principles of Economics*, 8th edn, London: Macmillan.

Marx, Karl (1867), *Capital: A Critique of Political Economy*, reprinted in Samuel Moore and Edward Aveling (ed. and trans.) (1954), Moscow: Progress Publishers.

Maslow, Abraham H. (1943), 'A theory of human motivation', *Psychological Review*, **50** (4): 370–96.

Masters, William H., Virginia E. Johnson and Robert C. Kolodny (1995), *Human Sexuality*, New York: HarperCollins.

Matthews, Justin L. and Teenie Matlock (2011), 'Understanding the link between spatial distance and social distance', *Social Psychology*, **42** (3): 185–92.

McCleary, Rachel M. and Robert J. Barro (2006), 'Religion and economy', *Journal of Economic Perspectives*, **20** (2): 49–72.

McClelland, David C. (1973), *The Achieving Society*, New York: Free Press.

McElroy, Marjorie B. (1990), 'The empirical content of Nash-bargained household behavior', *Journal of Human Resources*, **25** (4): 559–83.

McElroy, Marjorie B. and Mary Jean Horney (1981), 'Nash-bargained household decisions: toward a generalization of the theory of demand', *International Economic Review*, **22** (2): 333–49.

McLanahan, Sara and Larry L. Bumpass (1988), 'Intergenerational consequences of family disruption', *American Journal of Sociology*, **94** (1), 130–52.

Mehra-Kerpelman, K. (1996), 'Children at work: how many and where?', *World of Work*, **15**: 8–9.

Menchik, Paul L. (1980), 'Primogeniture, equal sharing and the US distribution of wealth', *Quarterly Journal of Economics*, **94** (2): 299–316.

Menchik, Paul L. and Martin David (1983), 'Income distribution, lifetime savings and bequests', *American Economic Review*, **73** (4): 672–89.

Michael, Robert T., John H. Gagnon, Edward O. Laumann and Gina Kolata (1994), *Sex in America: A Definitive Survey*, Boston, MA: Little, Brown.

Moav, Omer and Zvika Neeman (2012), 'Saving rates and poverty: the role of conspicuous consumption and human capital', *Economic Journal*, **122** (563): 933–56.

Modigliani, Franco (1986), 'Life cycle, individual thrift and the wealth of nations', *American Economic Review*, **76** (3): 297–313.

Modigliani, Franco (1988), 'The role of intergenerational transfers and life cycle saving in the accumulation of wealth', *Journal of Economic Perspectives*, **2** (2): 15–40.

Modigliani, Franco and Richard Brumberg (1954), 'Utility analysis and the consumption function: an interpretation of cross-section data', in Kenneth K. Kurihara (ed.), *Post-Keynesian Economics*, New Brunswick, NJ: Rutgers University Press, pp. 388–436.

Murstein, Bernard I. and Patricia Christy (1976), 'Physical attractiveness and marriage adjustment in middle-aged couples', *Journal of Personality and Social Psychology*, **34** (4): 537–42.

Nakane, Chie (1967), *Kinship and Economic Organization in Rural Japan*, London: Athlone.

Nangia, Parveen (1987), *Child Labour: Cause-Effect Syndrome*, New Delhi: Janak Publishers.

Nardinelli, Clark (1990), *Child Labor and the Industrial Revolution*, Bloomington, IN: Indiana University Press.

Nash, John F. (1950a), 'Equilibrium points in n-person games', *Proceedings of the National Academy of Sciences*, **36** (1): 48–9.

Nash, John F. (1950b), 'The bargaining problem', *Econometrica*, **18** (2): 155–62.

National Association of Realtors (1986), *The Homebuying and Selling Process*, Washington, DC.

Neal, Derek (1997), 'The effects of Catholic secondary schooling on educational achievement', *Journal of Labor Economics*, **15** (1): 98–123.

Nechyba, Thomas J. (2006), 'Income and peer quality sorting in public and private schools', in Eric A. Hanushek and Finis Welch (eds), *Handbook of the Economics of Education, vol. 2*, Amsterdam: Elsevier Science, pp. 1327–68.

Neumark, David and Postlewaite Andrew (1998), 'Relative income concerns and the rise in married women's employment', *Journal of Public Economics*, **70** (1): 157–83.

Nock, Steven L. (1992), *Sociology of the Family*, Englewood Cliffs, NJ: Prentice Hall.

Norton, Seth W. (2002), 'Population growth, economic freedom and the rule of law', PERC Policy Series No. 24, Population Growth, Economic Freedom, and the Rule of Law, February.

Nugent, Jeffrey B. (1985), 'The old-age security motive for fertility', *Population and Development Review*, **11** (1): 75–97.

O'Flaherty, Brendan and Aloysius Siow (1995), 'Up-or-out rules in the market for lawyers', *Journal of Labor Economics*, **13** (4): 709–35.

Okólski, Marek (2001), 'Incomplete migration: a new form of mobility in Central and Eastern Europe. The case of Polish and Ukrainian migrants', in Claire Wallace and Dariusz Stola (eds), *Patterns of Migration in Central Europe*, Basingstoke: Palgrave Macmillan, pp. 105–28.

Osberg, Lars (1984), *Economic Inequality in the United States*, New York: M.E. Sharpe.

Oswald, Andrew J. and Nattavudh Powdthavee (2010), 'Daughters and left-wing voting', *Review of Economics and Statistics*, **92** (2): 213–27.

Overland, Jody, Christopher D. Carroll and David N. Weil (2000), 'Saving and growth with habit formation', *American Economic Review*, **90** (3): 341–55.

Panayotou, Theodore (1994), 'The population, environment and development nexus', in Robert Cassen (ed.), *Population and Development: Old debates, New Conclusions*, New Brunswick, NJ: Transactions Publishers, pp. 149–80.

Parish, William L. and Robert J. Willis (1993), 'Daughters, education and family budgets: Taiwan experiences', *Journal of Human Resources*, **28** (4): 863–98.

Peters, Michael and Aloysius Siow (2002), 'Competing premarital investments', *Journal of Political Economy*, **110** (3): 592–608.

Peterson, John L. and Constance Miller (1980), 'Physical attractiveness and marriage adjustment in older American couples', *Journal of Psychology: Interdisciplinary and Applied*, **105** (2): 247–52.

Pitt, Mark M., Mark R. Rosenzweig and Nazmul Hassan (2012), 'Human capital investment and the gender division of labor in a brawn-based economy', *American Economic Review*, **102** (7): 3531–60.

Plug, Erik and Wim Vijverberg (2003), 'Schooling, family background and adoption: is it nature or is it nurture?', *Journal of Political Economy*, **111** (3): 611–41.

Polachek, Solomon W. and W. Stanley Siebert (1993), *The Economics of Earnings*, Cambridge: Cambridge University Press.

Pollak, Robert A. (1985), 'A transaction cost approach to families and households', *Journal of Economic Literature*, **23** (2): 581–608.

Pollak, Robert A. (1988), 'Tied transfers and paternalistic preferences', *American Economic Review*, **78** (2): 240–44.

Pollak, Robert A. (2003), 'Gary Becker's contributions to family and household economics', *Review of Economics of the Household*, **1** (1): 111–41.

Pollak, Robert A. and Michael L. Wachter (1975), 'The relevance of the household production function and its implications for the allocation of time', *Journal of Political Economy*, **83** (2): 255–77.

Posner, Richard A (1992), *Sex and Reason*, Cambridge, MA: Harvard University Press.

Qian, Nancy (2009), 'Quantity–quality and the one child policy: the only-child disadvantage in school enrollment in rural China', NBER Working Paper 14973, New York: National Bureau of Economic Research.

Rae, John (1834), *Statement of Some New Principles on the Subject of Political Economy: Exposing the Fallacies of the System of Free Trade and of Some Other Doctrines Maintained in the 'Wealth of Nations'*, reprinted (1964), New York: Augustus M. Kelley.

Ramey, Valerie A. (2011), 'Is there a "Tiger Mother" Effect? Time Use Across Ethnic Groups', mimeo, UCSD.

Rao, Vijayendra (1993), 'The rising price of husbands: a hedonic analysis of dowry increases in rural India', *Journal of Political Economy*, **101** (4): 666–77.

Rasmusen, Eric (1989), *Games and Information*, Cambridge, MA: Basil Blackwell.

Rawls, John (1971), *A Theory of Justice*, Cambridge, MA: Harvard University Press.

Ricardo, David (1817), *The Principles of Political Economy and Taxation*, London: Dent [1911 reprint].

Rosen, Sherwin (1981), 'The economics of superstars', *American Economic Review*, **71** (5): 845–58.

Rosenzweig, Mark R. (1977), 'The demand for children in farm households', *Journal of Political Economy*, **85** (1): 123–46.

Rosenzweig, Mark R. and Robert E. Evenson (1977), 'Fertility, schooling and the economic contribution of children in rural India: an econometric analysis', *Econometrica*, **45** (5): 1065–79.

Rosenzweig, Mark R. and Kenneth I. Wolpin (1980), 'Testing the quantity–quality fertility model: the use of twins as a natural experiment', *Econometrica*, **48** (1): 227–40.

Sacerdote, Bruce (2002), 'The nature and nurture of economic outcomes', *American Economic Review*, **92** (2): 344–8.

Sahota, Gian S. (1978), 'Theories of personal income distribution: a survey', *Journal of Economic Literature*, **16** (1): 1–55.

Salaff, Janet W. (1976), 'Working daughters in the Hong Kong Chinese family: female filial piety or a transformation in the family power structure?', *Journal of Social History*, **9** (4): 439–65.

Salaff, Janet W. (1981), *Working Daughters of Hong Kong: Filial Piety or Power in the Family?*, New York: Cambridge University Press.

Schoeck, Helmut (1987), *Envy: A Theory of Social Behaviour*, Indianapolis, IN: Liberty Press.

Schor, Juliet B. (1991), *The Overworked American: The Unexpected Decline of Leisure*, New York: Basic Books.

Schultz, Theodore W. (1974), 'The high value of human time: population equilibrium', *Journal of Political Economy*, **82** (2): S2–S10.

Segal, Carmit (2008), 'Classroom behaviour', *Journal of Human Resources*, **43** (4): 783–814.

Siow, Aloysius (1998), 'Differential fecundity, markets and gender roles', *Journal of Political Economy*, **106** (2): 334–54.

Smith, Adam (1759), *The Theory of Moral Sentiments*, reprinted in D.D. Raphael and A.L. Macfie (eds) (1976), *Glasgow Edition of the Works and Correspondence of Adam Smith, vol. 7*, Oxford: Oxford University Press.

Smith, Adam (1776), *An Inquiry into the Nature and Causes of the Wealth of Nations*, reprinted in Edwin Cannan (ed.) (1977), Chicago, IL: University of Chicago Press.

Stannard, Una (1971), 'The mask of beauty', in Vivian Gormick and Barbara K. Moran (eds), *Woman in Sexist Society*, New York: Basic Books, pp. 187–203.

Stark, Oded (1995), *Altruism and Beyond, An Economic Analysis of Transfers and Exchanges Within Families and Groups*, Cambridge: Cambridge University Press.

Stark, Oded and C. Simon Fan (2007a), 'The analytics of seasonal migration', *Economics Letters*, **94** (2): 304–12.

Stark, Oded and C. Simon Fan (2007b), 'Losses and gains to developing countries from the migration of educated workers: an overview of recent research and new reflections', *World Economics*, **8** (2): 259–69.

Stark, Oded and C. Simon Fan (2011a), 'Migration for degrading work as an escape from humiliation', *Journal of Economic Behavior and Organization*, **77** (3): 241–7.

Stark, Oded and C. Simon Fan (2011b), 'The prospect of migration, sticky wages and "educated unemployment"', *Review of International Economics*, **19** (2): 277–87.

Stark, Oded, Christian Helmenstein and Yury Yegorov (1997), 'Migrants' savings, purchasing power parity and the optimal duration of migration', *International Tax and Public Finance*, **4** (3): 307–24.

Stark, Oded, Marcin Jakubek and C. Simon Fan (2012), 'Can a Rawlsian and a Utilitarian See Eye to Eye?', mimeo, University of Bonn.

Stevenson, Betsey and Justin Wolfers (2006), 'Bargaining in the shadow of the law: divorce laws and family distress', *Quarterly Journal of Economics*, **121** (1): 267–88.

Strauss, John and Duncan Thomas (1998), 'Health, nutrition and economic development', *Journal of Economic Literature*, **36** (2): 766–817.

Suen, Wing (1995), 'Sectoral shifts: impact on Hong Kong workers', *Journal of International Trade and Economic Development*, **4** (2): 135–52.

Terry, Roger L. and Elizabeth Macklin (1977), 'Accuracy of identifying married couples on the basis of similarity of attractiveness', *Journal of Psychology: Interdisciplinary and Applied*, **97** (1): 15–20.

Tertilt, Michèle (2005), 'Polygyny, fertility and savings', *Journal of Political Economy*, **113** (6): 1341–70.

Thomas, Duncan (1990), 'Intra-household resource allocation: an inferential approach', *Journal of Human Resources*, **25** (4): 635–64.

Todaro, Michael P. (2000), *Economic Development*, Reading, MA: Addison Wesley.

Tsang, Su-ki and Yuk-shing Cheng (1997), 'The economic link-up of Guangdong and Hong Kong: structural and development problem', in Joseph C.H. Chai, Y.Y. Kueh and Clement A. Tisdell (eds), *China and the Asian Pacific Economy*, New York: Nova Science Publishers, pp. 51–74.

Tuttle, Carolyn (1999), *Hard at Work in Factories and Mines: The Economics of Child Labor During the British Industrial Revolution*, Boulder, CO and Oxford: Westview Press.

UNICEF (2002), *Trafficking in Human Beings in Southeastern Europe*, Belgrade: UNICEF.

van der Eyken, Willem (1977), *The Pre-School Years*, Harmondsworth: Penguin Books.

van der Klaauw, Wilbert (2008), 'Breaking the link between poverty and low student achievement: an evaluation of title I', *Journal of Econometrics*, **142** (2): 731–56.

van-Groezen, Bas, Theo Leers and Lex Meijdam (2003), 'Social security and endogenous fertility: pensions and child allowances as Siamese twins', *Journal of Public Economics*, **87** (2): 233–51.

Veblen, Thorstein (1899), *The Theory of the Leisure Class*, New York: Macmillan.

Vella, Francis (1999), 'Do Catholic schools make a difference? Evidence from Australia', *Journal of Human Resources*, **34** (1): 208–24.

Washington, Ebonya L. (2008), 'Female socialization: how daughters affect their legislator fathers', *American Economic Review*, **98** (1): 311–32.

Wei, Shang-Jin and Xiaobo Zhang (2011), 'The competitive saving motive: evidence from rising sex ratios and savings rates in China', *Journal of Political Economy*, **119** (3): 511–64.

Weil, David N. (1994), 'The saving of the elderly in micro and macro data', *Quarterly Journal of Economics*, **109** (1): 55–81.

Weil, David N. (2007), 'Accounting for the effect of health on economic growth', *Quarterly Journal of Economics*, **122** (3): 1265–306.

Weinberg, Bruce A. (2001) 'An incentive model of the effect of parental income on children', *Journal of Political Economy*, **109** (2): 266–80.

Weiss, Yoram (1997), 'The formation and dissolution of families: Why marry? Who marries whom? And what happens upon marriage and divorce?', in Mark R. Rosenzweig and Oded Stark (eds), *Handbook of Population Economics*, Amsterdam: Elsevier Science, pp. 81–123.

Weiss, Yoram and Robert J. Willis (1985), 'Children as collective goods and divorce settlements', *Journal of Labor Economics*, **3** (3): 268–92.

Weiss, Yoram and Robert J. Willis (1993), 'Transfers among divorced couples: evidence and interpretation', *Journal of Labor Economics*, **11** (4): 629–79.

Weiss, Yoram and Robert J. Willis (1997), 'Match quality, new information and marital dissolution', *Journal of Labor Economics*, **15** (1): S293–329.

Wellington, Alison J. (1993), 'Changes in the male/female wage gap', *Journal of Human Resources*, **28** (2): 381–411.

West, Stuart A., Curt M. Lively and Andrew F. Read (1999), 'A pluralist approach to sex and recombination', *Journal of Evolutionary Biology*, **12** (6): 1003–12.

Whitemore, Diane (2005), 'Resource and peer impact on girls' academic achievement: evidence from a randomized experiment', *American Economic Review*, **95** (2): 99–203.

Wilhelm, M.O. (1996), 'Bequest behavior and the effect of heirs' earnings: testing the altruistic model of bequests', *American Economic Review*, **86** (4): 874–92.

Willis, Robert J. (1973), 'A new approach to the economic theory of fertility behavior', *Journal of Political Economy*, **81** (2): S14–64.

Willis, Robert J. (1999), 'A theory of out-of-wedlock childbearing', *Journal of Political Economy*, **107** (S6): S33–S64.

Willis, Robert J. (2000), 'The economics of fatherhood', *American Economic Review*, **90** (2): 378–82.

Wilson, John (1978), *Religion in American Society: The Effective Presence*, Englewood Cliffs, NJ: Prentice-Hall.

Wright, Robert (1994), *The Moral Animal: Evolutionary Psychology and Everyday Life*, New York: Pantheon.

Wrigley, Edward Anthony and Roger S. Schofield (1981), *The Population History of England 1541–1871: A Reconstruction*, London: Edward Arnold.

Yi, Junjian and Junsen Zhang (2010), 'The effect of house price on fertility: evidence from Hong Kong', *Economic Inquiry*, **48** (3): 635–50.

Zagorsky, Jay L. (2005), 'Marriage and divorce's impact on wealth', *Journal of Sociology*, **41** (4): 406–24.

Zhang, Hongliang, Jere R. Behreman, C. Simon Fan, Xiangdong Wei, and Junsen Zhang (2013), 'The Impact of Parental Migration on Children Left Behind: Evidence from Rural China', mimeo, Chinese University of Hong Kong.

Zhang, Junsen (1994), 'Bequest as a public good within marriage: a note', *Journal of Political Economy*, **102** (1): 187–93.

Zhang, Junsen and William Chan (1999), 'Dowry and wife's welfare: a theoretical and empirical analysis', *Journal of Political Economy*, **107** (4): 786–808.

Zimmerman, David (2003), 'Peer effects in academic outcomes: evidence from a natural experiment', *Review of Economics and Statistics*, **85** (1): 9–23.

Zweig, David, Siu-Fung Chung and Donglin Han (2008), 'Redefining the brain drain: China's diaspora option', *Science, Technology and Society*, **13** (1): 1–33.

# Index